VR..
SECRETS OF THE
BLACK SUN

David Hatcher Childress

Adventures Unlimited Press

VRIL
SECRETS OF THE
BLACK SUN

Vril: Secrets of the Black Sun

ISBN 978-1-948803-66-3

Published by:
Adventures Unlimited Press
One Adventure Place
Kempton, Illinois 60946 USA
auphq@frontiernet.net

Cover by Terry Lamb

AdventuresUnlimitedPress.com

10 9 8 7 6 5 4 3 2 1

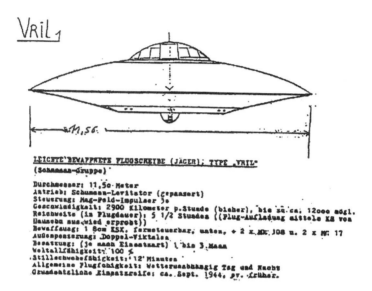

VRiL₁

LEICHTE BEWAFFNETE FLUGSCHEIBE (JÄGER); TYPE „VRIL"
(Schumann-Gruppe)

Durchmesser: 11,5o Meter
Antrieb: Schumann-Levitator (gepanzert)
Steuerung: Mag-Feld-Impulser 3e
Geschwindigkeit: 2900 Kilometer p.Stunde (bisher), bis zu ca; 12ooo mögl.
Reichweite (in Flugdauer); 5 1/2 Stunden ((Flug-Aufladung mittels KB von
Neumoda aus wied erprobt))
Bewaffnung: 1 8cm KSK fernsteuerbar, unten, + 2 x MK 108 u. 2 x MG 17
Außenpanzerung: Doppel-Viktalen
Besatzung: (je nach Einsatzart) 1 bis 3 Mann
Weltallfähigkeit: 100 %
Stillschwebefähigkeit: 12' Minuten
Allgemeine Flugfähigkeit: Wetterunabhängig Tag und Nacht
Grundsätzliche Einsatzreife: ca. Sept. 1944, ev. früher.

Plans for the Vril craft.

An early Vril craft in flight.

VRIL
SECRETS OF THE
BLACK SUN

David Hatcher Childress

The Black Sun signet.

TABLE OF CONTENTS

A photo of a Haunebu II taken during WWII.

Chapter 1

Secrets of the Black Sun

Look out at your children
See their faces in golden rays
Don't kid yourself they belong to you
They're the start of the coming race
—*Oh, You Pretty Things*, David Bowie

Bell flight fourteen you now can land.
See you on Aldebaran, safe on the green desert sand.
It's so very lonely, you're two thousand light years from home.
—*2000 Light Years From Home*, Rolling Stones

In my previous books, *Haunebu: The Secret Files, Andromeda: The Secret Files* and *Antarctica and the Secret Space Program*, I have discussed the missing submarines and secret bases in the Antarctic. I have discussed the German craft known as the Haunebu and the Andromeda. In this book I want to discuss the Vril craft, the Vril Society, the Black Sun and Vril power itself. We will also document Vril craft in flight in the many historic photos that have been taken over the years.

A certain amount of recap from my earlier books will occur as these are important points and photos that need to be repeated. The evidence for the Vril, Haunebu and Andromeda craft is overwhelming in my opinion. As the reader will see, the information on this comes from a variey of sources and—at least some parts of the overall story—are historical fact.

Was Germany developing electric-type Tesla craft in the 1930s

11

and creating what would be the natural outcome of such electric-vortex-gyro technology? Did they develop early saucer craft and then the mothership called the Andromeda to hold and transport these smaller discoid craft of various sizes? The answer seems to be an astounding "Yes!"

What is Vril? What is the Black Sun?

First of all, the Black Sun is a concept and symbol used by the German SS before and during WWII. It is still used today by the remnants of the SS in South America and by neo-Nazi and "far right" groups. It is not an ancient symbol, having been created by the SS, but it is similar to many ancient sun wheels, or sonnenrads. The symbol's design consists of twelve radial sig runes, similar to the symbols employed by the SS in its logo.

The symbol that later became known as the "black sun" originated in the early 20th century, with the first depiction being the Wewelsburg mosaic ordered specially by the head of the SS, Heinrich Himmler. Himmler acquired Wewelsburg, a castle near Paderborn in the German region of Westphalia, in 1933. He intended to make the building into a center for the SS, and between 1936 and 1942, Himmler ordered the building expanded and rebuilt for ceremonial purposes.

Himmler's remodeling included the Wewelsburg mosaic that was composed of twelve dark-green radially overlaid sig runes on the white marble floor of the structure's north tower. This tower is known as the "General's Hall" or "Obergruppenführersaal."

Himmler intended the castle at Wewelsburg to be a center for the SS and Black Sun mosaic was to be central to ceremonies at the castle. The exact "meaning" of the mosaic is unknown but it has become a symbol of the survival of the SS in its various forms and has come to replace the swastika as a symbol of the Nazis. The swastika is banned in Germany but the black sun symbol is not.

It should be noted that in the 2014 documentary entitled *Grey Wolf*, about

The Black Sun symbol.

The Black Sun mosaic on the floor of a room at Wewelsburg Castle.

Hitler's survival in South America, it is said that one woman was warned in a phone call that, "the SS was still active in Argentina." This group would presumably use the black sun symbol as their logo.

Says Wikipedia about the origins of the Black Sun symbol:

> Some scholars have suggested that the artist may have found inspiration from motifs found on decorative Merovingian period discs (Zierscheiben) from Central Europe, which have been suggested to represent the sun, or its passing through the year. Zierscheibe (German for "ornamental disk") in archaeology is the term for a kind

of metal jewelry dating to the European Iron Age. They are found in graves and are thought to have been worn as pendants attached to the tunica, or as part of a belt pouch. Early examples date to the Late Bronze Age (ca. 800 BC). They develop into characteristic designs notably attested from Alamannic graves from the migration period.

According to Wikipedia, there is an association with the Black Sun symbol with a 1991 German novel, *Die Schwarze Sonne von Tashi Lhunpo* ("The Black Suns of Tashi Lhunpo," yes plural), by the pseudonymous author Russell McCloud. The book links the Wewelsburg mosaic of the Black Sun with the neo-Nazi concept of the "Black Sun," in a novel that begins with Hitler holding the Spear of Destiny in Vienna and then committing suicide in Berlin. The rest of the novel consists of a diary of a journalist, presumably Russell McCloud, who makes a quest for other sacred artifacts and finding some of them at Wewelsburg Castle. It then has a Tibetan connection. The book is considered a "Nazi thriller."

Russell McCloud is in fact a German scholar and travel writer named Stephan Mögle-Stadel. His biography can be found on Wikipedia which states:

> Stephan Mögle-Stadel (born December 21, 1965) is a German educator, journalist and book writer. Together with Troy Davis, he is the chairman of a world citizenship group, of which he is the Founder and President and the author of the "Dag Hammarskjöld: Vision einer Menschheitsethik'" (Vision from a Human Ethic).
>
> He studied education, psychology, and history, partly at the C.G. Jung Institute for Depth Psychology, and he is a member of the Erich Fromm Society for Social Psychology. He trained as a journalist in the Axel Springer company and at the "Akademie für Publizistik" in Hamburg. After this he wrote as an independent journalist for different newspapers. In 1990 he became a correspondent at the United Nations in New York City. In 1992, while he did his alternative national service as a conscientious objector,

he took part in a UN internship program. In 1998 he took part as a journalist and NGO representative at the Berlin Conference for World Climate Change and in 1993 at the Preparation Conference for the World Summit in Rio. As a travel journalist he reported from Egypt, Israel, India, Japan and the USA. After that he worked within the range of human rights and globalization questions for non-governmental organizations and since 1998 he has been an honorary member of the board of the World Citizen Foundation New York.

He has written and published several books on globalization, human rights, united nations, governance, futurology, and psychohistory. His first book, the occult-Nazi thriller *Die Schwarze Sonne von Tashi Lhunpo*, was published in 1991 under the pen-name Russell McCloud. He was also the Editor of Boutros Boutros Ghali's book *UNorganisierte Welt*.

While Stephan Mögle-Stadel may have written a book about the Black Sun symbol and Wewelsburg Castle, he was not the first to write about the Black Sun symbol that began with novels published in Germany in the 1970s such as those by the former SS office Wilhelm Landig.

In my book, *Haunebu: The Secret Files*, I have a chapter on Miguel Serrano. Serrano was a former Chilean diplomat and esoteric writer who built on the works of Carl Jung, Otto Rahn, Wilhelm Landig, Julius Evola and Savitri Devi to bind together and develop already existing theories on Nazi survival, secret bases in Antarctica, and the Black Sun. Serrano had been a member of the National Socialist Movement of Chile in the 1930s and was able to work as an ambassador to numerous countries until the rise of Salvador Allende. In 1984 he published his book *Adolf Hitler: The Ultimate Avatar.* Serrano claimed that the Aryans were extragalactic beings who founded Hyperborea in the far north and lived the heroic life of Bodhisattvas, while the Jews were created by the Demiurge and were concerned only with coarse materialism. Serrano claimed that a new Golden Age can be attained if the Hyperboreans repurify their blood (supposedly the light of the Black Sun) and restore their "blood-memory."

Wilhelm Landig and the Landig Group

Wilhelm Landig and the so-called The Landig Group, a neo-völkisch group formed in 1950, that first gathered for discussions at the studio of the designer Wilhelm Landig in the Margareten district of Vienna. The circle's most prominent and influential members were Wilhelm Landig (1909–1997), Erich Halik (Claude Schweighardt) and Rudolf J. Mund (1920–1985). The circle has also been referred to as the Landig Circle (Landig Kreis), Vienna Group (Wien Konzern) and Vienna Lodge (Wien Lodge).

Landig was the founder of the group, which has since inspired decades of völkisch mysticism. He and his group revived the ariosophical, Ario-Germanic mythology of Thule, the supposed polar homeland of the ancient Aryans.

Landig, through his circle, popularized esoteric ideas current among the pre-Nazi völkisch movement and the SS relating to Atlantis, the World Ice Theory, pre-historic floods and secret racial doctrines from Tibet. Landig apparently coined the term Black Sun, which he said was a mystical source of energy capable of regenerating the Aryan race. However, it would seem that this term came from Himmler and his SS officers who had been initiated at Wewelsburg castle beginning in the late 1930s.

Wilhelm Landig was a former SS member who revived the ariosophical mythology of Thule. He wrote the Thule trilogy *Götzen gegen Thule* (1971), *Wolfszeit um Thule* (1980) and *Rebellen für Thule—Das Erbe von Atlantis* (1991). These books have also been published in French. *Götzen gegen Thule* which if translated directly into French would be "Les Petits Dieux contre Thulé" ("The Little Gods Against Thule"), but was published as *Combat pour Thule* in 1971, the same year it came out in German. Landig's books have not appeared in English as far as I can tell.

Landig's trilogy of books.

With Landig's death in 1997 a younger generation continued the development of the circle's ideas from the 1980s on. This younger generation consisted of members of the German/Austrian Tempelhofgesellschaft. Their publications demonstrate an exchange of ideas with the older generation, mainly revolving around the Black Sun concept. After the Tempelhofgesellschaft had been dissolved because of Landig's death, it was succeeded by a group called the Causa Nostra, a Freundeskreis (circle of friends) that reportedly remains active to this day.

Landig's books circulated amazing stories about secret German SS bases in Antarctica, Greenland, the Canadian Arctic and South America, where they developed flying saucers and miracle weapons such as Die Glocke (The Bell). These secret bases and colonies continued to operate and flourish after the war had ended and they were essentially staffed and directed by SS officers and their logo was the Black Sun, not the Nazi swastika. In the decades immediately after the war they believed that they would revive the Third Reich, in South America at least, and their superior technology—based on the concept of "Vril"—would be used for the good of mankind. This technology is manifested in the flying craft that are called "Vril," "Haunebu" and "Andromeda."

Landig began his first novel *Götzen gegen Thule* (1971) in the 1950s. The subtitle of this book was *Ein Roman voller Wirklichkeiten*, which translates as "a novel full of realities."

Says Nicholas Goodrick-Clarke in his book *Black Sun: Aryan Cults, Esoteric Nazism, and the Politics of Identity*,[28] about Landig's first book:

> *Götzen gegen Thule* is an allegory of the Landig circle's attempts to make contact with an esoteric center of Nordic

traditions, the legendary realm of Thule, the final bastion of the Germanic world in defeat. The story describes the world odyssey of a small group of SS soldiers and Luftwaffe airmen across four continents in the immediate aftermath of the Second World War. In the first part of the novel the two airmen, Recke ("berseker") and Reimer ("bard"), are sent from Norway [Banak air base] to Point 103, a secret base that has been established by the esoteric SS elite in Arctic Canada, unknown to the Allies and also to most German authorities. Point 103 is a large underground complex equipped with highly advanced technology, including flying saucers whose apparent mission is to maintain the spirit of German defense after the final surrender of the Reich.... Its symbol is the alchemical Black Sun, a round disk that is not exactly black but the deepest violet.

Like Landig's bloc of unaligned nations against the superpowers, Point 103 seeks to promote an international alliance for the ideals of the Black Sun. Many foreign delegates attend a great conference held in the assembly hall of the base decorated with astrological symbols and an enormous icon of Mithras slaying the Bull. The delegates have all been flown to the conference by means of the V-7, a German flying saucer with a speed of 4,000 kilometers per hour and a range of 2,000 kilometers. These include a Tibetan lama, Japanese, Chinese, and American officers, Indians, Arabs, Persians, an Ethiopian, a Brazilian officer, a Venezuelan, a Siamese and a full-blooded Mexican Indian. The Arabs speak darkly of secret Islamic brotherhoods, the Indians and Persians invoke old Aryan traditions, the Orientals allude to their occult orders and a mysterious world center. Attired in their uniforms or national dress, many of the delegates make speeches identifying their national myths and ideals with those of the Thule and pledge their full support when the time comes for action.

Nicholas Goodrick-Clarke[28] then tells us that a similar odyssey is described in Landig's second novel *Wolfszeit um Thule* (1980):

Here the narrative follows the adventures of two naval officers, Krall and Hellfeldt, and SS-Major Eyken, formerly stationed at Point 103. Assigned to a flotilla of German U-boats which leaves Norway in early May 1945, they achieve a devastating victory over an Allied naval convoy in the North Atlantic. The flotilla collects all equipment and personnel from Point 103, which is then evacuated and totally destroyed... The flotilla sets sail for the South Atlantic to make contact with the new bases of the Black Sun, the epithet of the shadow Reich government in exile. The geographical focus of this novel thus indicates the shift of Nazi survival toward Latin America and Antarctica, the new Thule of the Southern Hemisphere.

Thus, Landig claims that the secret base called Point 103 or the "Blue Island" in the Canadian Arctic is dismantled, and the important equipment is removed to new bases in South America and the facility effectively destroyed. The secret base in Greenland known as Beaver Dam is apparently still functioning. Once in South America the novel's heroes "find support in Buenos Aires" and continue their travels onward to La Paz, Bolivia.

Once in La Paz, the hero Eyken lectures the others on the work of the real-life personage, the German writer and adventurer Edmund Kiss. Edmund Kiss wrote a number of books and claimed to be an archeologist. Kiss was born in Germany 1886 and died in 1960. He studied architecture and became a writer of adventure fiction and then non-fiction books on cataclysms, Tiwanaku, Puma Punku and the World Ice Theory. He did some fascinating research at Tiwanaku and Puma Punku in Bolivia during the years before WWII.

In the 1920s Kiss started writing his first books on alternative archeology and ancient mysticism. In his 1933 book entitled *Die letzte Königin von Atlantis* (*The Last Queen of Atlantis*) he equated the mythical northern land of Thule to the origins of humanity. According to Kiss "The inhabitants of Northern Atlantis were led by their leader Baldur Wieborg, a native of the mythical Thule

19

who migrated all across the world." Clearly, Landig had read Kiss's books and was aware and sympathetic to his philosophy.

Kiss was a follower of the Welteislehre (World Ice Theory), a hypothesis created by an Austrian engineer named Hanns Hörbiger (1860-1931), and Philipp Johann Heinrich Fauth during the 1890s. Welteislehre suggests that the Earth and all other cosmic planetary bodies were made out of ice. One of the claims made in Hörbiger's book *Glacial-Kosmogonie* was that the Earth once had six satellite moons. He theorized that sometime in the ancient past, five of these moons were destroyed by crashing into the Earth. According to Hörbiger, this cataclysmic event would have caused global flooding and the formation of continent-spanning glaciers. According to Hörbiger, flora and fauna could only survive at high altitudes such as those found in the Himalayas and the Andes. Kiss was attracted by the claim of global ice and wanted to explore the Andes for evidence to prove Hörbiger's theory.

By his own account, Hörbiger was observing the Moon when he was struck by the notion that the brightness and roughness of its surface were due to ice. Shortly after this revelation he experienced a dream in which he was floating in space watching the swinging of a pendulum which grew longer and longer until it broke. "I knew that Newton had been wrong and that the sun's gravitational pull ceases to exist at three times the distance of Neptune," he concluded. He worked out his concepts in collaboration with amateur astronomer and schoolteacher Philipp Fauth whom he met in 1898, and published it as *Glazial-Kosmogonie* in 1912.

Hörbiger elaborated on his Welteislehre in the 1913 book *Wirbelstürme, Wetterstürze, Hagelkatastrophen und Marskanal-Verdoppelungen,* written in collaboration with Fauth. Hörbiger's theories were later popularized by H.S. Bellamy, and influenced Hans Robert Scultetus, head of the Pflegestätte für Wetterkunde (Meteorology Section) of the SS-Ahnenerbe. Scultetus believed that Welteislehre could be used to provide accurate long-range weather forecasts. Hörbiger died in 1931.

Publications on the Vril Society in German

Willy Ley was a German rocket engineer who had immigrated

to the United States in 1937. In 1947, he published an article titled "Pseudoscience in Naziland" in the magazine *Astounding Science Fiction*. He wrote that the high popularity of irrational convictions in Germany at that time explained how Nazism could have fallen on such fertile ground.

Among various pseudoscientific groups he mentions one that looked for the Vril:

> The next group was literally founded upon a novel. That group which I think called itself "Wahrheitsgesellschaft"— Society for Truth—and which was more or less localized in Berlin, devoted its spare time looking for Vril.

The existence of a Vril Society was alleged in 1960 by Jacques Bergier and Louis Pauwels. In their book *The Morning of the Magicians*, they claimed that the Vril-Society was a secret community of occultists in pre-Nazi Berlin that was a sort of inner circle of the Thule Society. They also thought that it was in close contact with the English group known as the Hermetic Order of the Golden Dawn. The Vril information takes up about a tenth of the volume, the remainder of which details other esoteric speculations, but the authors fail to clearly explain whether this section is fact or fiction. Historians have shown that there has been no actual historical foundation for the claims of Pauwels and Bergier, and that the article of Willy Ley has only been a vague inspiration for their own ideas. Nevertheless, Pauwels and Bergier have influenced a whole new literary genre dealing with the alleged occult influences on Nazis which have often been related to the fictional Vril Society.

In his book *Monsieur Gurdjieff*, Louis Pauwels claimed that a Vril Society had been founded by General Karl Haushofer, a student of Russian magician and metaphysician Georges Gurdjieff.

In his book *Black Sun*, Professor Nicholas Goodrick-Clarke refers to the research of the German author Peter Bahn. Bahn writes in his 1996 essay, "Das Geheimnis der Vril-Energie" ("The Secret of Vril Energy"), of his discovery of an obscure esoteric group calling itself the "Reichsarbeitsgemeinschaft." which revealed

21

itself in a rare 1930 publication *Vril. Die Kosmische Urkraft* (Vril, the Cosmic Elementary Power) written by a member of this Berlin-based group, under the pseudonym "Johannes Täufer" (German: "John [the] Baptist"). Published by the influential astrological publisher, Otto Wilhelm Barth (whom Bahn believes was "Täufer"), the 60-page pamphlet says little of the group other than that it was founded in 1925 to study the uses of Vril energy.

Other members of the "Reichsarbeitsgemeinschaft," were supporters of the theories of the Austrian inventor Karl Schappeller (1875–1947).

After World War II, a group referred to by Nicholas Goodrick-Clarke as the Vienna Circle elaborated an esoteric neo-Nazism that contributed to the circulation of the Vril theme in a new context. In their writings, Vril is associated with Nazi UFOs and the Black Sun concept. Julian Strube wrote that a younger generation related to the Tempelhofgesellschaft, has continued the work of the Vienna Circle and exerts a continuous influence on the most common notions of Vril. Those notions are not only popular in neo-Nazi circles but also in movies or computer games, such as *Iron Sky, Wolfenstein,* and *Call of Duty.*

The Ettl Photos and the Vril Saucers

Much has been written about German flying saucers since 1989. We learn from the plans given to Ralf Ettl that the names of the larger saucer is "Haunebu" and the smaller saucer is "Vril." The Vril was called the RFZ before and during the war and apparently named Vril only after the war. The plans also included the cigar-shaped mothership called the "Andromeda." Except for the one set of plans and the few photos, not much is known about the Andromeda craft. It seems to be the most secret and elusive of all the secret projects of Nazi Germany.

The Andromeda craft was said to be a 139-meter-long tubular craft that, according to plans released, had hangars for one Haunebu II, two Vril I's and two Vril II's.

There seems to have been different sizes of Andromeda craft, as some photos of it seem to show a very long craft while other photos show a shorter cigar-shaped craft. Some craft have had a flame coming out of the back, others not. The date on the plans is: 2 Dec 44.

The Andromeda craft had seats for at least 40 people, and probably could seat 50 to 60 people. There are various Vril sites on the Internet that give the specs for the various flying saucers developed by the Germans starting in the 1930s.

The one-man Vril I was said to come into service in September of 1944. It's statistics are:

Vril1 from Sept. 44
Diameter 11.5 m
Drive: Schuman levitator (antigravitation eqpm.)
Steuerung/steering: mag-field-impulser
Velocity: 2900-12000km/h
Capacity: 5.5 h in air

The larger of the saucers was known as the "Haunebu" which is reportedly the shortened form of Hauneburg Device. We are told that the Haunebu II craft held 9 people and the larger Haunebu III craft held 32 people. Says one of the Vril websites about the Haunebu:

Haunebu II from 1943-44
Diameter 26.3 m
Drive: Thule tachyonator 7b (antigravitation eqpm.)
Steuerung/steering: mag-field-impulser
Velocity: 6000-21000km/h
Capacity: 55 hrs in air
Crew 9 people

Haunebu III from sometime in 45
Diameter 71 m
Drive: Thule tachyonator 7b and Schuman levitators (antigravitation eqpm.)
Steuerung/steering: mag-field-impulser
Velocity: 7000-40000km/h
Capacity: 8 weeks in air
Crew 32 people

One Vril website, quoting from *Das Vril-Projekt. Der Endkampf um die Erde*[22] by Norbert Jürgen Ratthofer and Ralf Ettl, gives us some interesting information on the weapons used to arm the Haunebu as well as some information on the Andromeda craft. The Haunebu I was also called the RFZ 5. It was twenty-five meters across and carried a crew of eight. At first it reached a speed of 4,800 km/h, later up to 17,000 km/h. It was equipped with two 6 cm KSK ("Kraftstrahlkanonen," power ray guns in revolving towers) and four machine guns or cannons.

They also say that in early 1943 the Andromeda craft was being built in the Zeppelin works; it was 139 meters in length and could transport several saucer-shaped craft in its body for flights of long duration.

Ratthofer was the one who put a mystical spin on the documents that Ettl had received and interpreted much of the information from the Vril Society mystics and mediums being involved in the design and production of the craft. Many researchers see this as doubtful. Ratthofer apparently got hold of some documents that claimed the Vril Society mediums were attempting to contact exterrestrials on the planet Aldebaran.

Aldebaran is one of the easiest stars in the night sky to see. It is the brightest star in the constellation Taurus and is known as the "Eye of Taurus." The name Aldebaran is Arabic, which means "The Follower." This is because it appears to follow the Hyades star cluster that forms the head of the bull. Aldebaran is classified as a giant star and measured to be about 65 light-years from our sun. Aldebaran is believed to host, in it solar system, a planet several times the mass of Jupiter, named Aldebaran b. This large planet may have habitable moons.

Ratthofer says in *Das Vril-Projekt. Der Endkampf um die Erde* that Vril Society mediums had contacted extraterrestrials on a planet around the sun Aldebaran and would construct a craft to take them to that solar system by interdimensional means:

By Christmas 1943 an important meeting of the Vril-Gesellschaft took place at the seaside resort of Kolberg. The two mediums Maria Orsic and Sigrun attended. The

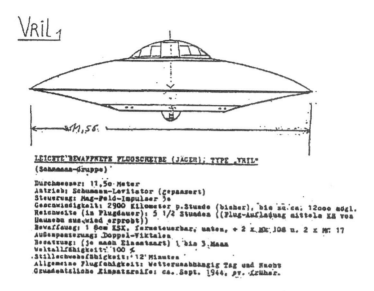

VRiL 1

LEICHTE BEWAFFNETE FLUGSCHEIBE (JÄGER): TYPE „VRIL"
(Schumann-Gruppe)

Durchmesser: 11,50 Meter
Antrieb: Schumann-Levitator (gepanzert)
Steuerung: Mag-Feld-Impulser 3e
Geschwindigkeit: 2900 Kilometer p.Stunde (bisher), bis zu ca. 12000 mögl.
Reichweite (in Flugdauer): 5 1/2 Stunden ((Flug-Aufladung mittels KS von
Hauneba aus wied erprobt))
Bewaffnung: 1 8cm KSK, ferngesteuert, unten, + 2 x MK 108 u. 2 x MG 17
Außenpanzerung: Doppel-Viktalen
Besatzung: (je nach Einsatzart) 1 bis 3 Mann
Weltallfähigkeit: 100 %
Stillschwebefähigkeit: 12 Minuten
Allgemeine Flugfähigkeit: Wetterunabhängig Tag und Nacht
Grundsätzliche Einsatzreife: ca. Sept. 1944, ev. früher.

VRIL 2 und VRIL 9 : Projektiert, aber nicht gebaut !

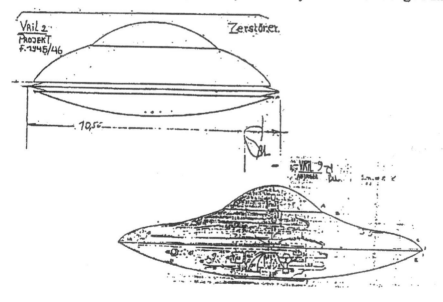

VRiL 2
PROJEKT
F. 1945/46

Zerstörer.

25

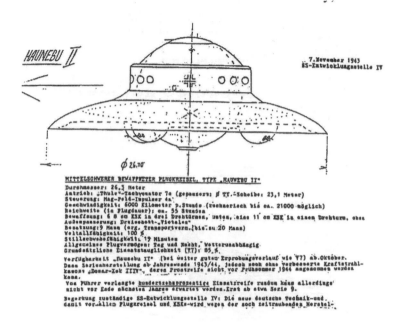

Plans for the Haunebu II.

main item on the agenda was the Aldebaran Project. The mediums had received precise information about the habitable planets around the sun Aldebaran and one began to plan a trip there. At a January 22, 1944 meeting between Hitler, Himmler, Kunkel (of the Vril Society) and Dr. Schumann this project was discussed. It was planned to send the VRIL 7 large-capacity craft through a dimension channel independent of the speed of light to Aldebaran.

A first test flight in the dimension channel took place in the winter of 1944. It barely missed disaster, for photographs show the Vril 7 after the flight looking "as if it had been flying for a hundred years." The outer skin was looking aged and was damaged in several places.

On February 14, 1944, the supersonic helicopter—constructed by Schriever and Habermohl under the V 7 project—that was equipped with twelve turbo-units BMW 028 was flown by the test pilot Joachim Roehlike at Peenemunde. The vertical rate of ascent was 800 meters per minute, it reached a height of 24,200 meters and in horizontal flight a speed of 2,200 km/h. It could also be driven with unconventional energy. But the helicopter never saw action since Peenemunde was bombed in 1944 and the subsequent move to Prague didn't work out either, because the Americans and the Russians occupied Prague before the flying machines were ready again.

In the secret archives of the SS the British and the Americans discovered during the occupation of Germany at the beginning of 1945—photographs of the Haunebu II and the Vril I crafts as well as of the Andromeda device. Due to President Truman's decision in March 1946 the war fleet command of the US gave permission to collect material of the German high technology experiments.

Under the operation Paperclip German scientists who had worked in secret were brought to the US privately, among them Viktor Schauberger and Wernher von Braun.

This same Vril website, quoting from *Das Vril-Projekt. Der Endkampf um die Erde*[22] continues to speak on the Vril and Haunebu craft and then suggests that a Vril-7 large capacity craft somehow attempted to reach the Aldebaran system just before the end of the war in the spring of 1945. Says the site:

A short summary of the developments that were meant to be produced in series:

The first project was led by Prof. Dr. mg. W. 0. Schumann of the Technical University Munich. Under his guidance seventeen disc-shaped flying machines with a diameter of 11.5 m were built, the so-called VRIL-1-Jager (Vril-1 fighters) that made 84 test flights. At least one VRIL-7 and one VRIL-7 large capacity craft apparently started from Brandenburg—after the whole test area had been blown up—towards Aldebaran with some of the Vril scientists and Vril lodge members.

The second project was run by the SS-W development group. Until the beginning of 1945 they had three different sizes of bell-shaped space gyros built: The Haunebu I,

25m diameter, two machines built that made 52 test flights (speed ca. 4,800 km/h). The Haunebu II, 32m diameter, seven machines built that made 106 test flights (speed ca. 6,000 km/h). The Haunebu II was already planned for series production. Tenders were asked from the Dornier and Junkers aircraft manufacturers, and at the end of March 1945 the decision was made in favor of Dornier. The official name for the heavy craft was to be Do-Stra (DOrnier STRAtospehric craft). The Haunebu III, 71 m diameter, only one machine built that made at least 19 test flights (speed ca. 7,000 km/h).

There are documents showing that the VRIL 7 large capacity craft was used for secret, still earth-bound, missions after it was finished and test flown by the end of 1944:

1. A landing at the Mondsee in the Salzkammergut in Austria, with dives to test the pressure resistance of the hull.

2. Probably in March and April 1945 the VRIL 7 was stationed in the "Alpenfestung" (Alpine Fortress) for security and strategic reasons, from whence it flew to Spain to get important personalities who had fled there safely to South America and "Neuschwabenland" to the secret German bases erected there during the war.

From this fascinating list of craft and their statistics, and information coming from the 1989 document dump in Britain that included all of the diagrams that we are seeing, we can gather that at the end of the war there were:

17 VRIL-1-Jager (Vril-1 fighters, seated crew of one)
2 (or more) VRIL-7 (Seated crew of 9 plus more?) There was also a large capacity Vril-7 that held more people.
2 Haunebu I (Seated 9 people?)
7 Haunebu II (The Haunebu II seated 9 crew, could hold up to 20)
1 Haunebu III (The Haunebu III seated 32 people, more may

have been built after the war)

2 or 3 Andromeda Craft (capacity 50 to 60, even more? Three craft were seen together over Finland in 1966, to be discussed later, and two craft were photographed together over Buenos Aires in 1965.

So we see that our Black Sun SS group has inherited not just a flotilla of black U-boats that have never surrendered, but they also have control of secret bases in various parts of the world, including Antarctica. On top of this they have some long-range aircraft and—incredibly—an assortment of flying saucers and cylindrical aircraft. These craft may well be fully functional submarines as well. They would seem to have at least 30 flying saucers and two cigar-shaped craft. More could have been built in the immediate years after the war at the secret factory-bases where parts of the craft were stored and could be assembled.

Ultimately, as we will see, the submarines and long-range aircraft were no longer useful to the Black Sun SS. But the flying saucers and cylindrical craft would prove to be very useful to them and allowed them to conduct a psychological war against the Western powers during the 40s, 50s, and 60s. This psychological warfare seemed to wane in the 1970s and 1980s, but was still present nonetheless. Naturally we will take a deep-dive in the

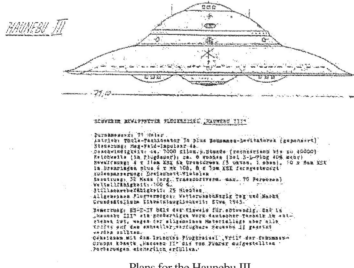

Plans for the Haunebu III.

UFO cases that seem to fit this narrative.

Hess, Haushofer and the Thule Society

Before the Vril Society was the earlier Thule Society, of which both Rudolf Hess and Karl Haushofer were members. Hess would go to Antarctica and then fly to Scotland in 1941 to convince the British to allow Hitler to have Europe while the Germans would guarantee Britain her colonial empire. Hess would later die in Spandau Prison in Berlin in 1987, its only prisoner. Haushofer would commit suicide with this wife in the months after the war.

Rudolf Hess was born in Alexandria, Egypt, on April 26, 1894, the son of a prosperous wholesaler and exporter. He came to Germany for the first time when he was fourteen. At the age of 20 he volunteered for the German Army at the outbreak of World War I in 1914. This was partly to escape the control of his domineering father who had refused to let him go to a university and instead wanted him to be part of the family business. Young Rudolf Hess had other ideas.

Hess was wounded twice during the war, and later became an airplane pilot. Hess was a large and powerful man, now a battle-hardened killer, and after the war he joined the Freikorps, a right-wing organization of ex-soldiers for hire. The Freikorps were involved in violently putting down Communist uprisings in Germany, often by having literal fistfights in the street.

Hess began attending the University of Munich where he studied political science. At the university he met Professor Karl Haushofer and joined the Thule Society, a secret society of sorts that espoused Nordic supremacy, mystical Germanic views of antiquity (such as a belief in Atlantis and Tibetan masters), and anti-Semitic views in the sense that the Jewish Old Testament was not the most important book in the world.

According to such authors as Nicholas Goodrick-Clarke[28] and Joscelyn Godwin[35] the Thule Society was originally a "German study group" headed by Walter Nauhaus, a wounded World War I veteran turned art student from Berlin who had become a keeper of pedigrees for the Germanenorden (or "Order of Teutons"), a secret society founded in 1911 and formally named in the following year.

30

Secret societies were booming in Germany during this period and Nauhaus moved to Munich in 1917 where his "Thule Society" was to be a cover name for the Munich branch of the Germanenorden, but a schism in the order caused events to develop differently. In 1918, Nauhaus was contacted in Munich by Rudolf von Sebottendorf who was an occultist and newly elected head of the Bavarian province of the schismatic offshoot known as the Germanenorden Walvater of the Holy Grail. The two men became associates in a recruitment campaign, and Sebottendorf adopted Nauhaus's Thule Society as a cover name for his Munich lodge of the Germanenorden Walvater at its formal dedication on August 18, 1918.

The logo of the Thule Society.

"Thule" was a land located by Greco-Roman geographers in the farthest north (often displayed as Iceland). The Latin term "Ultima Thule" is mentioned by the Roman poet Virgil in his pastoral poems called the *Georgics*. Thule may have been the original name for Scandinavia, although Virgil simply uses it as an expression for the edge of the known world to the north. The Thule Society identified Ultima Thule as a lost ancient landmass in the extreme north, near Greenland or Iceland, said by Nazi mystics to be the capital of ancient Hyperborea. Atlantis fitted into these myths as well and the Nazi mystics believed that Atlantis had existed in the Northern Sea, rather than in the Azores or the Caribbean.

Wikipedia says that Hitler biographer Ian Kershaw said that the organization's "membership list ...reads like a Who's Who of early Nazi sympathizers and leading figures in Munich," including Rudolf Hess, Alfred Rosenberg, Hans Frank, Julius Lehmann, Gottfried Feder, Dietrich Eckart, and Karl Harrer.

Joscelyn Godwin says in *Arktos*[35] that there was a similar group in France known as the Veilleurs (Vigilants) and that Hess may have met with them. Says Godwin:

> At the same time as Rudolf Hess was studying with Karl Haushofer, an Alsatian chemist called René Schwaller (1887-1961) was organizing some of his Theosophical friends in Paris into a group with the motto "Hierarchy, Fraternity, Liberty." Its first public appearance, in 1919, was with a review, *L'Affranchi*, numbered so as to seem like a continuation of the Theosophical Society's magazine of prewar days. The articles, signed by pseudonyms, treated the themes of social and spiritual renewal in the context of internationalist and somewhat mystical politics. There was praise for Woodrow Wilson's League of Nations, and discreet allusions were made to a coming Messiah.
>
> Within the Affranchis were two inner circles: one a "Centre Apostolique," Theosophical in nature; the other, formed in 1918, called the "Mystic Group Tala," a word that René Guénon translates as "the link." We know nothing of its activities, but can scarcely pass over the similarity of the name with Thule... in his first book, *Les Nombres* (1916), Schwaller had discussed just one symbol, besides the numbers and basic geometrical figures: the swastika, which he calls an accentuation of the cross within a circle, representing the archetypal formative movement of any body around it axis. There are other parallels between Schwaller's group, renamed in July 1919 "Les Veilleurs" (the Vigilants), and the Thule-descended parties organized by Hess and eventually headed by Hitler: their warrior mentality, their antijudaism, their uniform of dark shirts, riding breeches and boots (which Schwaller claimed to have designed), their messianism, and the tile of *Chef* given to their leaders.
>
> ...[Pierre Mariel] wrote that the young Rudolf Hess was a member of the Veilleurs. I cannot be sure whether to believed this or not; but it is worth considering. Hess, whose

movement in 1919 are virtually uncharted, was certainly aware of what was going on in Paris. The difference of language would have presented no difficulty either to Schwaller or to the young Hess, raised in Alexandria and educated in Switzerland. It is thinkable that, on his return to Germany, Hess set himself to create, upon the foundations of the Thule Society, a veritable parody of the Veilleurs. Likewise it is not merely thinkable but definite that Schwaller's world of ideas intersected at many points with that of Thule: a circumstance that has troubled more than one admirer of this Hermetic master.[35]

Whether Hess somehow helped start the Thule Society or not, Professor Karl Haushofer was certainly central to the secret society. He was a former general whose theories on expansionism and race formed the basis of the concept of Lebensraum—increased living space for Germans at the expense of other nations. He advocated extending Greater Germany to Moscow and the oilfields of Baku. Haushofer's teachings were very influential in Germany's ultimate invasion of Eastern Europe under the belief that the Germans needed to expand their territory and culture. Their allies in Japan had a similar belief in Japan's alarming Imperial expansion throughout eastern Asia and the Western Pacific.

Haushofer was well known to the German public. He was a prolific writer, publishing hundreds of articles, reviews, commentaries, obituaries and books, many of which were on Asian topics. He claimed to have been to Tibet and to have been initiated in secret Tibetan rites. If he had been to Tibet, he might have been instrumental in setting the SS airbase there. Perhaps he even flew on a Haunebu to the Tibetan SS base, as he was apparently very fond of the country. Haushofer also arranged for many leaders in the Nazi Party and in the German military to receive copies of his various works.

Louis Pauwels, in his book *Monsieur Gurdjieff*, describes Haushofer as a former student of George Gurdjieff. Gurdjieff also claimed to have been initiated in Tibet. Pauwels and others have said that Haushofer created the Vril Society from the Thule

Society.

The Nazi regime began to persecute Jews soon after its seizure of power. Hess's office was partly responsible for drafting Hitler's Nuremberg Laws of 1935, laws that had far-reaching implications for the Jews of Germany, banning marriage between non-Jewish and Jewish Germans and depriving non-Aryans of their German citizenship. Haushofer remained friendly with Hess, who protected Haushofer and his wife, who was part Jewish, from the strict racial laws implemented by the Nazis, which deemed her a "half-Jew." Hess issued documents exempting them from the new legislation.

During the prewar years, Haushofer was instrumental in linking Japan to the Axis powers, acting in accordance with the theories of his book *Geopolitics of the Pacific Ocean*. Haushofer apparently made several trips to Japan prior to 1941 and is said to have been part of a Japanese secret society known as the Black Dragon Society. Several American films and serials were made just prior to WWII and during the war that featured this alleged secret society. In some ways the Black Dragon Society was a Japanese version of the Vril Society (which Haushofer allegedly founded).

Along these lines, it is interesting to surmise that some of the UFO activity seen and photographed in Japan starting in the 1940s might have to do with Haunebu or Vril craft picking up members of the Black Dragon Society in the decades after the war. It may well be that Miguel Serrano was also a member of the Black Dragon Society and may have taken a Haunebu flight to Japan from India or even Chile.

In 1944, after the July 20 Plot to assassinate Hitler failed, Haushofer's son Albrecht (1903–1945), a close friend of Rudolf Hess, was implicated, in part because of his association with Hess. Albrecht went into hiding but was arrested on December 7, 1944 and put into the Moabit prison in Berlin. On the night of 22–23 April 1945, as Soviet troops were already reaching Berlin's eastern outskirts, he and other prisoners who were deemed part of the July 20 Plot, such as Klaus Bonhoeffer and Rüdiger Schleicher, were walked out of the prison with other prisoners by an SS-squad and killed with a gunshot wound to the neck. The only eyewitness to

34

Karl Haushofer with Rudolf Hess circa 1936.

these murders was another political prisoner, Herbert Kosney, who managed to move his head at the last moment so that the shot meant for his neck missed.

After the war Karl Haushofer continued to live at his Hartschimmelhof estate at Pähl/Ammersee in occupied West Germany. Starting on September 24, 1945, some four months after the war had ended, Haushofer was informally interrogated by Father Edmund A. Walsh on behalf of the Allied forces to determine whether he should stand trial for war crimes. After some time, Father Walsh determined that he had not committed any.

On the night of 10–11 March 1946, Karl Haushofer and his wife committed suicide in a secluded hollow on their estate. Both drank arsenic and his wife then hanged herself. In the book *The Morning of the Magicians*.[29] the authors claimed that Haushofer committed Japanese-style *hari-kari* suicide with a Japanese sword but Joscelyn Godwin in *Arktos*[35] says that this is one of a number of questionable things in that book.

Haushofer's influence on Rudolf Hess was considerable. Haushofer had befriended Hess and influenced him to join (or co-create) the Thule Society circa 1918. Then, on July 1, 1920,

35

Hess heard Adolf Hitler speak in a small Munich beer hall, and immediately joined the Nazi Party, becoming the sixteenth member. After his first meeting with Hitler, Hess said he felt "as though overcome by a vision." Hess was to become utterly devoted to Hitler and eagerly agreed with everything the shouting politician said. At early Nazi Party rallies, Hess was a formidable fighter who continually brawled with Marxist activists and others who violently attempted to disrupt Hitler's speeches.

In 1923, Hess took part in Hitler's failed Beer Hall Putsch. Hitler and the Nazis attempted to seize control of the government of Bavaria at this time and Hess was arrested and imprisoned along with Hitler at Landsberg Prison. While the two were in prison, Hess took dictation for Hitler's book, *Mein Kampf.* Hess also made some editorial suggestions regarding the organization of the Nazi Party, the notion of Lebensraum, plus material in the book about the historical role of the British Empire.

Both Hitler and Hess were released from prison in 1925 and Hess served for several years as the personal secretary to Hitler in spite of having no official rank in the Nazi Party. In 1932, Hitler appointed Hess an SS General and the Chairman of the Central Political Commission of the Nazi Party as a reward for his loyal service. On April 21, 1933, Hess was made Deputy Führer, a figurehead position with mostly ceremonial duties.

Hess was motivated by his loyalty to Hitler and a desire to be useful to him; he did not seek power or prestige or take advantage of his position to accumulate personal wealth. He and his wife Ilse lived in a modest house in Munich. Although Hess had less influence than other top Nazi officials, he was popular with the masses.

Hess then took part in the 1939 secret German expedition to Antarctica. In December of 1938 Hermann Göring launched an expedition to Antarctica in an effort to establish a naval base and whaling station on the polar continent. The New Swabia Expedition left Hamburg for Antarctica aboard MS *Schwabenland* on December 17, 1938. The MS *Schwabenland* was a freighter built in 1925 and renamed in 1934 after the Swabia region in southern Germany. The MS *Schwabenland* was also able to carry special aircraft that could be catapulted from the deck.

The expedition was top secret and was overseen by Göring himself. The Thule Society was also apparently involved. The expedition had 33 members plus the *Schwabenland*'s crew of 24. On January 19, 1939 the ship arrived at the Princess Martha Coast of Antarctica, in an area which had recently been claimed by Norway as Queen Maud Land, and began charting the region. Nazi German flags were placed on the sea ice along the coast. Naming the area Neuschwabenland after the ship, the expedition established a temporary base, and in the following weeks teams walked along the coast recording claim reservations on hills and other significant landmarks.

Upon his return in April of 1939 Hess reported to Göring and Hitler what had been discovered in Antarctica and whether they had found a suitable place for a German naval base. Such a base would serve commercial ships such as whalers as well as military ships and submarines.

This success must have one of the reasons that Hitler made Hess second in line to succeed him, after Hermann Göring, in September of 1939. During this same time, Hitler appointed Hess's chief of staff, Martin Bormann, as his personal secretary, a post formerly held by Hess. The German invasion of Poland happened at this time as well.

That Antarctica was part of Göring, Hess and Haushofer's plan for German expansion and the recreation of a global German colonial community is quite clear. Joseph Farrell quotes the German author Heinz Schön, who wrote a 2004 book in German called *Mythos Neuschwabenland: Für Hitler am Südpol: Die deutsche Antarktis-expedition 1938/39* and says:

> As commissioner for the Four-Year Plan, Göring knew the importance for Germany of whaling in Antarctica, and how essential it was to ensure this, and to open up new fishing grounds. It seemed high time for him to send a large expedition to Antarctica. On May 9, 1938, a plan for an Antarctic expedition, drawn up by the staff of his ministry, which was to be carried out in the Antarctic

summer of 1938/39, was presented to him. He approved, and commissioned Helmut Wohlthat as Minister-Director for special projects, with the preparation of the expedition, and conferred upon him all his powers of authority.[2]

As noted above, one of the main purposes of the secret expedition was to find an area in Antarctica for a German whaling station, as a way to increase Germany's production of fat. Whale oil was then the most important raw material for the production of margarine and soap in Germany and the country was the second largest purchaser of Norwegian whale oil, importing some 200,000 metric tons annually.

Germany did not want to be dependent on imports and it was thought that Germany would soon be at war, which would put a lot of strain on Germany's foreign currency reserves. The other goal of this secret expedition was to scout possible locations for a German naval base, and that would include a base for submarines.

Hess in Scotland and Aktion Hess

It is said that Hess was obsessed with his health to the point of hypochondria, consulting many doctors and other practitioners for what he described to his British captors as a long list of ailments involving the kidneys, colon, gall bladder, bowels and his heart. Hess was a vegetarian, like Hitler and Himmler, and he did not smoke or drink. He was a big believer in homeopathic medicines and Rudolf Steiner-type food that was "biologically dynamic." Hess was interested in music, enjoyed reading and loved to spend time hiking and climbing in the mountains with his wife, Ilse. He and his friend Albrecht Haushofer, Karl Haushofer's son, shared an interest in astrology, psychic powers, clairvoyance and the occult.

As the war progressed, Hitler's attention became focused on foreign affairs and the conduct of the war. Hess, who was not directly engaged in these endeavors, became increasingly sidelined from the affairs of the nation and from Hitler's attention. Martin Bormann had successfully supplanted Hess in many of his duties and essentially usurped the position at Hitler's side that Hess had once held. Hess later said that he was concerned that Germany would face a war on two fronts as plans progressed for Operation Barbarossa, the invasion of the Soviet Union scheduled to take place in 1941.

Hess decided to attempt to bring Britain to the negotiating table by travelling there himself to seek direct meetings with the members of the British government. He asked the advice of Albrecht Haushofer who suggested several potential contacts in Britain. Hess settled on fellow aviator

Himmler and Rudolf Hess at a rally, 1936.

Douglas Douglas-Hamilton, the Duke of Hamilton, whom he had met briefly during the Berlin Olympics in 1936.

On Hess's instructions, Haushofer wrote to Hamilton in September of 1940, but the letter was intercepted by MI5 and Hamilton did not see it until March of 1941. The Duke of Hamilton was chosen because he was one of the leaders of an opposition party that was opposed to war with Germany, and because he was a friend of Karl Haushofer. In a letter that Hess wrote to his wife dated November 4, 1940, he says that in spite of not receiving a reply from Hamilton, he intended to proceed with his plan to fly himself to Scotland and meet with Hamilton.

Hess began training on the Messerschmitt 110, a two-seater twin-engine aircraft, in October of 1940 under the chief test pilot at Messerschmitt. He continued to practice, including logging many cross-country flights, and found a specific aircraft that handled well—a Bf 110E-1/N—which was from then on held in reserve for his personal use. He asked for a radio compass, modifications to the oxygen delivery system, and large long-range fuel tanks to be installed on this plane, and these requests were granted in March 1941.

Hoping to save the Reich from disaster and redeem himself in the eyes of his Führer, Hess put on a Luftwaffe uniform and leather jacket (he was an SS General as well) and flew the fighter plane alone toward Scotland on a 'peace' mission on May 10, 1941, just before the Nazi invasion of the Soviet Union. After a final check of the weather reports for Germany and the North Sea, Hess took off at 17:45 from the airfield at Augsburg-Haunstetten in his specially prepared aircraft.

It was the last of several attempts by Hess to fly to Scotland, with previous efforts having been called off due to mechanical problems or poor weather. Wearing the leather flying suit, he brought along a supply of money and toiletries, a flashlight, a camera, maps and charts, and a collection of 28 different medicines, as well as dextrose tablets to help ward off fatigue, and an assortment of homeopathic remedies.

Hess flew north and when he reached the west coast of Germany near the Frisian Islands he turned and flew in an easterly direction for twenty minutes to stay out of range of British radar. He then took a heading of 335 degrees for the trip across the North Sea, initially at low altitude, but travelling for most of the journey at 5,000 feet (1,500 meters). At 20:58 he changed his heading to 245 degrees, intending to approach the coast of northeast England near the town of Bamburgh, Northumberland.

Flying north after reaching the west coast of Germany, Hess approached the coast of northeast England near the town of Bamburgh and realized that sunset was still nearly an hour away, and he needed darkness to fly past the coast. Hess backtracked, zigzagging back and forth for 40 minutes until it grew dark. Around this time his auxiliary fuel tanks were exhausted, so he released them into the sea. Shortly after that he was over Scotland and at 6,000 feet Hess bailed out and parachuted safely to the ground where he encountered a Scottish farmer and told him in English, "I have an important message for the Duke of Hamilton."

Now in captivity, Hess told his captors that he wanted to convince the British government that Hitler only wanted

Lebensraum for the German people and had no wish to destroy a fellow 'Nordic' nation. He also knew of Hitler's plans to attack the Soviet Union and wanted to prevent Germany from getting involved in a two-front war, fighting the Soviets to the east and Britain and its allies in the west.

During interrogation in a British Army barracks, Hess proposed that if the British would allow Nazi Germany to dominate Europe, then the British Empire would not be further molested by Hitler. Hess demanded a free hand for Germany in Europe and the return of former German colonies as compensation for Germany's promise to respect the integrity of the British Empire. Hess insisted that German victory was inevitable and said that the British people would be starved to death by a Nazi blockade around the British Isles unless they accepted his generous peace offer.

Before his departure from Germany, Hess had given his adjutant, Karlheinz Pintsch, a letter addressed to Hitler that detailed his intentions to open peace negotiations with the British. Pintsch delivered the letter to Hitler at the Berghof (Hitler's home in the Bavarian Alps where he spent a great deal of time during WWII and which became an important center of government) around noon on May 11. After reading the letter, Hitler let loose an angry yell that was heard throughout the entire Berghof, and sent for a number of his inner circle as he was concerned that a putsch (an attempt to overthrow the government) might be underway.

Hess's odd flight out of Germany, but not his destination or fate, was first announced by Munich Radio in Germany on the evening of May 12. On May 13 Hitler sent Foreign Minister Joachim von Ribbentrop to give the news in person to Mussolini, and on the same day the British press was permitted to release full information about the events. Ilse Hess finally learned that her husband had survived the trip when news of his fate was broadcast on German radio on May 14. Hitler publicly accused Hess of suffering from "pacifist delusions."

Hitler was worried that his allies, Italy and Japan, would perceive Hess's act as an attempt by Hitler to secretly open peace negotiations with the British. Hitler contacted Mussolini specifically to reassure him otherwise. Hitler ordered that the

41

German press should characterize Hess as a madman who made the decision to fly to Scotland entirely on his own, without Hitler's knowledge. Subsequent German newspaper reports described Hess as "deluded, deranged," indicating that his mental health had been affected by injuries sustained during World War I.

Some members of the government, such as Göring and Propaganda Minister Joseph Goebbels, believed this only made matters worse, because if Hess truly were mentally ill, he should not have been holding such an important government position, second in line to succeed the Führer.

Hitler stripped Hess of all of his party and state offices, and secretly ordered him shot on sight if he ever returned to Germany. He abolished the post of Deputy Führer, assigning Hess's former duties to Bormann, with the title of Head of the Party Chancellery. Bormann used the opportunity afforded by Hess's departure to secure significant power for himself. Meanwhile, Hitler initiated Aktion Hess, a flurry of hundreds of arrests of astrologers, faith healers and occultists that took place around June 9 and 10. The campaign was part of a propaganda effort by Goebbels and others to denigrate Hess and to make scapegoats of occult practitioners.

This process involved rounding up and imprisoning Hess's associates, including his wide-ranging network of occultists, astrologers, and ritualists. By positioning himself squarely at the center of the occult movement and then falling from grace so spectacularly, Hess doomed his fellow practitioners to a very sudden end. Everything from fortunetelling to astrology was outlawed, and the Nazi party's infatuation with the occult was over. However, the occult undercurrent remained in the SS, of which Hess had been a General.

One man who believed in Hitler's almost mythical status was a college professor named Johann Dietrich Eckhart. He was a member of the mysterious Thule Society, and he and many of the group's members believed that a German messiah was prophesied to enter history in the near future. This German leader would return the nation to its former glory, and avenge its defeat in the First World War, undoing the humiliation imposed upon the country with the Treaty of Versailles. Eckhart was a student of eastern mysticism and developed an ideology of a "genius superman," based on writings by the Völkisch author Jörg Lanz von Liebenfels. Eckhart met Hitler in 1919 and was certain that this man was the savior he believed Germany had been promised. The man went on to shape Hitler's ideologies considerably, sculpting the beliefs and worldview of the Nazi party. Eckhart died in 1923 before Hitler and the Nazis could come to power.

Hitler has often been seen as the subject of various prophecies and the Nazis had sought to use the prophecies of Nostradamus for their own benefit. Perhaps most notable is the Nostradamus verse in which he wrote, "Beasts ferocious with hunger will cross the rivers; the greater part of the battlefield will be against Hister," along with references to a "Child of Germany."

One person arrested during Aktion Hess was Karl Ernst Krafft, an astrologer and psychic who claimed he was clairvoyant. He was a committed supporter of the Nazi regime, but in 1939 he made a prediction of an assassination attempt against Adolf Hitler between the 7th and 10th of November of that year.

At the time his claims received little attention, but following the detonation of a bomb in the Munich Beer Hall on November 8, everything changed. Hitler had already left the building by the time the explosion occurred. It killed seven people and injured almost 70 more, but the target of the attack escaped unscathed. Soon afterward, word of Krafft's prophecy reached Rudolf Hess, and the fortune-teller was arrested. However, he managed to convince his interrogators that he was innocent of any wrongdoing and that his gifts of prophecy were genuine.

Krafft was well-liked by Hitler himself, and was ordered to begin an evaluation of the prophecies of Nostradamus that would favor the Nazi worldview. However, his own gifts were his undoing; as mentioned above, following Rudolf Hess's flight to Scotland, he was swept up in Aktion Hess. Krafft was arrested in 1941 and died in prison in 1945.

Vril Power and the Vril Staff

One has to wonder if Aktion Hess made the Vril Society become more secretive. The Thule Society had become inactive before Aktion Hess, barely surviving into the 1930s, and now it was the Vril Society that commanded the ear of powerful SS Generals such as Heinrich Himmler and Martin Bormann. All of these men were familiar with the concept of "vril." Vril was an energy and there was also a "Vril Staff."

The concept of an energy called vril comes from an 1871 novel titled *The Coming Race* by Edward Bulwer-Lytton, published anonymously in Britain. It has also been published as *Vril, the Power of the Coming Race.*[53] Vril was a fabled source of free and infinite energy, a sort of electricity all around us—similar to ether—that could be utilized. Something like static electricity but much more powerful and useful. The term vril was first used in the 1871 novel by Edward Bulwer-Lytton, *Vril: The Coming Race.*[53] The book is about an inner-earth dwelling race of superhumans called the Vril-ya, who master this vril energy for its healing, positive and destructive properties.

The novel centers on the narrator, who is an unnamed young, wealthy traveller who visits a friend who is a mining engineer. They explore a natural chasm in a mine that has been exposed by an exploratory shaft using a rope. The narrator reaches the bottom of the chasm safely, but the rope breaks and the mining engineer is killed. The narrator then finds his way into a subterranean world occupied by beings who seem to be advanced humans. He befriends the first being he meets, and this person guides him around a city that has features similar to ancient Egyptian architecture. The explorer meets his host's wife, two sons and daughter who learn to speak English by way of a makeshift dictionary. His guide comes toward him, and he and his daughter, Zee, explain who they are and how they function.

The narrator discovers that these beings, who call themselves Vril-ya, have great telepathic and other parapsychological abilities, such as being able to transmit information, get rid of pain, and put others to sleep.

The narrator soon discovers that the Vril-ya are descendants of an antediluvian civilization called the Ana, and live in networks of caverns that are linked by tunnels. Originally surface dwellers, they fled underground thousands of years ago to escape a massive

44

flood and gained greater power by facing and dominating the harsh conditions of the Earth. The place where the narrator descended houses 12,000 families, one of the largest groups. Their society uses vril and those that are spiritually elevated are able to master this power—an extraordinary force that can be controlled at will.

The uses of vril in the novel amongst the Vril-ya vary from destruction to healing. The Vril Staff can be used in focusing vril energy. According to Zee, the daughter of the narrator's host, vril can be changed into the mightiest agency over all types of matter, both animate and inanimate. It can destroy like lightning or replenish life, heal, or cure. It is used to rend ways through solid matter. Its light is said to be steadier, softer and healthier than that from any flammable material. It can also be used as a power source for animating mechanisms. Vril can be harnessed by use of the Vril Staff or mental concentration. In many ways it is similar to "the Force" talked about by Jedi Knights in the *Star Wars* movies.

The book describes a Vril Staff as an object in the shape of a wand or a staff that is used as a channel for vril. The narrator describes it as hollow with "stops," "keys," or "springs" in which vril can be altered, modified, or directed to either destroy or heal. The staff is about the size of a walking stick but can be lengthened or shortened according to the user's preferences. The appearance and function of the Vril Staff differs according to gender, age, etc. Some staves are more potent for destruction; others, for healing. The staves of children are said to be much simpler than those of sages; in those of wives and mothers, the destructive part is removed while the healing aspects are emphasized.

It seems that the Vril Staff is similar to the Egyptian staves and pillars such as the *Was* staff or the *Djed* pillar. An early version of this is also seen in Sumeria. In Bolivia, the figure of Virococha on the Sun Gate at Tiwanaku is holding two staffs on either side of his body and the first Inca, Manco Capac was said to carry a staff; he sunk it into the ground at Cuzco when he arrived at that place and declared it the capital of the new Inca Empire. We might also envision this staff as functioning in a similar manner to a caduceus, the symbol of a staff with two snakes intertwined around it and sometimes with wings at the top (the medical staff symbol—the

Rod of Asclepius—has only one snake on it). The caduceus is the staff carried by Hermes in Greek mythology and consequently by Hermes Trismegistus in Greco-Egyptian mythology. It is also depicted being carried in the left hand of Mercury, the Roman messenger of the gods.

Vril, the Power of the Coming Race was an important and popular book when it was published, and when it was learned that the anonymous author was actually the well-liked royal figure, Lord Edward Bulwer-Lytton, the book became even more popular. Other occultists of the time immediately recognized the imagery and concepts in the book as esoteric Atlantean science thinly veiled in a novel. These occultists, including Helena Blavatsky, accepted the book as based on occult truth, but did not believe in the civilization living in caverns beneath the planet (though they did believe in an underground world) as much as they did in ancient civilizations and the use of some electric force that was also able lift huge blocks of stone that weighed hundreds of tons each. Surely, only a force like vril could lift such massive blocks of granite with a force of anti-gravity that could magically float these blocks into place.

We see such gigantic blocks of stone all over the world and they are always very ancient. Such places as Baalbek, Egypt, Carnac, Stonehenge, Teotihuacan, Sacsayhuaman, Tiwanaku, Easter Island contain megalithic structures or statues that defy the logic of a modern engineer and make the idea of levitation a reality. Is vril power the ability to control gravity and the space around us?

The book and the concept of vril inspired the creation of the Vril Society out of the Thule Society. It was taught that vril was a "Cosmic Primal Force"—an exotic spiritual technology that would bring about a new Utopian era for humanity: the Rebirth of Atlantis. But little is known of the Vril Society and some historians doubt that it ever existed.

Godwin says that Willy Ley, a German rocket engineer who emigrated to the United States in 1937, published an article titled "Pseudoscience in Naziland" in 1947 in the magazine *Astounding Science Fiction*. He wrote that the high popularity of irrational convictions in Germany at that time explained how National Socialism could have fallen on such fertile ground. Among various pseudoscientific groups he mentions is one that looked for the power of vril:

> The next group was literally founded upon a novel. That group which I think called itself 'Wahrheitsgesellschaft'— Society for Truth—and which was more or less localized in Berlin, devoted its spare time looking for Vril. Yes, their convictions were founded upon Bulwer-Lytton's "The Coming Race." They knew the book was fiction, Bulwer-Lytton had used that device in order to be able to tell the truth about this "power." The subterranean humanity was nonsense, Vril was not. Possibly it had enabled the British, who kept it as a State secret, to amass their colonial empire. Surely the Romans had had it, enclosed in small metal balls, which guarded their homes and were referred to as *lares*. For reasons which I failed to penetrate, the secret of Vril could be found by contemplating the structure of an apple, sliced in halves.
>
> No I am not joking, that is what I was told with great solemnity and secrecy. Such a group actually existed, they even got out the first issue of a magazine which was to proclaim their credo.[35]

As far as the vril apple meditation, Godwin mentions that Rudolf Steiner suggests such a meditation in his books, which is to slice an apple in half across the middle which would reveal a five-pointed star. If an apple is sliced down the center starting from the stem, down through the middle, it reveals what some might visualize as a vortex-toroid. Either could be part of some "vril" meditation.

The Vril Society was discussed in 1960 by Jacques Bergier and Louis Pauwels in their book *The Morning of the Magicians*[29] originally published in French. In the book they claimed that the Vril Society was a secret community of occultists in pre-Nazi Berlin that was a sort of inner circle of the Thule Society, of which

Rudolf Hess was a member. They also thought that it was in close contact with the English group known as the Hermetic Order of the Golden Dawn. They also mention the Tibetans living in Berlin as discussed earlier. They do not mention a Nazi base in Tibet or Tibetans at any Arctic base as per Landig.

In a separate book, only published in French, *Monsieur Gurdjieff*, Louis Pauwels claims that a Vril Society was "founded by General Karl Haushofer, a student of Russian magician and metaphysician Georges Gurdjieff."

In *Black Sun,*[28] Nicholas Goodrick-Clarke refers to the research of the German author Peter Bahn. Bahn writes in his 1996 essay, "Das Geheimnis der Vril-Energie" ("The Secret of Vril Energy"), of his discovery of an obscure esoteric group calling itself the Reichsarbeitsgemeinschaft Das Kommende Deutschland (Imperial Working Society of the Coming Germany), or RAG for short. RAG taught its readers to meditate on the image of an apple sliced vertically in half, representing the map of universal free energy available from Earth's magnetic field. Using this knowledge they would harness vril, the "all-force of the forces of nature" by using "ball-shaped power generators" to channel the "constant flow of free radiant energy between outer space and Earth." This was just as Willy Ley recalled.

RAG published several small booklets on vril energy. One of the booklets was published in 1930 and entitled *Vril, Die Kosmische Urkraft* (Vril, the Cosmic Elementary Power) written

A photo of a Haunebu on the ground. Date unknown.

by a member of this Berlin-based group, under the pseudonym "Johannes Täufer" which in German translates to "John [the] Baptist."

The booklets describe Atlantean dynamo-technology superior to modern mechanistic science, saying that their spiritual technology and limitless vril energy is what enabled Egyptians and Mayans to build massive pyramids. Nikola Tesla spoke of similar things in his interviews with reporters at his apartment in New York. All manners of electrical power and uses were being examined by the Nazis, including "vril."

The booklets on vril were issued by the influential German astrological publisher by the name of Otto Wilhelm Barth (whom Bahn believes was "Täufer"). The 60-page pamphlet says little of the group other than that it was founded in 1925 to study the uses of vril energy.

So we see how RAG was really what we call "the Vril Society" and that it was a real organization. They became known as the Vril Society because of the early Willy Ley article in 1947. It was the publication of the notable booklet on vril that caught people's notice at the time, in professor Ley, who left Germany in 1937 like many academics. The 1925 date is interesting as that date is often given as to the vague when the Thule Society stopped its meetings. It seems that the inner core of the Thule Society became RAG and was nicknamed the Vril Society. They apparently operated from 1925 until the end of the war in 1945.

At this time, with Germany being overrun by the Allies from the east and west, this society apparently dissolved and some members literally flew off in flying saucers to secret SS bases around the world (Karl Haushofer committed suicide). The SS airbase in Tibet would have been a safe place in 1945 when Tibet was still an independent country. Any relationship that the SS had with Tibet would have continued as it was—even after the war— at least for a few years and probably into the 1950s. China invaded Tibet—a de facto country allied with Germany during the war—in October of 1950, but it took years to secure even the most basic parts of the country, such as border areas and major towns that are stretched out over vast unpopulated areas, similar to Patagonia.

So, we see that the Vril Society was a real secret society that published at least two booklets on "vril power." When one adds the work of Nikola Tesla and the many designs for electric aircraft, including descriptions by Tesla, one can see that the war machine of the Nazis could use some technology like this if it were shown to be practical. Other scientists in Germany, Austria and elsewhere were working on exotic technologies as has been alleged of Guglielmo Marconi and his associates. Death rays were popular during the 1920s and 1930s and the Nazis were aware of these technological studies and theories, and wanted to pursue them. Allegedly the Americans were working on the so-called Philadelphia Experiment, which is beyond the scope of this book.

Once elements of the SS were interested in such devices as "the Bell" and electric flying saucers, funding for these programs would be delivered, and prototypes—at great expense—were created. It seems to have been in the 1930s that money was invested in the creation of the Haunebu and Vril craft, as well as in other experiments such as the Bell. Meanwhile, the development of V-1 rockets, long-range bombers and the atomic bomb proceeded on a separate track.

That a Haunebu craft was already being tested in the 1930s can be seen in a YouTube video of a 1939 flight test. The video can be seen at https://youtu.be/jywwCaph25c (or do a search for Haunebu Test Flight) and it is an amazing piece of film. The YouTube video is one minute and ten seconds in length but the footage of the Haunebu is only about 13 seconds long. The rest of the video shows it over and over again, zoomed and slowed down. The video shows a Haunebu lifting off in an area where there are hangars and other buildings, hovering in the air for a few seconds, and then landing. A banner beneath the video says: HAUNEBU Test Flight, NAZI Germany, 1939.

The footage looks authentic and it adds credence to the early creation of the Haunebu and Vril craft before the war. As long as we can agree that many UFO photos and descriptions are valid and that something is clearly going on in this regard, then we see how the stories, including photos, diagrams and film footage, of German flying saucers comprise a credible subject. The Vril

Society is also a credible subject, whatever its activities were.

Some stories of the Vril Society may not be so credible however, such as the tales of the Vril Maidens. Nicholas Goodrick-Clarke tells us in his scholarly book *Black Sun*[28] that the story of the Vril Maidens supposedly begins in 1919 when an inner group of Thule and Vril Society members held a meeting in Vienna, where they met with a psychic named Maria Orsic. She allegedly presented transcripts of automatic writing she received in a language that she didn't understand. The language was found to be ancient Sumerian, allegedly channeled from a planet in the Aldebaran solar system—Aldebaran being the brightest star in the constellation of Taurus—68 light years away from Earth.

The Vril Maidens—an inner circle of young female psychic mediums, led by the beautiful Maria Orsic—kept their hair long because they believed it to be an extension of the nervous system which acted as an antenna when telepathically communicating between worlds.

The Vril Maidens

The Vril Maidens were said to channel blueprints for time travel machines, anti-gravity technology, and more. Over the decades this supposedly led to the development of the Vril and Haunebu series of anti-gravity flying saucers.[28]

According to information on a "vril site" that promotes Maria Orsic on the Internet, the Vril Society was formed by a group of female psychic mediums led by the Thule Gesellschaft medium Maria Orsitsch (Orsic) of Zagreb. She claimed to have received communication from Aryan aliens living on Alpha Centauri, in the Aldebaran system. Allegedly, these aliens had visited Earth and settled in Sumeria, and the word "vril" was formed from the ancient Sumerian word "Vri-Il" ("like god"). Says the text:

> A second medium was known only as Sigrun, a name etymologically related to Sigrune, a Valkyrie and one of Wotan's nine daughters in Norse legend. The Society allegedly taught concentration exercises designed to awaken the forces of Vril, and their main goal was to

51

achieve Raumflug (Spaceflight) to reach Aldebaran. To achieve this, the Vril Society joined the Thule Gesellschaft to fund an ambitious program involving an inter-dimensional flight machine based on psychic revelations from the Aldebaran aliens. Members of the Vril Society are said to have included Adolf Hitler, Alfred Rosenberg, Heinrich Himmler, Hermann Göring, and Hitler's personal physician, Dr. Theodor Morell. These were original members of the Thule Society which supposedly joined Vril in 1919. The NSDAP (NationalSozialistische Deutsche ArbeiterPartei) was created by Thule in 1920, one year later. Dr. Krohn, who helped to create the Nazi flag, was also a Thulist. With Hitler in power in 1933, both Thule and Vril Gesellschafts allegedly received official state backing for continued disc development programs aimed at both spaceflight and possibly a war machine.

After 1941 Hitler forbade secret societies, so both Thule and Vril were documented under the SS E-IV unit. The claim of an ability to travel in some inter-dimensional mode is similar to Vril claims of channeled flight with the Jenseitsflugmaschine (Other World Flight Machine) and the Vril Flugscheiben (Flight Discs).

It is difficult to verify this information on the Vril Society or Maria Orsic. Some believe that she was born in Zagreb on October 31, 1894 and visited Rudolf Hess in Munich in 1924. She is said to have disappeared in 1945. An Internet biography of her states:

> In December 1943 Maria attended, together with Sigrun, [another psychic, even more mysterious than Orsic] a meeting held by Vril at the seaside resort of Kolberg. The main purpose of the meeting was to deal with the Aldebaran project. The Vril mediums had received precise information regarding the habitable planets around the sun Aldebaran and they were willing to plan a trip there. This project was discussed again the 22nd January 1944 in a meeting between Hitler, Himmler, Dr. W. Schumann

(scientist and professor in the Technical University of Munich) and Kunkel of the Vril Gesellschaft. It was decided that a *Vril 7 Jaeger* would be sent through a dimension channel independent of the speed of light to Aldebaran. According to N. Ratthofer (writer), a first test flight in the

A supposed photo of Maria Orsic.

dimension channel took place in late 1944.

Maria Orsic disappeared in 1945. The 11th of March of 1945 an internal document of the Vril Gesellschaft was sent to all its members; a letter written by Maria Orsic. The letter ends: "niemand bleibt hier" [no one stays here]. This was the last announcement from Vril. It is speculated they departed to Aldebaran.

It seems that the Vril Society was real but the stories about Maria Orsic and the contact with the planet Aldebaran are doubted by many including Nicholas Goodrick-Clarke.[28] Some researchers claim that nothing can be found about Maria Orsic before 1990. However, it does seem that one of the saucer craft built by the Germans was given the name Vril. Henry Stevens says:

> The late Heiner Gehring wrote to me that he had been told that the efforts of the Vril Society at channeling continued after the war, until 1946. It is no secret that in the lore propounded by Ralf Ettl and Norbert Juergen-Ratthofer elements of the Nazi regime allegedly associated with the Vril Society launched an interdimensional flight to an extraterrestrial world seeking help in the Second World War. This flight communicated, allegedly, via medial transmission (or channeling). This medial contact, according to Heiner's source, continued until 1946 with the living crew of that ship when it was abruptly terminated. Of course, there is no way to verify any of this.[46]

More likely, Vril craft were not sent through some interdimensional doorway to Aldebaran, nor did members of the Vril Society probably escape to this planet. Far more likely, if members of the Vril Society had something to do with the actual manufacture and operation of these flying saucers, they would have escaped to various SS bases still in operation at the end of the war and afterward. Since the SS was clearly in control of these craft, plus some long-range aircraft and submarines, any Vril Society members wanting to escape from Germany at the end of the war would have had to hitch a ride on one of these SS special craft. It is likely that most Vril Society members in Germany and Austria at the end of the war remained where they were, like Professor Karl Haushofer, allegedly one of the founding members of the Vril Society.

What seems to be powering the Haunebu and the Vril is some sort of plasma (electrified gas such as mercury) that is gyroscopic and anti-gravity within a closed system. The foo fighters were apparently miniature versions of these pulsing, brightly lit balls that were flying through the sky. A Haunebu contained one central plasma gyro and three smaller ones around it as directional gyros.

With the Third Reich collapsing—the failure to take the oilfields at Baku a major turning point—many Germans faced the destruction of their country and more loss of life. Some Vril Society members must have been in the parties that fled via Haunebu or Vril—maybe even in the very large Andromeda Craft. They could have gone north, to still-functioning bases in Norway, like Banak, and on to Greenland or the Blue Island in the Canadian Arctic. But in these places they would be stuck in military bases, not the ideal spot for people trying to restart their lives. They might have gone by a southern route, one that ultimately took them to South America. Here they could live a fairly normal life, with restaurants, homes, parks, movie theaters, and other recreation. And, they would be working to reconstitute the Reich in Latin America, particularly in Argentina, Chile and Paraguay.

These agents and others were now part of the Black Sun underground world. There were U-boats, flying saucers, secret bases in Antarctica and elsewhere that still functioned in this extra-territorial Reich. While some of the members tried to live a semi-normal life in Argentina and elsewhere, they were always looking over their shoulders, walking down back alleys, hiding in doorways, wondering if they were being followed. They had mistresses and friends, they carried guns, they met with other Black Sun operatives in cafes, bars, city parks, or hotel rooms. Perhaps they were picked up from time to time to take part in some operation or to visit some of the bases still operational to keep them loyal subjects of the Black Sun network.

The systematic take over of Latin American countries is a theme in many of the books and articles on the SS and Nazi activities after the war. They could use the Haunebu or the Vril craft for various smuggling operations, and as vehicles for their constant psyops against the West. They had a need to keep most of these bases operational for some years after the war, but it seems that many were ultimately abandoned, especially the submarine bases. We see this in the story of the Canary Islands U-boat base.

The Secret Flights of Squadron 200

Aiding in the preparation for these "secret cities of the Black Sun" was Squadron 200 which made secret flights from Germany and Norway to Japan and from Europe to the Canary Islands. Stevens says that the Ju-390 flew to Japan, over the polar route, from a secret base in Norway. The Ju-390 left Norway from a base in the far north at Bardufoss, flew over the north pole, over the Bering Strait, then down the east side of the Kamchatka Peninsula to the island of Pamushiro which was within the Japanese Empire. From there it flew over Japanese-controlled Manchoutikuo to Tokyo. Stevens says confirmation of this flight comes from a radio report by the Japanese Attachés for Marine Aircraft in Germany, dated March 21, 1945. Says Stevens:

> The purpose was to transport German high-tech weaponry secrets and some personnel involved with this work. This was exactly the same purpose as the famous U-234 voyage and the two methods of communication can be considered complimentary, each part of a larger whole. There may have been and probably were more flights involving the Ju-390 to Japan just as there were probably other U-boats delivering technology to Japan besides U-234.[46]

Stevens says that the Focke-Wulf Fw-200 Condor was also used in the many long-range flights. This was originally a four-engine passenger aircraft but the Luftwaffe adapted it for long-range reconnaissance and even as an anti-shipping bomber.

Besides extensive work in the North Sea and polar regions surrounding Norway, this aircraft also transported supplies all the way to Stalingrad in 1942.

Stevens also says that in 1944 there was a conference at Strasbourg of SS officers and other Nazi officers at which it was agreed that blueprints, machine tools, secret weapons, specialty steel, gold, money and scientists were to be transported outside the Reich for future use. The means of this transfer was the deployment of Geschwader 200 (Squadron 200), an elite flying group of young men, many of whom had lost their families. British intelligence was known to use orphans as part of their most dangerous operations (Agent 007 is said to be an orphan by author Ian Fleming). On both sides, the most dangerous missions were best done by those without families.

Geschwader 200 was the first choice of the Luftwaffe for truly dangerous missions. Geschwader 200 was, at one point, scheduled to fly the manned version of the V-1 rocket to high value targets. This would have certainly meant the loss of almost all of the pilots, as the men themselves knew. They were, briefly, the Kamikaze squadron of the Third Reich. This project was abandoned but Geschwader 200 was involved in a suicide attack on a bridge spanning the Oder River in the final stages of the war in an attempt to slow the Soviet advance. Says Stevens about the transfer of people and goods out of the Third Reich:

> In the transfer specified in the Strasbourg agreement, the goods and people necessary were loaded aboard Condor aircraft by Geschwader 200 and flown from points within the Reich to Madrid, then on to Cadiz. Cadiz is on the Mediterranean Sea. From there transport to South America was accomplished using both Fw-200 Condors of Geschwader 200 and U-boats. Additionally, the Azores or the Canary Islands were used as a stopover base.[46]

These Focke-Wulf Condors could make long journeys, but could not fly as far as the Amerika-bomber-type planes, such as the Ju-390, being developed at the end of the war. But flights to

Spain and then to the Canary Islands or the Spanish Sahara were easily within their range, and the Condors could even fly from the Canary Islands to South America where they would probably land at a private airfield in Argentine Patagonia where Germans had large tracts of land.

Stevens says that the researcher/writer Friedrich Georg claimed the following tasks for the Ju-390 aside from being a long-range bomber:

1. Secret intelligence operations.
2. An escape vehicle for the Nazi leadership.
3. A long-distance delivery vehicle connecting to Japan.

Stevens mentions that the idea of giving the design for the long-range plane to the Japanese is included in number three above. The Nazis were happy to give the Japanese their technology and the Japanese would have found the Ju-390 aircraft useful, as it would have traversed the Pacific just as it would the Atlantic. Stevens also mentions that the SS commander Dr. Hans Kammler was said to have escaped Germany at the end of the war in a Ju-390, supposedly flying to South America.

Such high commanders in the SS would have had the ability to get the latest in aerospace to get them where they wanted to go. In the case of the end of the war catastrophe scenario these high ranking SS officers—and there were hundreds of them, even thousands—they would be given priority on the many escape vehicles used by the SS at the end of the war, including submarines, long-range aircraft, and even flying saucers.

Chapter 2

The Extra-Territorial Reich

Though I've flown one hundred thousand miles
I'm feeling very still
And before too long I know it's time to go
Our commander comes down back to earth, and knows
—*Space Oddity*, David Bowie

Even before WWII began, the Germans started creating special secret bases for their use outside of Germany. These secret bases were said to be in Antarctica, Tibet, Greenland, the Canary Islands, the Canadian Arctic, Norway, and Finland among other places. These secret bases soon expanded into Argentina, Chile, and other South American countries in the years immediately after the war.

Also immediately after the war, there was a lot of activity in Scandinavia, mainly in Sweden and Finland, involving unidentified flying objects looking like rockets or large airplanes. I have discussed in my other books the secret bases in Greenland, the Canadian Arctic, the Canary Islands and Antarctica, but not really the secret base that was apparently in northern Finland.

It is still largely a mystery what went on in the very north of Norway and Finland during the war. Norway was occupied by the Germans but Finland was a willing partner of the Third Reich and was an enthusiastic partner in the Axis powers during WWII along with Romania, Hungary and other countries. Finland's primary enemy was Russia, then the Soviet Union, and they were glad to join the Germans in their fight on the Eastern Front.

Let us look at the German involvement in northern Scandinavia.

The Mystery of Northern Finland

Finland joined the Axis powers in 1941 in order to fight against Russia and the Soviet Union. But on September 19, 1944 Finland signed the Moscow Armistice which made peace with the Soviet Union, and Finland was obligated to break diplomatic ties with Germany and expel or disarm any German soldiers remaining in Finland.

There was actual fighting between Germany and Finland—effectively from September to November 1944—in Finland's northernmost region, Lapland. It should be noted that Finland does not have a coast on the Arctic Ocean and essentially Norway and Russia landlock the country.

The German Wehrmacht had anticipated this turn of events and planned an organized withdrawal to German-occupied Norway, as part of Operation Birke (Birch). The evacuation proceeded peacefully at first but the Finns escalated the situation into warfare on September 28, 1944 because of Soviet pressure to adhere to the terms of the armistice. After a series of minor battles, the war came to an effective end in November 1944, when all of the German troops had reached Norway or the border area and took fortified positions. The last German soldiers left Finland on April 27, 1945, shortly before the end of World War II in Europe, which was May 8.

The XVIII Mountain Corps in northern Finland attacking behind Panzer cover, 1942.

As early as the summer of 1943, the German high command Oberkommando der Wehrmacht (OKW) began to plan for the eventuality that Finland might negotiate a separate peace agreement with the Soviet Union. The Germans planned to withdraw their forces northward in order to shield the nickel mines near Petsamo. During the winter of 1943–1944, the Germans improved the roads from northern Norway to northern Finland by extensive use of prisoner-of-war labor in certain areas. Casualties among the laboring prisoners were high, partially because many of them had been captured in southern Europe and were still in summer uniform. The Germans declined to give them warmer clothing.

The Germans surveyed defensive positions in northern Finland and Norway and planned to evacuate as much materiel as possible from the region, and meticulously prepared for withdrawal. In June of 1944, the Germans started to construct fortifications against a possible enemy advance from the south.

The German 20th Mountain Army had been fighting the Soviet Karelian Front since Operation Barbarossa along the 430-mile (700-km) stretch from the Oulu River to the Arctic Ocean. By 1944 the division was comprised of 214,000 soldiers, a considerable amount of them under SS formations. The number of active troops in Finland decreased quickly as they withdrew to Norway. The army had 32,000 horses and mules and 17,500–26,000 motorized vehicles as well as a total of 200,000 tons in rations, ammunition and fuel to last for six months.

As the Finns wanted to avoid devastation of their country, and the Germans wished to avoid hostilities, both sides strove for the evacuation to be performed as smoothly as possible. By September 15, 1944, a secret agreement had been reached by which the Germans would inform the Finns of their withdrawal timetable, and the Finns would then allow the Germans to use Finnish transportation for evacuation as well as to destroy roads, railroads and bridges behind their withdrawal.

The lack of Finnish aggression against the Germans did not go unnoticed by the Allied Control Commission monitoring adherence to the Moscow Armistice and the USSR threatened to occupy Finland if the terms of expelling or disarming the Germans were not met. Therefore on September 28, 1944, Finnish advance

61

A sign from the SS in northern Finland during their withdrawal, 1944.

units first issued a surrender demand and then opened fire on a small German rear-guard contingent.

This took the Germans by surprise as the Finns had previously agreed to warn them should they be forced to take hostile action against them. After the incident, the Germans told the Finns they had no interest in fighting them, but would not surrender. Another incident took place on September 29 at a bridge crossing the Olhava River between Kemi and Oulu. Finnish troops, who had been ordered to take the bridge intact, were attempting to disarm explosives rigged to the bridge when the Germans detonated them, demolishing the bridge and killing, among others, the Finnish company commander.

When Allied advances in Germany continued, German high command OKW and 20th Mountain Army leadership asserted that it would be perilous to maintain positions in Lapland and east of Lyngen municipality in northern Norway. The Minister of Armaments and War Production, Albert Speer, had determined that German nickel stores were sufficient and holding the nickel mines at the town of Petsamo in northern Finland was unnecessary. Preparations for further withdrawal from Finland into Norway began.

On October 4, 1944 Hitler accepted the proposal for the withdrawal from northern Finland. The plan was codenamed

Operation Nordlicht. Operation Nordlicht called for a rapid and strictly organized withdrawal to an area directly behind Lyngen Fjord in Norway, which would take placce under pressure from harassing enemy forces, both Russian and Finnish. As the Germans withdrew towards the town of Rovaniemi, a road junction point in Lapland, and Norway, movement was mostly limited to the immediate vicinity of Lapland's three main roads, which constricted military activities considerably. As Finnish infantry

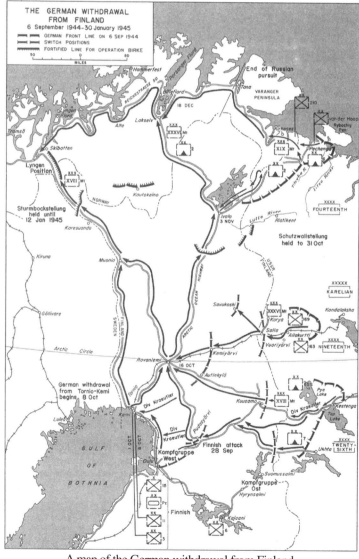

A map of the German withdrawal from Finland.

63

A map of the Arctic.

slowly picked their way through the dense woods and marshland, the motorized German units would simply drive away and take up positions further down the road.

The Germans initially concentrated on destroying governmental buildings in the Finnish town of Rovaniemi, but the fire spread and destroyed housing beyond that. German attempts to fight the fire failed and a train loaded with ammunition caught fire at the railroad station on October 14, resulting in an explosion that spread the fire throughout the primarily wooden buildings of the

64

town. Most of the town of Rovaniemi was destroyed.

For most practical purposes, the war in Lapland between Finland and Germany concluded in early November 1944. After holding the town of Tankavaara, the Germans swiftly withdrew from northeastern Lapland at Karigasniemi on November 25, 1944. The Finnish Jaeger Brigade pursuing them had by then been mostly demobilized. In northwestern Lapland, only four battalions of Finnish troops were left on November 4 and by February 1945, there were a mere 600 soldiers.

The Germans continued their withdrawal in early November 1944, ultimately moving to the fortified Sturmbock-Stellung position along the Lätäseno River, which was 62 miles (100 kilometers) from Norway, on November 26.

The German 7th Mountain Division held these positions until January 10, 1945 when positions at Lyngen Fjord in Norway were manned. Some German positions defending Lyngen extended over to Kilpisjärvi on the Finnish side of the border, but no major activity occurred.

The 20th Mountain Army successfully withdrew most of its over 200,000 men as well as supplies and equipment from Lapland to continue defending the occupied Finnmark province from the USSR. The casualties of the conflict were relatively limited with Finland suffering 774 killed, 262 missing and around 2,904 wounded while Germany experienced around 1,000 deaths and 2,000 wounded. 1,300 German soldiers became prisoners of war and were handed over to the USSR according to the terms of the armistice. However, the German operations of a delayed retreat left Lapland devastated. In addition to 3,100 buildings demolished elsewhere in Finland, estimates of destroyed infrastructure in Lapland include 14,900 buildings representing around 40–46 percent of Lapland's property; 470 km (290 miles) of railway; 9,500 km (5,900 miles) of road; 675 bridges; 2,800 road storm drains; and 3,700 km (2,300 miles) of phone and telegram lines.

The reconstruction of Lapland lasted through the 1950s, and the railway network was not functional until 1957. In addition to the demolished infrastructure, the Wehrmacht extensively laid mines and explosives in the area.

The Wehrmacht completely withdrew from Finland by April

27, 1945 and a Finnish battle patrol raised the flag on the three-country cairn between Norway, Sweden and Finland to celebrate the end of the wars. Germany would surrender 13 days later on May 8. There was never an official peace agreement signed between Finland and Germany. In 1954 the Finnish Government noted that "hostilities had ceased" and thus "the war has ended."

However the UFO activity and "ghost rocket" activity was just beginning. It would seem that during the years that Germany occupied both Norway and northern Finland (by invitation) they were busy constructing one of their secret bases somewhere in the mountains along the border of the two countries, an area that they exclusively controlled. They may have originally had a railroad spur that went to this secret hangar inside of a mountain but this track was removed along with all of the railway track on the Finnish side. Inside of this secret mountain hangar would be the Haunebu, Vril and Andromeda craft.

This secret base may have still been in use as late as the 1960s. In my book *Andromeda: The Secret Files* I describe the curious sighting of three cigar-shaped objects over Finland in December of 1966.

During that sighting three different Finnair crews observed a formation of three cigar-shaped objects accompanied by 10 lighter and darker round objects. This strange grouping of UFOs was first observed flying over Hamburg, Germany, and then later over Mariehamn (formerly Maarianhamina), Finland. Mariehamn is the capital of Åland, a Finnish island west of Helsinki between Finland and Sweden. Later, another Finnair Caravelle jetliner spotted the same formation near Helsinki-Oulu, Finland, 250 miles from Mariehamn.

It is thought that these objects were flying north, possibly to the secret base in the very far north. That three of the large cigar-shaped Andromeda craft were flying together with what appears to be three Haunebu and seven of the smaller Vril craft is remarkable. A photo does exist of two cigar-shaped Andromeda craft over Buenos Aires taken in 1965. The two objects hung together over the city for ten minutes and then departed.

Also in 1966, six objects were seen by the flight crew of an East African Airways DC-3 flying between Mombasa and Nairobi,

A famous photograph of a Vril craft taken at Varnamo, Sweden on March 21, 1974.

Kenya. This sighting apparently included at least one of the large cigar-shaped Andromeda craft. (Source: Bill Yenne, *UFO: Evaluating the Evidence*.[26])

One of the most famous color photos of a flying saucer was taken at Varnmo, Sweden, on March 21, 1974. The photo was taken by Christer Sundström, 15 years old, who was lying in his bed, home from school with chickenpox. He was looking out the window of his room towards the neighbor's house. All he could see was a dark grey sky. But then a dark object, which he at first thought was an eagle, started to circle above the roof of the neighbor's house. It disappeared into a cloud and then came back again. He went to the window and managed to get one good photo of the small saucer very much like a Vril craft. (Source: *UFO Sweden*, Claus Svahn, 2000.)

And finally from that same year, we have the claim that on March 20, 1974, a salesman named Adrian Sanchez was making the rounds visiting his customers in Spain when he encountered a cigar-shaped airship hovering in the air that he calculated to be between 150 to 200 meters long. The Andromeda craft was 139 meters according to the plans from the Ettl documents. Said Sanchez:

I noticed how a large door opened in the tail end of the ship and how a formation of three smaller ships, in the shape of yo-yos, approximately 8 meters long, proceeded to enter the larger one; but the last one turned and came slowly towards me.[22]

This sighting in broad daylight in a rural part of Spain, near Seville in the south, indicates that the back part of the Andromeda opens up into a great door and the Vril-like craft are able to fly inside and dock. This operation in 1974 is particularly intriguing because Spain, though neutral, was always a pro-Nazi country and many ex-Nazis lived in Spain after the war including Otto Skorzeny.

In Landig's first novel, *Götzen gegen Thule* (1971), the two protagonists, both SS officers, are flown from the Banak airbase in the Finnmark area of Norway to Point 103, a secret facility that had been built in the Canadian Arctic. At this secret base delegates from around the world have been flown via the large Haunebu saucer for a special conference. It is a submarine base and an airbase. One wonders if Point 103 had a long runway for large aircraft? If not, it was only accessible via submarine or flying saucer. Later in Landig's novel the base is dismantled and its contents moved to South America.

So, Landig's men may have taken a Haunebu to the secret base called Point 103. This craft may have taken off from the base at Banak but it may have been housed at the secret mountain hangar in the mountains of northern Norway or Finland.

It was claimed that flights from Banak took place to Japan on several occasions. These flights would have been polar flights that later landed on the northern Japanese island of Hokkaido.

Other flights from the Banak airbase may have been to Svalbard also called Spitsbergen. Svalbard may have contained a secret Nazi submarine base. Banak seemed to be an important base for long-range flights and patrolling the northern Arctic route to Russia. It is intriguing to think that an undiscovered U-boat base may be on the island of Svalbard. Was Svalbard the destination of the curious flight of three cigar-shaped and ten disc craft that was seen over Finland in 1966?

Svalbard, known to both the British and Germans as Spitsbergen, is directly north of Norway and has a very small population, mainly coal miners and weather monitors. The islands were little affected by the German invasion of Norway in April 1940. The small settlements continued to operate as before, mining coal and monitoring the weather without a German military invasion.

In July 1941, following the German invasion of the Soviet Union, Britain's Royal Navy reconnoitered the islands with a view to using them as a base of operations to send supplies to northern Russia, but the idea was rejected as impractical. Instead, with the agreement of the Soviets and the Norwegian government in exile, the British military evacuated the Norwegian and Soviet settlements on Svalbard in August 1941. The British called this Operation Gauntlet and most of the facilities were destroyed to keep the Germans from using them.

Meanwhile, the Germans responded to the destruction of the weather station by establishing a reporting station of their own, codenamed "Banso," in October 1941. This was chased away in November by a visit from four British warships, but later returned. A second German station, "Knospel," was established at Ny-Ålesund in 1941, remaining until 1942.

The Norwegian government in exile decided it would be important politically to establish a garrison in the islands, which was done in May 1942 during Operation Fritham. After the arrival of the Fritham force in May 1942, the German unit at Banso was evacuated.

In September 1943 Operation Zitronella launched a German task force, which included the battleship Tirpitz, to attack and destroy the settlements at Longyearbyen and Barentsburg.

In September 1944, the Germans set up their last weather station under Operation Haudegen. This station functioned until after the German surrender on May 8. It was still functioning on September 4, 1945, when the soldiers were picked up by a Norwegian seal hunting vessel and surrendered to its captain. This group of men were the last German troops to surrender after the Second World War.

So the big question is whether the SS in their "Nordic Ice" fascinations decided to build a secret base on Svalbard? We know

69

it was visited by German battleships. Was the island also visited by submarines? Was a submarine base built secretly at a remote site in the islands such a granite cliff face that drops into the water? The regular German soldiers may have never known about such a base as it was too dangerous for them to have this knowledge. Were the ghost rockets and other craft going to a secret base in northern Finland and then on to the secret base at Svalbard? It is an intriguing subject.

Foo Fighters and Secret Voyages to Japan

At the very end of WWII the Allies encountered balls of light over Germany. They were called foo fighters by the Allies. Author Renato Vesco revived the wartime theory that the foo fighters were a Nazi secret weapon in his work *Intercept UFO*, reprinted in a revised English edition as *Man-Made UFOs: 50 Years of Suppression* in 1994.[16] According to Vesco the foo fighters were in fact a form of ground-launched automatically guided jet-propelled flak mine called the Feuerball (Fireball).

The device, operated by special SS units, supposedly resembled a tortoise shell in shape, and flew by means of gas jets that spun like a Catherine wheel around the fuselage. Miniature klystron tubes inside the device, in combination with the gas jets, created the foo fighters' characteristic glowing spheroid appearance. A crude form of collision avoidance radar ensured the craft would not crash into another airborne object, and an onboard sensor mechanism would even instruct the machine to depart swiftly if it was fired upon.

According to Vesco, the purpose of the Feuerball was two-fold. The appearance of this weird device inside a bomber stream would (and indeed did) have a distracting and disruptive effect on the bomber pilots. Vesco alleges that the devices were also intended to have an offensive capability. Electrostatic discharges from the klystron tubes would interfere with the ignition systems of the bombers' engines, causing the planes to crash or at least drop their bombs before their

The control tower at Banak in Norway.

70

target destination and return to their home airfield. according to Vesco,

In his recent, very thick book *UFOs Before Roswell*,[1] the British author Graeme Rendall recounts numerous foo fighter incidents. Rendall claims that foo fighters began as early as 1940 and ended in 1945, the year the war ended. He has chapters on flying cylinders, RAF sightings, the Horton Flying Wing, American nocturnal sightings in Europe, involvement of the Luftwaffe, Renato Vesco, the Feuerball, the Kugelblitz, a technology transfer to Japan, and other topics. His last chapter is "What Were the Foo Fighters?"

In this last chapter Rendall essentially dismisses the idea that foo fighters were a German secret weapon, but concludes that many of them are real phenomena, as mysterious to the Germans as to the British and Americans. He feels that all the claims of German flying saucers are hoaxes but thinks that the Foo Fighters might have something to do with the Luiz Elizondo videos released in 2017 that show similar lights and small drones. He admits he does not know what Foo Fighters were. He never discusses the SS, Antarctica bases, or UFOs in South America—or anywhere for that matter—except for a few incidents. His book is heavily weighted with RAF reports and magazine articles written after the war. He admits that as hostilities ceased in 1945 the interest in foo fighters waned considerably with the RAF and the Americans, although the Allies apparently worried about "foo fighter technology" being transferred to Japan, as the Nazis had similarly transferred jet engine technology to the Japanese.

Rendall discusses a fascinating 1970 book in French called *Le Livre noir des soucoupes volantes* (*The Black Book of Flying Saucers*) by Henry Durant. Durant's first case in the book is about a Luftwaffe fighter pilot based at the Banak airfield in Norway who sees a large cigar-shaped craft near the airfield on March 14, 1942. The "machine" was flying silently near the Banak airfield on the evening of that day and the pilot, Hauptmann Fischer, took off in a Messerschmitt Bf 109 to intercept the craft.

Fisher reached the cigar-shaped craft at 3,500 meters, and provided a commentary to his controllers on the ground about what he was seeing above the airbase, which was an enormous object probably over 100 meters long. He told them:

A huge, tapering body, without any means of support, without any visible opening, its length is about 100 meters and its diameter about 15 meters—at one end a group of rods resemble radar antennae.

This large cylindrical airship, approximately the size of the Andromeda craft (which was slightly larger) maintained horizontal flight until suddenly rising vertically at high speed and disappearing out of sight. Rendall dismisses this incident as a fabricated story.[1]

So here we have the sighting of what was probably an Andromeda mothership that was hovering and maneuvering above the Banak airfield. It had obviously not originated from the Banak airfield and came from a secret base somewhere else—unless it was extraterrestrial.

This secret base may have been nearby, or it could have come from its home base in Germany somewhere. What was its mission? Perhaps it was on its way to a secret base on Svalbard or even Greenland. A secret base on the northeast coast of Greenland would be best served from a flight from Banak or somewhere else near northern Norway, such as the proposed base in northern Finland along the Norwegian border.

Rendall tells another tale from Durrant's book that involves two German Folk-Wulf Fs 190 single-seat piston-engined fighter aircraft. Durrant claimed that on December 18, 1943 a strange

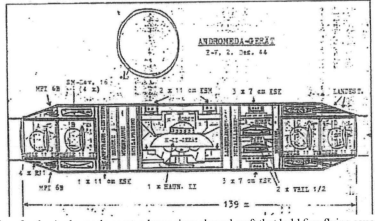

Plans for the Andromeda gerat, a large cigar-shaped craft that held five flying saucers.

object had been detected by radar stations located in Heligoland, Hamburg, Wittenberg and Neustrelitz in the morning. The speed was calculated as 3000 km/hour, so this was obviously a craft travelling at high speed. The pilots spotted the craft at about 11:15 in the morning so it was broad daylight when this occurred. According to Durrant the object was:

> …a cylindrical body with a warhead in the front, a large hole in the back with a panel. It seemed to be composed of a large number of rings, the surface of which seemed convex.[1]

The pilots attempted to follow the cylindrical craft but could only do so for a short distance before the object disappeared at high speed. Rendall apparently dismisses these incidents as hoaxes and generally dismisses advanced German aircraft and weaponry and appears to dismiss the many flying saucers seen after the war which he does not discuss at all, as his book is essentially about 1940 to 1945. He does not discuss Ghost Rockets either, sightings of which officially began in 1946. He dismisses Renato Vesco[16] and his claims as fabricated stories. It is difficult to make sense of these many stories if one does not believe that Germany was capable of making such devices as foo fighters, flying saucers and cylindrical craft (motherships).

Rendall also has a fascinating discussion of German and Japanese submarines going to each other's countries or meeting at a point somewhere in between. These submarine meetings were to exchange technicians, technology, gold, diamonds and other valuable and rare commodities including mercury. British and American blockades had made it impossible for surface cargo ships to make it across the Indian Ocean to Malaysia, so submarines became the only other viable option. He discusses the Japanese submarine (Imperial Japanese Navy) *I-30* which arrived at the Nazi U-boat base in northern France at Lorient in August 1942. It had a cargo of mica and shellac together with the plans for the Japanese Type E14Y aerial torpedo. On the return trip the *I-30* carried plans for the Wurzburg air defense radar, eight German torpedoes, a complete Hs 293 air-to-surface missile, several PAK

40 anti-tank guns, one million yen's worth of industrial diamonds and 50 Enigma coding machines. The submarine arrived in Singapore on October 13, 1941 and departed that same day but hit a British mine shortly after leaving the harbor and was sunk.[1]

In February 1943 the *U-80* left Brittany and rendezvoused with the *I-29* in the Indian Ocean somewhere. The *U-80* was carrying Subash Chandra Bose, the leader of the Indian National Army who had raised a force in occupied Europe of 3,000 Indian soldiers who had been captured by the Germans. They would now fight Britain under German and Japanese supervision. The Indian leader was to go to Japanese-controlled Asia to raise a similar army of captured Indian soldiers who had been fighting for the British.

The *I-29* transferred bullions of gold to the German submarine to pay for earlier blockade running ships that had brought cargo to Japanese occupied areas. They also transferred two Japanese engineers who were to study submarine construction in Germany.

Then in August 1943 the new Type IXC submarine *U-511* reached Kure in Japan from France. The craft was handed over to the Japanese and became their submarine *RO-500*. The vessel survived the war and was transferred to the Americans two years later.

Another Type IXC submarine *U-1224* was transferred to Japanese control at the Kiel naval yard in Germany and sailed under a Japanese crew in February 1944 for Japan. This submarine, with various plans and blueprints on board was sunk off the Cape Verde Islands in the Atlantic by a US destroyer on May 13, 1944.[1]

The Italian Navy got into the act by sending their German-built submarine *Commandante Cappellini* from Bordeaux, France to Japan in May 1943 with a cargo of mercury, aluminum, military equipment and blueprints for battle tanks. The submarine reached Singapore in mid-July and discharged its cargo and had planned to bring back a cargo of raw rubber, tin, opium, and spices. However, just as it was to depart for Germany in September of 1943 the Italian surrender to the Allies occurred, and the submarine was taken over by the German Kriegsmarine as *UIT-24*.

This submarine finally left Penang, Malaysia in February 1944 with a mixed German-Italian crew on board. However, it had to return to Penang when its supply ship was attacked by British destroyers in the middle of the Indian Ocean. This German supply ship had come from the secret base in Neuschwabenland on the coast of Antarctica opposite South Africa. The submarine then remained in Penang until the Japanese Navy took control of the craft when the Third Reich collapsed in May of 1945.

Rendall tells us that the last Japanese submarine to depart for Europe was the *I-52* in March 1944 with a cargo of passengers who were to study German anti-aircraft techniques, plus precious metals and uranium. This uranium would have come from the uranium mines that are today in North Korea. The *I-52* made a successful rendezvous with the *U-530* but was sunk by attack aircraft from the USS *Bogue* three months later off the Cape Verde Islands.

Rendall then tells about two further submarine voyages out of Germany with very interesting cargos. On December 5, 1944 the *U-864* departed from Bergen in Norway with a cargo containing 65 tons of mercury and parts for a Me 262 jet fighter. The submarine ran aground off the Norwegian coast and had to return to port for repairs. It then set off again in February 1945. Three days after leaving its berth in Bergen it was attacked by a British submarine and sunk with all hands.

The last U-boat mission to Japan was the *U-234* which left from the German port of Kiel on March 26, 1945. It carried various blueprints for advanced technology including examples of the Hs 293 air-to-surface guided missile and technical drawings related to the Me 262 jet fighter. It also carried 1,210 pounds (550 kg) of uranium oxide contained in 50 lead tubes. Among the 12 passengers was a production director for a Me 262 assembly plant, several other Messerschmitt employees and Fritz von Sandrart, an authority in anti-aircraft strategy. The U-boat made its way to the submarine base at Kristiansand, Norway and then left that port on April 15, 1945 for Japan. The U-boat was in the mid-Atlantic when Admiral Karl Donitz ordered the surrender of Germany to the Allies and for all naval crews to surrender.

The *U-234* surrendered to the destroyer escort USS *Sutton* after the two Japanese passengers had committed suicide, and was escorted by the US Navy to the Portsmouth Naval Shipyard in Kittery, Maine. Portsmouth Naval Shipyard is the Navy's main submarine manufacturer and over the course of World War II over 75 submarines were constructed there. Following World War II, Portsmouth Naval Shipyard was the Navy's center for submarine design and development. Rendall says that the uranium oxide was probably taken to the Oak Ridge facility in Tennessee where a diffusion plant was in operation as part of the Manhattan Project.[1]

What is fascinating about these accounts is that the cargo typically was of technical plans, technicians, and cargos of mercury and sophisticated jet engine and weapons parts. Why the large amount of mercury? What was it to be used for? I maintain that mercury—an element that is a metal, liquid, and a conductor—was used in the mercury gyros that were part of the anti-gravity technology that allowed the German saucer craft as well as the cigar-shaped Andromeda craft to fly in the manner that they did. Part of this was "Vril" power which we will discuss in a later chapter.

While Rendall only mentions two U-boats with a cargo of mercury, it is known that there were many other U-boats carrying cargos of mercury to Japanese areas as well as to the Antarctic base and probably Argentina. One U-boat with a cargo of mercury was apparently sunk off Indonesia in 1944. In order to explain the mystery of why mercury is the main cargo of a submarine it has been suggested that the mercury was "ballast" for the craft. However, this does not seem to be the case as other U-boats do not use this as ballast and such a submarine would essentially have no cargo if the mercury was not a product being moved from one port to another.

It has been estimated that from 58 to 100 U-boats did not surrender after the war and were used for decades for journeys around the Atlantic and Antarctica and out of the secret U-boat bases that I have outlined in my other books, such as in the Canary Islands, the Spanish Sahara, Greenland, Arctic Canada and Trindade Island, a remote island far off the coast of Brazil.

Ghost Rockets and the Secret Base in Northern Finland

During the war we had foo fighters and immediately after there war was the mystery of the "ghost rockets." Ghost rockets were rocket- or missile-shaped flying objects sighted mainly in

1946, but some were sighted earlier, mostly in Sweden, Finland and other nearby countries. Wikipedia says that the first reports of ghost rockets were made on February 26, 1946, by Finnish observers. This was about nine months after the war in Europe had ended. About 2,000 sightings were logged between May and December 1946, with peaks on 9 and 11 August 1946.

In 1946 it was thought likely that ghost rockets—so-called because people thought they were rockets— originated from the former German rocket facility at Peenemünde. It was supposed they were long-range tests by the Russians of captured German V-1 or V-2 missiles, or perhaps another early form of cruise missile because of the ways they were sometimes seen to maneuver. Basically the Swedish thought that the Russians were test-firing actual rockets over Scandinavia.

This prompted the Swedish Army to issue a directive stating that newspapers were not to report the exact location of ghost rocket sightings, or any information regarding the direction or speed of the objects. This information, they reasoned, was vital for evaluation purposes to the nation or nations performing the tests. Essentially they thought that these were early, crude rockets being fired toward the Arctic which would eventually crash into the Arctic Ocean.

But why would the Russians be doing this? They could move them to their own territory and then fire them into the Arctic Ocean and did not need to fire these weapons over Scandinavia. Also, the rockets seemed to slow down at times and sometimes they were seen to crash into a lake.

This leads me to believe that a secret SS UFO base was in northern Finland beneath a lake! This secret base would have an access to the underground base from the surface via a carefully hidden door in a remote mountain area that was unpopulated. A granite mountain might be nearby. The main hangar would open up into the lake, from which the Haunebu or Vril craft would depart, first by navigating the lake water as a submarine and then taking off into the atmosphere as a discoid craft under the electric power of "anti-gravity mercury gyros."

The early Russian-origins theory was rejected by Swedish, British, and US military investigators because no recognizable

77

rocket fragments were ever found. The objects usually left no exhaust trail, and usually flew horizontally. They sometimes traveled and maneuvered in formation, some moved slowly and they were usually silent. They were apparently not rockets at all and didn't behave as such.

The sightings most often consisted of fast-flying rocket- or missile- shaped objects, with or without wings, visible for mere seconds. Instances of slower moving cigar shaped objects are also known. A hissing or rumbling sound was sometimes reported.

Crashes were not uncommon, almost always in lakes. Reports were made of objects crashing into a lake, then propelling themselves across the surface before sinking, as well as ordinary crashes. The Swedish military performed several dives in the affected lakes shortly after the crashes, but found nothing other than occasional craters in the lake bottom or torn off aquatic plants.

Wikipedia reports that the best known of these crashes occurred on July 19, 1946, at Lake Kölmjärv, Sweden. Witnesses reported a gray, rocket-shaped object with wings crashing in the lake. One witness interviewed heard a thunderclap, possibly the object exploding. However, a 3-week military search conducted in intense secrecy again turned up nothing.

Immediately after the investigation, the Swedish Air Force officer who led the search, Karl-Gösta Bartoll, submitted a report in which he stated that the bottom of the lake had been disturbed but nothing was found, and that: "...there are many indications that the Kölmjärv object disintegrated itself... the object was probably manufactured in a lightweight material, possibly a kind of magnesium alloy that would disintegrate easily, and not give indications on our instruments." Wikipedia continues: When Bartoll was later interviewed in 1984 by Swedish researcher Clas Svahn, he again said their investigation suggested the object largely disintegrated in flight and insisted that "what people saw were real, physical objects."

Wikipedia says that on October 10, 1946, the Swedish Defense Staff publicly stated:

> Most observations are vague and must be treated very skeptically. In some cases, however, clear, unambiguous

observations have been made that cannot be explained as natural phenomena, Swedish aircraft, or imagination on the part of the observer. Echo, radar, and other equipment registered readings but gave no clue as to the nature of the objects.

It was also stated that fragments alleged to have come from the missiles were nothing more than ordinary coke or slag.

On December 3, 1946, a memo was drafted for the Swedish Ghost Rocket committee stating, "nearly one hundred impacts have been reported and thirty pieces of debris have been received and examined by Swedish National Defense Research Institute" (later said to be meteorite fragments). Of the nearly 1,000 reports that had been received by the Swedish Defense Staff to November 29, 225 were considered observations of "real physical objects" and every one had been seen in broad daylight.

The Americans became interested in the ghost rockets as well. On August 20, 1946, the *New York Times* reported that two US experts on aerial warfare, aviation legend General Jimmy Doolittle and General David Sarnoff, president of RCA, arrived in Stockholm, ostensibly on private business and independently of each other. Doolittle and Sarnoff were briefed that on several occasions the ghost rockets had been tracked on radar. Sarnoff was later quoted by the *Times* on September 30 saying that he was "convinced that the 'ghost bombs' are no myth but real missiles."

On August 22, 1946, the director of the Central Intelligence Group (CIG), Lt. Gen. Hoyt Vandenberg, wrote a Top Secret memo to President Truman, perhaps based in part on information from Doolittle and Sarnoff. Vandenberg stated that the "weight of evidence" pointed to Peenemünde as origin of the missiles, that US MA (military attaché) in Moscow had been told by a "key Swedish Air Officer" that radar course-plotting had led to a conclusion that Peenemünde was the launch site. CIG speculated that the missiles were extended-range developments of V-1 being aimed for the Gulf of Bothnia for test purposes and "do not overfly Swedish territory specifically for intimidation; [and] self-destruct by small demolition charge or burning."

Nevertheless, there are no reports of rocket launches at

Peenemünde or the Greifswalder Oie after February 21, 1945.

Wikipedia says that while the official opinion of the Swedish and US military remains unclear, a Top Secret USAFE (United States Air Force Europe) document from November 4, 1948 indicates that at least some investigators believed the ghost rockets and later "flying saucers" had extraterrestrial origins. Declassified only in 1997, the document states:

> For some time we have been concerned by the recurring reports on flying saucers. They periodically continue to pop up; during the last week, one was observed hovering over Neubiberg Air Base for about thirty minutes. They have been reported by so many sources and from such a variety of places that we are convinced that they cannot be disregarded and must be explained on some basis which is perhaps slightly beyond the scope of our present intelligence thinking.
>
> When officers of this Directorate recently visited the Swedish Air Intelligence Service, this question was put to the Swedes. Their answer was that some reliable and fully technically qualified people have reached the conclusion that "these phenomena are obviously the result of a high technical skill which cannot be credited to any presently known culture on earth." They are therefore assuming that these objects originate from some previously unknown or unidentified technology, possibly outside the earth.

The document also mentioned a flying saucer crash search in a Swedish lake conducted by a Swedish naval salvage team, with the discovery of a previously unknown crater on the lake floor believed caused by the object. The document ends with the statement that "we are inclined not to discredit entirely this somewhat spectacular theory [extraterrestrial origins], meantime keeping an open mind on the subject."

So it appears that the ghost rockets were not rockets at all, nor were they coming from the Peenemünde space center that Wernher von Braun famously worked at. These appear to be manned craft that were being flown by pilots. The above document seems to be an early diversion to the "extraterrestrial hypothesis" under which no earthly power had such technology to produce cigar-shaped craft or discoid craft that can hover in the air, dive into lakes, come out of lakes, and fly in a seemingly erratic fashion.

What we seem to have is considerable evidence that flying saucers and cylindrical craft were flying through the skies of Europe, particularly Scandinavia, in the months and early years after the surrender of Germany. It is my opinion that while some of these may have been extraterrestrial in origin, some of them were manufactured using Nazi technology. Some of these flights may have originated in Germany, although one would think that the SS, now in control of whatever was left of the Reich, would avoid Germany on their many flights because of the occupying armies and many airfields that the British, Americans and Soviets now controlled.

We can only speculate as to how many craft were involved in these ghost rocket flights but it would seem that there were at least a handful of the larger cigar-shaped craft around immediately after the war. Because these craft are now thought to be piloted craft—and fairly large at that—we can now see how the same craft could have generated many of the sightings that are recorded. However, it seems that there are just too many sightings of ghost rockets than could be created by just one craft, so there must have been a few. This brings us to the question of whether there were five or six or even more of these manned cylindrical craft, that we now call Andromeda, flying over Scandinavia and elsewhere during 1946 and 1947. It would seem so.

Ghost Rockets in Greece and Italy

Wikipedia has an interesting entry under Ghost Rockets that refers to the Greek government's investigation into the occurrence of ghost rockets over its country and how the US military apparently got the Greeks to stop the investigation. Says Wikipedia:

> The "ghost rocket" reports were not confined to Scandinavian countries. Similar objects were soon reported early the following month by British Army units in Greece, especially around Thessaloniki. In an interview

on September 5, 1946, the Greek Prime Minister, Konstantinos Tsaldaris, likewise reported a number of projectiles had been seen over Macedonia and Thessaloniki on September 1. In mid-September, they were also seen in Portugal, and then in Belgium and Italy. The Greek government conducted their own investigation, with their leading scientist, physicist Dr. Paul Santorinis, in charge. Santorinis had been a developer of the proximity fuze on the first A-bomb and held patents on guidance systems for Nike missiles and radar systems. Santorinis was supplied by the Greek Army with a team of engineers to investigate what again were believed to be Russian missiles flying over Greece.

In a 1967 lecture to the Greek Astronomical Society, broadcast on Athens Radio, Santorinis first publicly revealed what had been found in his 1947 investigation. "We soon established that they were not missiles. But, before we could do any more, the Army, after conferring with foreign officials (presumably U.S. Defense Dept.), ordered the investigation stopped. Foreign scientists [from Washington] flew to Greece for secret talks with me." Later Santorinis told UFO researchers such as Raymond Fowler that secrecy was invoked because officials were afraid to admit of a superior technology against which we have "no possibility of defense."

So, what were the Greeks told about these cylindrical aircraft that were not missiles but cigar-shaped craft that moved slowly through the sky at times? Were they told that these were extraterrestrials from Mars or Venus? Were they told that they were secret craft developed by the Germans? At the time the war had only just ended and the activity of Russian and remnant German forces was likely suspected and this is what the Americans probably told the Greeks. A sort of, "We'll handle it," approach.

Was there a secret base in North Africa or Greece—both areas controlled by the Nazis during the war—from which these craft were coming? It seems that the Germans had multiple cigar/ missile-shaped craft immediately after the war that were probably transferring people and possibly special technology to or from northern Finland or Norway in the months and early years after the war.

This activity may have been largely to evacuate personnel from a secret northern base to a secret base in the Western Sahara, immediately opposite the Canary Islands, both controlled by Spain. From there they could make the journey to Argentina or Antarctica, perhaps by submarine.

But why the ghost rockets over Greece? Was it just a flyover country for airships to journey to other countries, or did they have something to do with a secret base in Greece? Greece has many granite mountains and hidden bays. Was there a secret submarine base built somewhere in Greece during the war? Perhaps it was a secret airbase in the mountains of Greece that had a hangar for flying saucers. In my other books I have discussed the secret airbase in Tibet that is isolated from all but aircraft. Other secret airbases in mountainous areas probably exist, especially in South America. With the ghost rockets over Greece and Italy we cannot discount that there was a base in the Libyan Desert during the war, perhaps a temporary one that was above ground. This may have been the origin of the cylindrical aircraft seen over Greece immediately after the war.

Pre-War Ghost Rockets and Mystery Airplanes

Some researchers maintain that sightings of ghost rockets and similar ghost aircraft began in the 1930s, before the real beginning of WWII. If true, this would help to show that the Nazis in the early 1930s had already begun their expansion to extra-territorial military bases that were completely outside of Germany and typically unknown to the country on whose territory these secret bases were being created. Although expensive, Germany had the money, power, and technical capability to do create these bases and then supply them with submarines, long-range aircraft, or even flying saucers and cigar-shaped craft.

In his privately published book, *The Secret to Rational Space Travel*, German author Klaus-Peter Rothskugel says that secret bases were set up as early as the 1930s in northern Finland. Says Rothskugel:

At the beginning of the 1930s, especially in the northern part of Europe, huge multi-engine aircraft with a dull painting and no national markings emerged mainly at night or in severe weather conditions and circled over cities but also over remote areas, sometimes switching on one or several search-lights.

So during the winters 1933-34 and 1936-37 many such reports came from Sweden, Norway and Finland. Even the Swedish Air Force tried to hunt down these mysterious airplanes.

The hunt resulted in the crash of a total of six Swedish bi-plane fighters, while the aircraft they were hunting seemed to have no problems in flying at night and in severe snow storms or in extreme coldness.

There were many theories what kind of airplane cruised over the Scandinavian countries. One explanation was that the planes could have come from Germany. A certain quantity of German personnel from some German aircraft companies (Junkers) were indeed working in Sweden to test new aircraft types or to sell German technology to the Swedish military.

I should point out that Hitler came to power in 1933, the same year that these mystery flights over Scandinavia occurred. Rothskugel says that one witness who saw such a ghost flyer told a Swedish researcher:

> I am still steadfastly convinced that the airplane my father and I saw at a moonlit winter's night in 1934 was a large, low-winged, four-engined monoplane. Such did not exist in Germany at that time... I might add that my father got the outline of the airplane verified by other people who had also observed it.

Rothskugel says that Swedish and Norwegian military commanders were of the opinion that the planes came at least temporarily from a mobile base in the west of Norway and that the numerous reports from the Gulf of Bothnia, between Sweden and Finland, pointed to bases in Finland. He says that this would indicate that these countries could have secretly agreed to use certain airfields or remote landing strips for clandestine tests. If such a secret agreement was made, it was probably between Germany and Finland, as these two countries would fight the Russians together only a few years later.

On 30 April 1934, Swedish Major General Reutersward released the following press declaration:

> Without doubt there is an illegal air traffic going on within our restricted airspace. There are many reports of reliable persons who watched the mysterious craft very well. And there were always the same observations: All the airplanes had no national markings nor any identification numbers…

So, it seems that Finland and Norway may have had secret SS bases as early as 1934. Also, it is interesting that one of the ghost flyers was said to be a four-engine aircraft. Such aircraft are typically large bombers, but supposedly no four-engine airplanes had been built at this time—but why not?

The Messerschmitt Me 264 is said to be the first of the long-range strategic bombers developed for the German Luftwaffe. The design was later selected as Messerschmitt's competitor in the Reichsluftfahrtministerium's (the German Air Ministry) Amerikabomber program, a program to develop a strategic bomber capable of attacking New York City from bases in France or the Azores.

An Me 261 long-range aircraft.

85

The origin of the Me 264 design came from Messerschmitt's long-range reconnaissance aircraft project, the P.1061, of the late 1930s. These designs were also successfully used in the long-range Messerschmitt Me 261, itself originating as the Messerschmitt P.1064 design of 1937. The first flight of a four-engine Me 261 officially took place on December 23, 1942 and only three were supposedly built.

But these aircraft all have their origins in long-range reconnaissance aircraft projects that go back to the 1930s. Because of the secret nature of the war buildup in Germany in the 1930s, and all the preparations made for war on France and the Soviet Union, it seems that many secret projects were already underway in the early 1930s and that four-engine long-range craft had been built already as experimental craft.

It seems that the SS was creating its own special air force. We must conclude that all of these experimental craft were controlled by the SS starting in 1934. The incredible power of the German war machine was behind them including all of the aircraft, ship and submarine factories. An incredible economy and industrial force was at their disposal.

This also lends credibility to some of the Vril Society claims that the Vril craft were developed and flown in the 1930s. It would seem that the secret technology and experimental aircraft were already being developed in the early 1930s, an era when Nikola Tesla was the most famous inventor in the world and continually promoted his wireless power, anti-gravity airships, ray guns and death rays to the world press.

Rothskugel says that in 1936 the unknown aircraft returned again on the same routes they used in 1934, coming from the far north in a southerly direction, flying over the northern part of Norway, across Sweden and back again. He says that another theory was that a Soviet heavy bomber wing, based in the Murmansk area, was conducting training missions with their four-engined TB-3 bombers or testing new equipment. Says Rothskugel:

> This could indeed explain the violation of the airspace
> of the three Scandinavian countries but not the inactivity
> of these countries to solve the mystery that occurred twice

(1933-34 and 1936-37, always in wintertime!).

One might assume that some special evaluation flights were conducted under extreme weather conditions, especially in cold and dark nights. These could have been secret tests of some new flight navigation systems working under these bad circumstances. And strangely the same (?) air bases might have been used some ten years later, possibly again with the agreement of the three Scandinavian countries. In 1946 and 1947 this time unconventional and still unknown airplanes circling in the northern airspace, later widening their flight path to other parts in Europe.

One probable explanation could be that a certain equipment (withstanding cold and freezing conditions) with special converted multi-engined airplanes was tested in the 1930s. These operations were totally shrouded in secrecy and could have been undertaken with the participation of several nations to prepare an even more secret mission in an area where cold and icy conditions prevail and where visibility and orientation is difficult even under normal daylight conditions.

Such a field of operation could be for example the Artic or the Antarctic region. After WWII in this very Antarctic region UFOs, flying cigars and flying spheres were frequently seen and the famous Antarctic pioneer Admiral Byrd ran into trouble while on a secret mission at the South Pole (at least the official version is explaining this. Byrd, who was in Hamburg, Germany before WWII to lecture about the South Pole was probably part of a highly secret mission which is still today covered-up). Even during WWII there were rumors that Germany transferred in secrecy personnel and equipment to the South Pole.

More reports of ghost rockets and ghost flyers were made after the war. On February 26, 1946, Finnish observers saw a rocket-like object in the sky that they could not explain. Was it one of the Andromeda craft that had been built? About 2,000 sightings were logged in the skies above Sweden and Finland between May and December 1946.

Again, what was the purpose of the ghost flyer flights? It must have been to move personnel and certain technology from place to place—secret base to secret base. These secret bases in the Arctic Circle seem to be in northern Finland, Greenland, possibly Svalbard, and the secret Canadian base known as the Blue Island.

A Haunebu Lands in Patagonia 1949

In my earlier books I spoke about the lore of the postwar SS activities that has them producing and storing craft at the "Beaver Dam" super-base in Greenland. From here these craft began to fly to all parts of the world, including the secret base in Tibet and suspected saucer bases in the Canary Islands and the former Spanish colonial possession called Spanish Sahara, on the north African coast just opposite the easternmost island of the Canary Islands.

The main gathering place of the Black Sun SS officers and their craft immediately after the war seems to be Antarctica where Germany's only official colony was undisturbed until Operation High Jump arrived in December of 1946. They departed in February 1947. The SS officers there probably arrived by submarine or as passengers in a cigar-shaped Andromeda craft. But many of the men (and women) went straight to Argentina via Italy or Spain. From Argentina many dispersed to other South American countries, now with Argentinian passports. It has been written that Juan Peron gave 100,000 Argentinian passports to the Germans who arrived there.

Starting in 1945, if not earlier, there must have been considerable submarine and airship traffic between Neuschwabenland and Argentina. Haunebu and Andromeda activity must have been occurring during 1947 and 1948 in Argentina but there are very few public reports. The book *Hitler es vivo* was published in 1947 in Buenos Aires.[19] This is the first book to mention the German Antarctic base in Neuschwabenland and that Hitler had escaped to South America.

There is a report from 1947 of a cigar-shaped object—probably an Andromeda craft—seen from a cruise ship steaming to South Africa reported by Coral Lorenzen,[17] and the crash of cylindrical craft at the secret facility in Russia in 1948, but it seems that

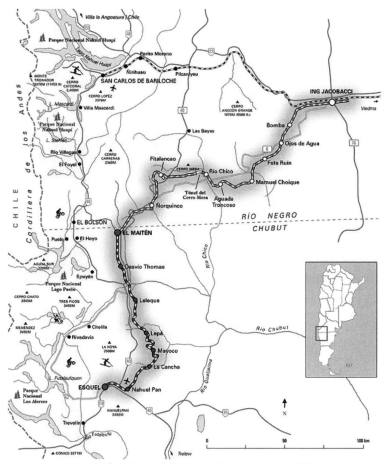

A route map of the Patagonia train to Esquel through El Maiten.

the postwar Nazis and the SS kept pretty quiet until 1949. The Nuremberg Trials ended in 1946 and those not executed that same year were transferred to Spandau Prison in 1947. The Nazi trial and punishment phase of Germany's defeat was over and many Germans could return to a relatively normal life.

Nazi UFO activity in the late 1940s seems to have been focused on remote areas of Patagonia from whence little information was likely to leak at any time. Possibly on large ranches in Patagonia that are owned by Germans there was some saucer activity. The remnant of the Reich couldn't just exist in the icy and remote bases in the Arctic and Antarctic. It needed real territory where there were farms, ranches and factories. For postwar Nazis, this was Patagonia, other areas of Argentina, Paraguay and Chile, all

89

A locomotive at the workshop in El Maiten, Patagonia.

of which have large German populations. There are also large German populations in Uruguay and southern Brazil.

In February of 1949 the first flying saucer media report in Argentina occurred, four years after the end of the war. This incident happened near a town called El Maitén in Chubut province in northern Patagonia.

El Maitén started as a rural community but was influenced greatly by the arrival of the General Roca railroad in the area in 1939, on a branch that continued to Esquel, a Welsh-speaking town in Patagonia. This branch was completed and opened in 1945, and El Maitén was selected as the site of its maintenance sheds and locomotive warehouse. This was one of the southernmost stations for the extensive railway network in Argentina. El Maitén is in Chubut Province which encompasses the Chubut River Valley, an area with many German ranches. The Chubut Valley also has a large population of Welsh who immigrated in 1865. The train that ran through El Maitén to Esquel became known as the Old Patagonian Express.

According to an article in the national newspaper *La Razon*, published in Buenos Aires on March 13, 1970, on February 20, 1949, a very excited salesman came to a police officer at his military station. This officer held the information as confidential until he retired. He claimed that he was told by the salesman that about 20 kilometers (12.4 miles) from the town, he had met a UFO.

After the flying saucer landed, three normal-looking men walked out of the craft. The three human figures were dressed in strange suits (uniforms) and they had something flashing in their headgear. They also seemed to be connected to the UFO by something like cords. They signaled the witness to stop his car. Not much more is known. This incident had been in the Wikipedia article "UFOs in Argentina" but has been removed. The cases sited there now start in 1962.

The occupants of the saucer may have been there to inspect the relatively new locomotive warehouse and maintenance sheds in El Maitén. It would seem that the area around this small town along the Andes near the border with Chile was a safe place to land a craft and have a look around. Perhaps someone was waiting for the craft in this remote locale, or the occupants had simply stopped their craft here for other reasons.

Was this a Haunebu craft coming from a base further south in Patagonia or even from Antarctica? One would think that the Germans would want some secret mountain base somewhere in Patagonia and the area south of El Maitén and Esquel, the terminus of the railway, would seem a logical location. As one goes further south from these towns it is a remote countryside indeed. Towns

The inaugural trip to Esquel from El Maiten on May 25, 1945.

like El Maitén and Esquel with their rail links could be important towns for supplies.

This area of the world—Patagonia, and Argentina in general—was just developing and held great promise. It was far removed from the destruction and atrocities of WWII and opinions in Argentina in general were neutral toward the war, and in fact largely pro-German.

Argentina's next big UFO encounter was about a year later with the sighting of a flying saucer on April 18, 1950 in Resistencia, a city in the northeast, very near to Paraguay. The local paper reported that the craft was seen by virtually the whole town, and many people expected it to land since they knew about the previous encounter in Patagonia.

So, by 1949 the SS was beginning to land their craft in remote towns in Patagonia and things would move farther north in 1950. Here we have the postwar SS slowly moving from their established bases in Antarctica, Tierra del Fuego and Patagonia northward through Argentina and into Brazil, Paraguay, Bolivia and Peru. The activity of the SS in South America would continue to build with ultimately a UFO factory functioning in the industrial city of Cordoba in northern Argentina.

We need to remember that in the late 1940s and early 1950s there were dozens of daylight sightings of small and large flying saucers, especially in South America. They were also seen in Central America, Canada and the USA as well as in Europe and Africa. It was literally a time of "saucermania" as photos, news articles, and Hollywood movies got the public very interested. Everyone heard about the flying saucers. What were they and where did they come from? We have to think that a Black Sun SS remnant of the Third Reich was waging a flying saucer publicity war and wanted their craft seen by as many people as possible in some cases.

On a fascinating site called BibleUFO.net, they have a list of some of the flying saucers and cylindrical craft incidents from 1948, 1949, and 1950, which was a year with many sightings. Most of these sightings are taken from Project Bluebook. Some of these sightings are very curious such as the first example from BibleUFO.net:

• Canada, Swastika, Ontario. In 1948, Mr. Galbraith twice saw an object land. The first time, it was a disk-shaped craft with a humanoid figure. The second time, it was a cigar-shaped craft with three human figures. The small mining town of Swastika is in northern Ontario near Kirkland Lake. It is curious that a town with this name should be visited by a flying saucer with one occupant and then by a cylindrical craft with three occupants. Was this an Andromeda craft and a visit by one of the small Vril craft? Did they land in Swastika out of curiosity?

• USA, Alabama, Montgomery. In 1948, an Eastern Airlines DC-3 piloted by Captain Clarence S. Chiles was narrowly missed by a UFO while flying over Montgomery on July 24.

• USA, Indiana, Indianapolis: In 1948, an object swept over a road at 10 m altitude.

• USA, Kentucky, Louisville. In 1948, Capt. Thomas Mantell lost his life on January 7 while attempting to chase a UFO. This is the first fatality on record directly connected with a UFO chase. Reports from private citizens were made to the Kentucky State Highway Patrol describing a strange, saucer-shaped flying object, 200-300 feet in diameter. It was also seen by several other witnesses, including the base commander, at the control tower of Godman AFB, outside Louisville. Official explanations concluded that he was chasing the planet Venus in the bright afternoon sky or a secret Navy balloon. Was it in fact a Haunebu?

• USA, Ohio, Maplewood. In 1948, a farmer observed a silvery sphere of large dimension rise from a wooded area and hover above his farm, dropping a silvery substance that disintegrated before touching the ground.

• In 1948, Carl Mitchell, a physicist, saw three luminescent greenish discs, one-second apart, pass across the sky from north to south on March 20.

• In 1948, Seymour L. Hess, a meteorologist and astronomer, saw a disc or sphere in apparent "powered" flight. Project Blue Book classified this as "Unknown."

• Oct. 15, 1948; Fusuoka, Japan. 11:05 pm. A pilot named Halter and a radar operator named Hemphill of a P-61 "Black Widow" night fighter, saw up to six objects tracked on radar, only one seen

93

visually. It was a dull or dark object shaped like a dirigible with a flat bottom and clipped tail end. Six seen on radar separately. Pilot attempted to close on visual object, but it dove away fast.

• USA, California, Dec. 3, 1948; Fairfield-Suisan AFB. 8:15 pm. A USAF Sgt., control tower operator, saw one round, white light fly for 25 seconds with varying speed, moving in a bouncing motion, finally make a rapid erratic climb.

• USA, Indiana July 31, 1948; Indianapolis. 8:25 am. Mr. and Mrs. Vernon Swigert saw an object that was shaped like a cymbal, or domed disc, about 20 feet across and 6-8 feet thick. It was white without any shine. It flew straight and level from horizon to horizon in about 10 seconds, shimmering in the sun as if spinning. This small saucer was probably a Vril craft.

• USA, New Mexico, April 5, 1948; Holloman AFB. Afternoon. Geophysics Lab balloon observers Alsen, Johnson, and Chance saw two irregular, round, white or golden objects. One made three loops then rose and disappeared rapidly; the other flew in a fast arc to the west during the 3O-second sighting. Why make three loops unless you want to show off what your craft can do?

• USA, Virginia July or August, 1948; vicinity of Marion. Shortly after sunset. Max Abbott, flying a Bellanca Cruisair four-passenger private airplane, saw a single bright white light that accelerated and turned up a valley.

• Clyde W. Tombaugh, astronomer, saw a circular pattern of rectangular lights, keeping fixed interval in August 1948.

• USA, Arizona, April 28, 1949; Tucson. 5:45 pm. Howard Hann, Mr. Hubert, and Tex Keahey saw one bright, sausage-shaped object for 40 minutes while it rolled and flew fast.

• USA, Arizona, May 9, 1949; Tucson, 2:30 pm. M/Sgt. Troy Putnam saw two round, flat silvery objects, estimated to be 25 feet in diameter, flying 750-1,000 m.p.h. in a banked but steady manner.

• USA, California, April 4, 1949; Merced. 10:20 pm. William Parrott, former Air Force pilot and major, saw one generally round object with a curved bottom and dull coloring. The object gave off a clicking sound until overhead. Parrott's dog reacted. The sighting lasted 35 seconds.

• USA, California, May 6, 1949; Livermore. 9:35 am. C. G.

Green watched while two shiny, disc-like objects rotated around each other and banked. Then one shot upwards with a grey trail and rejoined the other. The sighting lasted 5 minutes.

• USA, Florida, Jan. 27, 1949; Cortez-Bradenton. 10:20 pm. Capt. Sames, acting chief of the Aircraft Branch, Eglin AFB, and Mrs. Sames, watched for 25 minutes while a cigar-shaped object as long as two Pullman cars and having seven lighted square windows and throwing sparks, descended and then climbed with a bouncing motion at an estimated 400 mph.

• USA, Hawaii, Jan. 4, 1949; Hickam Field. 2 pm. USAF pilot Capt. Paul Storey on ground saw one flat white, elliptical object with a matte top circling while oscillating to the right and left, and then speeding away.

• USA, Idaho, July 24, 1949; Mountain Home, 12 noon. Henry Clark, manager of a flying service, flying a Piper Clipper, saw seven delta-shaped objects, 35-55 feet in span, 20-30 feet long, 2-5 feet thick. They were light colored except for a 12-foot diameter dark circle at the rear of each. They flew in a tight formation of twos with one behind, and made a perfect, but unbanked, turn. During the 10-minute sighting, they displayed decreasing smooth oscillations. Clark's engine ran rough during the sighting, and upon landing was found to have all its spark plugs burned out. This would appear to a formation of seven Vril craft.

• USA, Montana, April 3, 1949; Dillon. 11:55 am. A construction company owner, Gosta Miller, and three other unnamed persons saw one object shaped like two plates attached face-to-face. It was described as having a matte bottom and a bright aluminum top with 20 foot diameter, 4-5 foot thickness. It rocked or rotated in six cycles, descended, rocked, flew, rocked; all this was very fast.

• USA, New Mexico, April 24, 1949; Arrey, l0:30 am. General Mills, meteorologist and balloon expert C.B. Moore and others on a balloon launch crew saw one white, round ellipsoid, about 2.5 times as long as wide.

• USA, South-central Oregon, May 27, 1949. 2:25 pm. Joseph Shell, ferrying SNJ trainer for North American Aviation from Red Bluff, California to Burns, Oregon saw five to eight oval objects, twice as long as wide, and 1/5 as thick. They flew in trail formation, with an interval equal to 3 to 4 times their length, except that the second and third were closer together.

• USA, Oregon, July 30, 1949; Mt. Hood, 9 pm. Northwest Airlines Capt. Thrush, two Portland control tower operators, and one flying instructor saw one object with one white light and two red lights which maneuvered and hovered.

• USA, Texas, March 17, 1949; Camp Hood. 7:52 pm. Guards of the 2nd Armored Division, while awaiting the start of a flare firing, watched for an hour while eight large, green, red and white flare-like objects flew in generally straight lines.

• USA, Texas, May 5, 1949; Ft. Bliss. 11:40 am. Army officers Maj. Day, Maj. Olhausen and Capt. Vaughn saw two oblong white discs flying at an estimated 200-250 mph.. They made a shallow turn during the 30-50 second observation.

• Argentina, Lago Argentino: At some period during 1950, a rancher, Wilfredo H. Arevalo, saw two objects, one of which landed. He walked within 150 m of the aluminum-looking craft which gave off a greenish-blue vapor and "an intense smell of burning benzine." A large, flat section on top was revolving above a glass cabin in which could be seen four tall men, dressed in something like cellophane, working at various instruments. They saw him and shone a light in his direction while a blue light illuminated the craft; the vapor increased and flames (alternately reddish and greenish) shot out of the base while the object rose with a faint hum. Both craft flew away toward Chile, leaving bluish trails.

• Brazil, Porto Novo, In 1950, Mr. Campello and several others in a car saw two large, silvery objects by the side of the road, one on a hillock, the other on flat ground, about 50 meters away from each other. They came within 600 meters of the objects, which went away at "an incredible speed," causing a rush of air that rocked the car.

• Canada, Steep Rock Lake, In 1950, a man and his wife saw a double saucer with portholes and a rotating antenna come to rest on the surface of the lake. Ten figures, 1.2 meters tall, dressed in shiny clothing, emerged and walked on deck like robots "changing direction without turning their bodies." Their faces could not be seen. One of them wore a red cap, had darker arms and legs and

96

"seemed to be their chief." They immersed a hose in the lake, then took off. Fishermen later reported a green moss forming on the lake. UFOs are often seen in and around freshwater lakes. This is a typical incident where they have taken fresh water with a hose from a lake.

• Italy, Abbiate Guazzone. In 1950, Bruno Facchini heard and saw sparks coming from a dark, hovering object, near which a man dressed in tight-fitting clothes and wearing a helmet seemed to be making repairs. Three other men were seen near the craft. When the work was finished, a trap through which light had been shining was closed and the thing took off. The witness had the time to note many details of the machine and its occupants. This would seem like a Black Sun SS pilot with three others making some adjustments to a Haunebu craft.

• USA, Alaska, Juneau. In 1950, Mikel Konrad made a movie of eight disks he saw landing and taking off 60 km north of town.

• USA, Arkansas, Stuggart: In 1950, Chicago & Southern Airlines Capt. Jack Adams and First Officer G. W. Anderson, Jr. reported witnessing one 100-foot circular disc with 9-12 portholes along the lower side emitting a soft purple light, and a light at the top which flashed 3 times in 9 seconds. The craft flew at not less than 1,000 mph. It was seen for 25-35 seconds.

• USA, California, Pasadena. In 1950, a producer for Metro-

Four photos of a Haunebu in flight. Date unknown.

Goldwyn-Mayer, was driving home with his wife when they said they witnessed three revolving discs traveling at great speed. The next day, a group at Caltech reported seeing the same objects.

• USA, Colorado, South Table Mountain. In 1950, a Mr. Quintana of Denver saw a silvery-green ovoid object hovering about 15 meters above a slope and landing slowly in a small ravine. Then it shot upward at very high speed. Its diameter was about 20 meters, and it had a revolving middle band. A greenish light flashed under it, and the witness felt a rush of air and smelled a pungent odor.

• USA, Illinois, Red Bud. On April 23, 1950, Mr. Dean Morgan, a part-time photographer, was coming down the south side of a wooded hill from Red Bud, in southern Illinois, northwest of Carbondale, when he saw a small flying saucer and got one photograph of it. It appears to be a Vril craft.

• USA, Indiana, Kokomo. In 1950, a metal worker was awakened by his dog and observed an object 60 meters away at low altitude. It was a gray metal disk, 5 meters in diameter, shaped like a top with a kind of turret. It was oscillating, spinning slowly, and had three portholes shining with a blue-white light. It hovered for about two minutes, then left toward the north, very fast.

• USA, Nevada, Ely. In 1950, a couple and their grandson were returning from a picnic when, about 14 km south of town, they saw a silvery-white object at treetop level. It hovered for 10 minutes, then oscillated "as if attempting to rise" and suddenly flew out of sight at high speed.

• USA, Oregon, McMinnville. Just after dinner on May 11, 1950, Evelyn Trent was out feeding her rabbits when she noticed a disc-like craft hovering in the sky just to the northwest of her. She called out to her husband, Paul, who came out and took a picturesof the object, rewound the manual rewind as rapidly as possible, and took another picture 30 seconds or so later. Afterwards, he put the camera away as the film roll was not used up yet. He later finished the role on Mothers Day activitie's. Paul Trent then took the role of film to town for developing at a drug store on Third Street. The day Trent had the film developed the film he told banker Ralph Wortman about what had happened out on his property and about the pictures he took. Mr. Wortman later told Editor Phil Bladine of the local paper, the *Telephone-Register*, who in turn, put journalist Bill Powell on the story. It wasn't long before the story had gone nationwide, being called by many publications the first authentic UFO pictures to be published.

• USA, Texas, Amarillo. In 1950, David and Charles Lightfoot, aged 12 and 9 saw a disc land behind a hill and ran over and touched it. It was the size of a car tire; about 30 cm high, with a rounded top that rotated and a pivot between the base and the top. It took off very fast. The faces and arms of the boys later became red.

• USA, Texas, Lufkin. In 1950, Jack Robertson was driving about 13 km west of town when he saw a round object about 3 meters in diameter hovering about 7 meters above him with a dull red glow. It took off with a "swooshing roar" as sparks flew from a slot under it. Minutes later the witness felt a burning sensation on his face.

• Bermuda, August 25, 1950; Approximately 250 mi. SW of Bermuda. 8 pm. A B-29 radarman S/Sgt. William Shaffer made a radar observation of a UFO, plus a possible blue streak three minutes later. A B-29 followed the unidentified target, then passed it at a quarter mile distance. The target followed for 5 minutes, then passed the B-29 and sped away. Total time of tracking: 20 minutes.

• Chile, March 28, 1950; Santiago. 3:15 pm. M/Sgt. Patterson, of the office of the US Air Attaché saw one white object that he observed for 5-10 seconds through binoculars while it flew high and fast, crossing the sky.

• Cyprus, Aug. 20, 1950; Nicosia. 1:30 pm. USAF MATS liaison officer Lt. William Ghormley, Col. W.V. Brown, and Lt. Col. L.W. Brauer saw one small, round, bright object fly fast, straight and level for 15-20 seconds.

• Kenya, Dec. 2, 1950; Nanyika. 10:50 am. Mr. and Mrs. L. Scott saw one pearly, iridescent object with a flattened top spin while hovering. It made a sound like bees buzzing.

• Okinawa, March 27, 1950; Motobo. 10:30 am. USAF radar operator Cpl. Bolfango tracked a craft on radar for two minutes while it was stationary and then moved at 500 mph.

• USA, Alabama, July 13, 1950; Redstone Arsenal. 5 pm.

Two skilled Arsenal employees including a Mr. Washburn saw one object, shaped like a bowtie, and cover with what looked like polished aluminum. It flew straight and level, then one triangle of the bowtie rotated 1/4 turn in the opposite direction and returned to its original position. The object then made a right-angle turn and accelerated away after at least 30 seconds. This would seem like some sort of test flight out of the Redstone Arsenal, home to Wernher von Braun.

• USA, Colorado, Sept. 20, 1950; Kit Carson. 10:49 am. A witness identified only as a "reliable source" observed two large, round, glowing objects and three smaller, internally lit objects. Two objects hovered for one minute, moved, and then three smaller ones came from behind or from within the two larger objects, and all sped upward and away. This appears to be two Haunebu craft and three Vril craft flying over Colorado.

• USA, Florida, Dec. 6, 1950; Ft. Myers. 5 pm. A former aircraft purchasing agent named Harry Lamp and four boys, using 10-power binoculars observed one 75 foot object, 3-4 feet thick, with a bubble on top. It was silver with a red rim, having two white and two orange jets along it. The center revolved when the object hovered; then it flew away very fast.

• USA, Indiana, April 8, 1950; Kokomo. 2 am. A man named Earl Baker saw a grey metallic disc, 50 feet in diameter, 15 feet thick. It was top-shaped with a "conning tower" at the top and three ports on the rim giving off a blue light. It hovered for two minutes, then flew away. Baker was aroused from sleep by his dog.

• USA, Michigan, March 3, 1950; Selfridge AFB. 11:05 pm. 1st Lt Frank Mattson saw an intense, dull yellowish light descend vertically, then fly straight and level very fast for four minutes.

• USA, Massachusetts, Feb 5, 1950; Teaticket. 5:10 pm. Marvin Odom, former US Navy fighter pilot, USAF Lt. Philip Foushee, a pilot from Otis AFB, and two others saw two thin, illuminated cylinders, one of which dropped a fireball. The craft maneuvered together and then disappeared high and fast after five minutes.

• USA, Nevada, May 7, 1950; Nine miles south of Ely. 6:45 pm. Mr. and Mrs. George Smith and their grandson saw a silvery white object that hovered at 100 feet altitude. It moved back and forth for 10 minutes and then flew up and away.

• USA, New Jersey, April 14, 1950; Ft. Monmouth. 2:30 pm. Army M/Sgt. James saw four rectangular, amber objects, about 3 foot by 4 foot, that changed speed and direction rapidly; the group of objects rose and fell during the 3-4 minute sighting.

• USA, New Mexico, Feb. 24, 1950; Albuquerque. 1:55 pm. Municipal Airport Weather Observers Luther McDonald and Harrison Manson saw a white, slightly elongated oval. They watched for 1.5 minutes through a theodolite while it flew straight and level.

• USA, New Mexico, Feb. 25, 1950; Los Alamos. 3:55 pm. Twelve Atomic Energy Commission security inspectors saw a cylinder with tapered ends, silver and flashing, that flew slow and then fast, fluttered and oscillated, and changed course. Observations by individuals varied from three seconds to two minutes. This is a classic description of the Andromeda craft.

• USA, North Carolina, Oct. 23, 1950; Bonlee. 12:42 pm. An ex-USAF pilot Frank Risher saw an aluminum object shaped like a dirigible or Convair C-99 cargo plane, with 3 portholes, that arrived from the southeast, hovered 3-5 seconds and flew away to the south- south-east at the end of the 40 second sighting. Clearly a cigar-shaped craft like the Andromeda.

• USA, Tennessee, March 29, 1950; Marrowbore Lake. 7 am. Two real estate salesmen, Whiteside and Williams, saw six to twelve dark objects shaped like 300-lb. bombs, estimated to be five feet long. They flew at about 500 mph and descended, making a noise like wind blowing through the trees.

• USA, Tennessee, Oct. 15, 1950; Oak Ridge. 3:20 pm. Atomic Energy Commission Trooper Rymer, J. Moneymaker, and Capt. Zarzecki saw two shiny silver objects shaped like a bullet or bladder. They dove with a smoke trail and one vanished. The other hovered at about six feet in altitude, 50 feet away, left and then returned several times somewhat further away.

• USA, Texas, June 27, 1950; Texarkana. 7:50 am. Terrell and Yates, employees of Red River Arsenal, saw an object, bright and shaped like two dishpans face-to-face, that flew fast, straight and level, for four to five seconds.

• USA, Washington, Sept. 3, 1950; Spokane. 2 pm. Maj R.J. Gardiner, Mrs. Gardiner and a neighbor saw three objects that were metallic bronze discs, 20 to 30 feet long, and two to six feet thick. They moved independently and erratically for five minutes. These small saucers would seem to be three Vril craft.

As we can see, flying saucers and the cigar-shaped craft were being seen all over the place in the late 40s and early 50s. They were often around military bases. They didn't need to worry about the fighter jets scrambled after them as they could easily outmaneuver them and zoom off to a higher altitude in a few seconds. So, it would appear that these craft—probably coming from South America or some secret base in the Arctic—were harassing the American Military Bases that eluded them during the war.

Yet, it was psychological warfare using new tactics rather than conventional weapons. The saucers themselves did not have destructive weapons such as cruise missiles as part of their meager arsenal. The destructive power of bombers—atomic bombers at that—and the missiles that fighter jets could fire was much more than any of these craft had. Their advantage was the Tesla anti-gravity engines that allowed them to hover and fly off at any angle at tremendous speeds. Except for a few cases, no UFO has ever attacked a military facility. Yet, UFOs of all types are often seen around military facilities as we see from the accounts above.

Haunebu and Vril Craft All Over the World

In his book *The CIA UFO Papers,*[40] investigator Dan Wright says that CIA reports from 1953 indicate that there was a great deal of UFO activity around the world that year. He says a document refers to the Danish Defense Command remarking that the "flying saucer traffic" over Scandinavia was of immense aero-technical interest.

This would seem to be a continuation of the "ghost rocket" activity of the 1940s. This would also seem to validate the secret base in northern Finland and that this base was still being used in the 1950s. Also, any craft going from Germany to Greenland or Svalbard would probably pass over Scandinavia.

Another CIA paper dated August 18, 1953 conveyed accounts of anomalies from newspapers in Athens, Greece; Brazzaville, Congo; and Tehran, Iran. Wright then mentions another CIA paper from that year that said:

A famous photograph of three Vril craft taken in northern Italy on September 26, 1960.

...a German engineer claimed that flying saucer plans, drawn up by Nazi engineers before World War II's end, had come to be in Soviet hands. The source claimed German saucer blueprints were already underway in 1941. By 1944, three experimental models were ready, one in disc shape. All could take off vertically and land in a confined space. After a three-month siege of the German's Breslau (now Wroclaw, Poland) facility at the war's conclusion, Soviets stole the plans on saucer construction.

Wright then describes another curious CIA document with an account from November 22, 1952:

103

A missionary and five companions in French Equatorial Africa had had a close encounter. Driving at night, they had witnessed four motionless discs overhead that lit up like suns when in motion but were silvery when stationary. Over 20 minutes the four moved about the area, seemingly performing tricks, then hovered momentarily before leaving non-uniformly. Later the six witnesses saw four objects forming a square at cloud level. One lit up vivid red and rose vertically; the other three joined it to form a square again. Luminous aerial objects were seen in the same time period above Homs, Syria, and the oil fields at Abadan in west-central Iran.[40]

Wright mentions two strange cases in Africa from 1952 in the CIA documents. One incident took place on June 1, 1952 when the master and first mate of a cargo ship just off of Port Gentil, in the West African country of Gabon, witnessed an orange luminous object rise up behind the port, do two right-angle turns, pass overhead, and continue out of sight. Was this a craft picking up or letting off passengers in a field behind the port?

This craft might have then departed for Laâyoune (or El Aaiún) that at the time was the capital of the colony of Spanish Sahara. It became a modest city in the 1930s and in the year 1940, Spain designated it as the capital. Because Spain was a neutral country, but pro-Nazi (like Argentina), its colonial lands were used as proxy territory by the Third Reich, and U-boats and aircraft made routine stops at locations where supplies were available and transactions could take place. The country was disestablished in 1976 and today is part of Morocco. The Spanish Sahara was a known haven for Nazis and one early report said that Hitler was living in Laâyoune immediately after the war.[33]

Wright then discusses a CIA document on UFO activity in July of 1952 in Algeria. Starting on July 11 in Lamoriciere, several UFOs were seen including a longish, fiery oval. Then four days later a flying saucer was seen at the town of Boukanefis. Then on July 25, at 2:35 in the afternoon, UFOs were seen over a factory and other places near the coastal city of Oran. The same night near the Algerian town of Lodi, southwest of Algiers, several UFOs were seen.

The next morning at 10:45 in broad daylight in Tiaret, Algeria, five persons saw a shining cigar-shaped UFO with a darkened center silently traversing the sky. A similar UFO was seen later that night in the Algerian town of Eckmuhl. The CIA documents say that a few days later, on July 30 in Algiers, a black disk was seen by a woman to descend from the sky and then suddenly move horizontally out of sight. Later that night, in the early hours of July 31, UFOs were seen in the sky by multiple people around Algiers, the main city of the country, and in other areas like Oued and Tlemcen. Finally, later that morning in broad daylight (11:30 am) a couple driving just outside of the major city of Oran saw a UFO cross the sky at great speed.

So with these last sightings in Algeria in 1952 we seem to have a Haunebu or Vril craft along with a cigar-shaped craft. Did these craft depart for a secret base in the Spanish Sahara or nearby? The CIA seemed particularly interested in the activities in Algeria.

The postwar activities of the SS were being carefully followed by the CIA and probably Naval Intelligence. While we have been able to see many of the CIA and FBI files concerning UFOs because of the Freedom of Information Act, this does not apply to files from Naval Intelligence which would no doubt show much more than these CIA files do. I would like to remind the reader that virtually only the United States has a method for citizens to request former Top Secret files on certain topics.

A Secret Underwater Base in Argentina?

In my book *Haunebu: The Secret Files* I chronicle a number of UFO incidents in South America during the year 1954. That year there were dozens of reports of various types of craft including flying saucers and cylindrical craft. October of 1954 saw UFO sightings in Buenos Aires, the Chicama Valley of Peru near Trujillo, and in Curitiba and Puerto Alegre, Brazil. Then in November UFOs were seen in Buenos Aires and Berna, Argentina.[52, 17]

There is the famous 1965 incident and photograph chronicled by Bill Yenne in his book *UFO: Evaluating the Evidence*[26] of two cylindrical UFOs, identical to the Andromeda craft, that hovered

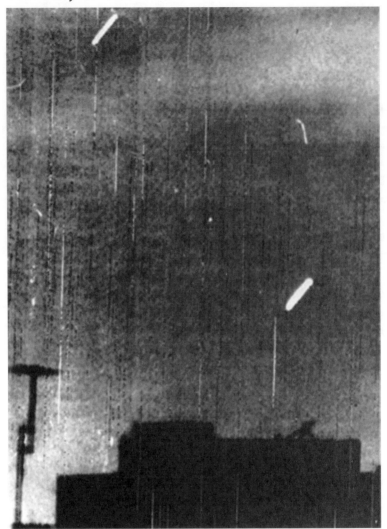

Two cigar-shaped craft hovered over Buenos Aires for 10 minutes in 1965.

for 10 minutes over Buenos Aires one evening. The two cigar-shaped craft hovered in place for so long that a photographer was able to make a two-minute exposure of the craft with his camera on a tripod. The objects, after hovering motionless for a long period, suddenly departed at a very high speed.

In *The CIA UFO Papers,* author Dan Wright mentions briefly a curious incident when a young man saw a flying saucer move silently over pastures near the Argentinian port city of Bahia Blanca on September 19, 1971. Says Wright:

The object stirred up whirlwinds of dust, while cows appeared to change color in its presence. Afterward, his face was severely burned and he suffered from a persistent migraine headache.[40]

In the book *UFO Contact from Undersea*,[3] Wendelle Stevens has an interesting appendix that discusses unusual sightings, all in Argentina, of disk-shaped craft emerging from under water and flying away. He mentions how he was investigating a case where an abductee from Rio Salado in northern Argentina was told by the occupants of the flying saucer that their base was under water. Asks Stevens in the 1982 book:

> Is there, in fact, a submarine UFO base in the South Atlantic off the Patagonia Coast of Argentina? More and more incidents seem to point that way.
> Ever since ten years before [in] February 1960 when the Argentine and United States Navys' combined forces tried for two weeks, with uncounted tons of explosives, to bring two unidentified objects maneuvering under the waters of Golfo Nuevo, an area of only 20 by 40 miles, to the surface, reports of UFOs in that area have continued.
> Near the end of June 1959, Sr. Romero Ernesto Suarez, walking the coastal road between Rio Grande and San Sebastian in the Territory of Tierra del Fuego, late, about 23:00 hours, suddenly heard the sound of turbulent water, which increased and became more violent. He was puzzled and became a little frightened. There was no wind, storm, or water currents that could explain this noise. He peered into the darkness in that direction, and suddenly a huge, luminous, oval-shaped object emerged from the sea about 500 meters from shore. It ascended vertically to a certain altitude, made a quick 90-degree turn and disappeared rapidly to the northwest, toward Rio Gallegos.
> Fifteen days later, again at night, when he was between Rio Gallegos and Santa Cruz, ascending a hill near Puerto Coyle in the province of Santa Cruz, he witnesses a similar

107

occurrence. This time four small luminous domed discs surged up out of the water vertically, in perfect formation, leveled off and flew up the coastline a ways and then turned left in the direction of the Cordillera de Los Andes.

Two years after that, and even 2-1/2 years after the February 1960 case so well reported in *Flying Saucer Review* Vol. 6, Number 3 and Vol. 10, Number 4, UFOs were seen to enter and also to leave the water again. In August 1962, Sr. Vicente A. Bordoli, a truck driver from Mar del Plata, while in the South, driving along National Highway Route #3 bordering the Atlantic Coast, with his son Hugo, observed strange formations of lights in the sky that entered the water in the Golfo San Matias, Province of Rio Negro. A few minutes later they emerged and ascended into the sky and disappeared. San Matias is a deep gulf with 500-foot depths in some places.

Two hundred miles south is another deep gulf, the Golfo San Jorge. On 28 July 1964, at 21:24, the subprefectura at Puerto Madryn, Chubut Province, received a message from the Argentine tanker "Cazador," saying that at 21:10 the captain and crew had sighted a strange light that fell into the water. They had plotted its bearings as latitude 45 degrees, 56 minutes and 06 seconds South and 64 degrees, 00 minutes and 00 seconds West longitude. They and another tanker, the "San Antonio" searched a five-mile circle looking for survivors and debris. In the afternoon of the next day, the Norwegian ship "Sumber" arrived in port and the captain reported to the authorities, "Yesterday at about 21:10, as we were approaching the Argentine coast, we observed the fall of an aerial object or small comet (into the waters of the Gulf). It came from the northeast, horizontally, towards shore. It radiated a brilliant light."

Two months later, in the same Golfo San Jorge, a public personality known for his honesty, who prefers to remain anonymous, declared that on 20 September 1964, while driving at night to the city of Comodoro Rivadavia, as he was leaving the town of Caleta Olivia, northbound up the coastal highway, he saw four small luminous lens-shaped objects describing a parabola in the sky as they flew in perfect formation. Suddenly they dipped, and still in formation plunged into the waters of the gulf and disappeared. He stopped his car and got out but could see nothing more.

A little later, while driving north of that position, he saw four similar luminous objects, possibly the same ones, emerge from beneath the sea, veer in his direction as they accelerated, and climb out at a steep angle at prodigious speed and disappear into space above.

Also in the Golfo San Jorge, on 18 March 1966, Sr. Carlos Corosan, a well-known resident of the area, walking the beach 15 kilometers north of Puerto Deseado, at 16:00 heard a strange rumbling sound. Looking up, he saw a strange cigar-shaped craft 18 to 20 meters long, moving about 30 meters above the waves offshore. A grayish vapor was coming from the rear of the object. It was dark gray colored and its surface shined with a metallic finish. The finish was completely smooth with no wings, windows, ports, or breaks of any kind and no markings. Suddenly it stopped ten meters above the water, commenced to vibrate with the rumbling sound increasing in intensity, and then he heard a muffled explosion. The smoke from the rear became denser and very black. The nose came up and it began a slow ascent to the north northeast, though visibly erratic. He heard another explosion followed by a reduction in the rumbling, and it descended rapidly and entered the water with a splash and disappeared beneath the waves.

Farther north, off Buenos Aires, in front of the Pinamar District, at night on 31 May 1971, psychologist Zulema Bruno, driving her car along the shoreline road, saw a strange luminous lens-shaped object surge from the sea as it rotated on its vertical axis and radiated orange rays of light. It followed her automobile for some 300 meters and then, putting on a burst of prodigious speed ascended and disappeared into the sky above.

Stevens then discusses the photograph that shows a dark disk-shaped object emerging from the ocean while two young men stand on a beach in front of several dead seals. Says Stevens:

> On 2 December 1971, at Punta Norte, on the Valdez Peninsula, in the Golfo San Matias, Province of Chubut, at 15:00, mid-afternoon, Sr. Ricardo Jorge Espindola and several companions were hunting seals in the cold clear deep waters off the north cape of Punta Norte. They had taken a number of seals and he was shooting a picture of two of his friends with some of the seal carcasses. He had color slide film in his camera. Suddenly the water about a quarter of a mile off shore began to roil violently and a large circular craft emerged from the turbulence coming directly towards them, and then curved away and flew out to sea and disappeared. He snapped the picture and lowered the camera in stunned surprise. The object was far away before he recovered his composure and remembered to try for another. He decided it was too distant and did not take the second picture. The object was circular and of a

A photo from Chubut, Patagonia of a Haunebu exiting the water, December 2, 1971.

dark color, and was closely surrounded by a reddish haze or halo effect that gave the whole craft a reddish cast. The object was soundless and left no trail.

The photo is remarkable and the many stories of UFOs coming in and out of the water in Argentina, mainly in the large Patagonia region, are credible. While UFO researchers for years believed that these incidents must be of extraterrestrial craft exiting or entering the water, we now know that the Germans were active in Antarctica and Argentina after the war and they designed and built craft such as the Haunebu and Vril saucers that could function as aerial craft and submersible craft.

Stevens was partially aware of German flying saucers when this book was written in 1982, but it wasn't until after 1989 that he collected the many plans and photos of the Haunebu and Vril craft. In fact, Wendelle Stevens put nearly all of these photos and plans onto CD disks that he burned one by one and sold at UFO conferences. I purchased one of these CDs from him at a UFO conference in Laughlin, Nevada circa 2004. Wendelle was a very approachable person and I chatted with him about the Haunebu and Vril photos; he believed them to be authentic and very important. I think that Stevens would have agreed with me that some of the reports above are likely to be of Haunebu or Vril craft.

Wendelle Stevens gives us one last curious encounter in Patagonia, this one in 1974, which was also photographed:

> Two hundred and sixty miles south of the Valdez Peninsula, along the coastline of Golfo San Jorge, which has figured prominently above, another new case developed. At 19:40 on 23 March 1974, near coastal highway Route #3 just before reaching the town of Caleta Olivia, Sr. Cesar Elorda saw a silvery metallic domed disc approaching from the east, from the Golfo San Jorge. It was moving west on a steady course at low altitude and he could see it very clearly. He had time to get his camera ready and take one beautiful color picture on Ektachrome film. It was completely symmetrical and smoothly finished in a low conical form almost like a "coolie hat." It had

111

no projections, ports or windows of any kind and no markings. The dome rose in a smooth unbroken curve from the flange of the disc to the top, and was smoothly rounded. It flew almost directly overhead and to the west into the sunset sky. By the time he got his camera ready it had already passed over and he shot the picture at an angle into the sunset. He could still see the silvery finish when he snapped the picture but when the slides came back he was surprised to see that it had photographed completely black.

It is interesting to note that in several of the cases the flying saucers came out of the water, which is the eastern Atlantic coast of Argentina, and then flew west towards the Andes. It seems that there is a Black Sun base somewhere in the Argentine Andes, south of the town of Esquel.

Somewhere in these bleak, snow-covered mountains is a hidden base, probably inside a mountain, where Haunebu, Vril and other craft are stationed. In my book *Antarctica and the Secret Space Program*[10] I propose that there is a submarine and UFO base run by the SS in the Antarctic Peninsula (also called Palmer Peninsula, Graham Land, or Tierra de O'Higgins in Chile). This peninsula has been claimed by the United Kingdom, Chile, and Argentina.

The peninsula forms an 800-mile (1,300-km) extension of Antarctica northward toward the southern tip of South America. The peninsula is ice-covered and mountainous, the highest point being Mount Jackson at 10,446 feet (3,184 meters). Marguerite Bay indents the west coast, and Bransfield Strait separates the peninsula from the South Shetland Islands to the north. Many other islands and floating ice shelves lie off the coast. I surmise in the last chapter of that book that a secret base is actually located on the island of King George in the South Shetland Islands off the northwest coast of the Antarctic Peninsula.

This island is actually one of the closest islands in Antarctica to the southern tip of South America so it is well located in regard to Argentina and Chile, and it can be a remote station while still being fairly accessible to flying craft or submarines.

On top of the mysterious Haunebu base in the Argentine

Andes of central or southern Patagonia, we have the curious case of the Cerro Uritorco near the small town of Capilla del Monte in northern Argentina. I have already discussed this in my previous books[36] but it is so important to the case that Argentina is harboring a Black Sun SS unit that possesses flying saucers and cigar-shaped aircraft since WWII up until this very day. Indeed it has been stated that the "SS is still active in Argentina." This very much seems to be the case, although their activity has diminished somewhat.

During the 1980s in Argentina the UFO activity centered around the northern city of Capilla del Monte. Capilla del Monte is a small city in the northeastern part of the province of Cordoba. The main tourist attraction of this town is the Cerro Uritorco, a small mountain only three kilometers from Capilla del Monte, famed around Argentina as a center of paranormal phenomena and UFO sightings. One famous incident happened on January 9, 1986. On that day a flying saucer was seen near Capilla del Monte by hundreds of residents. The astonished crowd watched the craft land on a nearby hill known as El Pajarillo. Later, residents rushed to the scene where they found a mysterious footprint on the ground where the flying saucer had landed. The mountains around Capilla del Monte has been a major UFO area since the 1950s. There has also been a lot of activity in the area involving "Men in Black." It seems likely that both of these mysterious occurrences are related to postwar German activity in the area.

About three years later on the sunny afternoon of December 26, 1988, a silver UFO flew over the northern Buenos Aires suburb (barrio) of Villa Urquiza. It is considered the most spectacular UFO incident to occur in Argentina, with more than 7,500 witnesses. The local airport reported an object flying to the west, towards General Paz Avenue, seen on radar.

In 1991 a major flap of UFO sightings occurred around the town of Victoria, a city located in the southwestern part of the province of Entre Ríos, Argentina, just west of Buenos Aires. Victoria is located on the eastern shore of the Paraná River, opposite the major city of Rosario, which is in Santa Fe province. The Paraná River here is quite wide and commercial fishing is a major activity in the area. Flying saucers were seen coming out of the river and flying with bright floodlights over the homes in the

113

area. Said one witness named Andrea Pérez Simondini, who saw the saucers and commented on the frequent UFO flights and bright floodlights:

> Regarding the objects, they said that their luminosity was so great that many of their homes had dark drapes over the windows, since the objects could bathe the ranches in light. It is somewhat humorous to see all these little houses with black curtains.

So, what of this amazing flying saucer light show over an area not too far from the capital megacity of Buenos Aires? It appears that the craft, seen coming out of the water at times, made deliberate passes over ranches and other areas with its powerful lights on full blast to illuminate people's houses in the middle of the night. Why would sneaky extraterrestrials be so overt about their activities in this area?

The pilots wanted people to know that they were there. Were they trying to frighten people? It doesn't seem like it. Were they completely unafraid of the Argentine authorities? It does seem that way. Were they trying to be noticed in order for people to realize that the flying saucer phenomenon was real, and not just a fantasy coming out of the media? This maybe the idea.

Indeed, having spent years travelling around South America, starting in the mid-1980s, I have found that people on this continent have a high degree of belief in the UFO phenomenon. People on the street, the media, and even the governments, all largely admit that UFOs, called Ovnis in Spanish, are very real.

The reader should have a pretty good idea of just how strange things have gotten in Argentina, Chile, Brazil and other countries since the end of the WWII. Much of this activity seems to be from a remnant of the SS and the Black Sun group with their Haunebu, Vril and cigar-shaped Andromeda craft. Other incidents might be attributed to hoaxes and genuine extraterrestrial activity.

114

Chapter 3

The Rise of the SS

Bang! Bang! Shoot em' up, destiny
Bang! Bang! Shoot em' up to the Moon
Bang! Bang! Shoot em' up one, two, three
—*Spaceman*, Harry Nilsson

Understanding the SS is crucial to understanding the enigma of the German saucers and why these craft would remain a secret for so many decades. Let us have a quick look at who comprised the SS and how the organization came into power.

The term SS is an abbreviation of Schutzstaffel which means "Protective Echelon" in German. They were the black-uniformed elite corps and self-described "political soldiers" of the Nazi Party. Founded by Adolf Hitler in April 1925 as a small personal bodyguard, the SS grew with the success of the Nazi movement, ultimately gathering immense police and military powers. The SS became virtually a state within a state.

Beginning in 1929 until its dissolution in 1945, the SS was headed by Heinrich Himmler (Oct. 7, 1900—May 23, 1945). Heinrich Himmler was the son of a Roman Catholic secondary-school master. He studied agriculture after World War I and joined rightist paramilitary organizations. As a member of one of these organizations he participated in Adolf Hitler's November 1923 abortive Beer Hall Putsch in Munich. Himmler joined the Nazi Party in 1925, rose steadily in the party hierarchy, and was elected a deputy to the Reichstag (German parliament) in 1930.

Himmler was appointed as Reichsführer of the SS, Hitler's elite bodyguard, which was nominally under the control of the Sturmabteilung (SA; "Assault Division" or "Storm Troopers").

115

SS officers wore sleek black uniforms and special insignia: the lightning-like runic S's, death's head badges, and silver daggers. They also wore the Death's Head ring on the third finger of their left hand. In these uniforms the men of the SS felt superior to the brawling brown-shirted Storm Troopers of the SA, to which initially they were nominally subordinate. However, Himmler masterminded the June 30, 1934 purge in which the SS eliminated the SA as a power within the Nazi Party.

With the purge of the SA in 1934 and its reduction in political

A portrait of Heinrich Himmler in his SS uniform.

importance, the SS became an independent group responsible, via Himmler, to Hitler alone. Between 1934 and 1936 Himmler and his chief adjutant, Reinhard Heydrich, consolidated SS strength by gaining control of all of Germany's police forces and expanding their organization's responsibilities and activities. At the same time, special military SS units were trained and equipped along the lines of the regular army.

Himmler built up the SS from fewer than 300 members to more than 50,000 by the time the Nazis came to power in 1933. Himmler screened applicants for their supposed physical perfection and racial purity and recruited members from all ranks of German society. By 1939 the SS, now numbering about 250,000 men, had become a huge bureaucracy, divided mainly into two groups: the Allgemeine-SS (General SS) and the Waffen-SS (Armed SS).

The Allgemeine-SS dealt mainly with police and "racial" matters. Its most important division was the Reichssicherheitshauptamt (RSHA; Reich Security Central Office), which oversaw the Sicherheitspolizei (Sipo; Security Police). This, in turn, was divided into the Kriminalpolizei (Kripo; Criminal Police) and the dreaded Gestapo under Heinrich Müller. The RSHA also included the Sicherheitsdienst (SD; Security Service), a security department in charge of foreign and domestic intelligence and espionage.

The Waffen-SS was made up of three subgroups: the Leibstandarte, Hitler's personal bodyguard; the Totenkopfverbände (Death's-Head Battalions) which administered the concentration camps and a vast empire of slave labor drawn from the Jews and the populations of the occupied territories; and the Verfügungstruppen (Disposition Troops), which swelled to 39 divisions in World War II and which, serving as elite combat troops alongside the regular army, gained a reputation as fanatical fighters.

SS men were schooled in racial hatred and admonished to harden their hearts to human suffering. Their chief "virtue" was their absolute obedience and loyalty to the Führer, who gave them their motto: "My honor is loyalty." As ruthless guards and soldiers during the war the SS carried out mass executions of political opponents, Jews, Roma (Gypsies), Polish leaders, communist authorities, partisan resisters, and Russian prisoners of war, including officers.

117

The extreme actions of the SS were mostly on the Eastern Front against the Soviets, who were declared the real enemy of Germany. It was in Eastern Europe and western Russia that Germany hoped to annex land that would be part of Greater Germany. This Greater Germany included the important oil fields at Baku in Azerbaijan and such cities as Kiev and Moscow. The vast Siberian forest and plains to the east of Moscow were not to be part of Greater Germany.

Heinrich Himmler with an SS helmet.

I discuss the importance of the oil fields at Baku and Germany's reliance on the oil fields in Romania for most of their oil in my book *Haunebu: The Secret Files*. I explain how much of WWII was an oil war in which the Germans strategically sought to capture and control the vast oil fields at Baku while the Allies desperately sought to destroy the Ploesti oil fields in Romania in two separate bombing raids a year a part in 1942 and 1943. The second bombing raid, Operation Tidal Wave, was the largest bombing raid during all of WWII. Both of the bombing raids on the Ploesti oil fields were considered failures and production from these oil fields did not significantly fall.

But on the other hand, the Germans were forced to retreat from Baku (and their push southward through the Caucasus region) because of other Soviet victories, and were never to obtain the oil fields they so desperately needed. The German war machine was running out of gas and the German government sought more and more alternative energy supplies and methods. Ultimately Germany lost the war and German officers desperately wanted to surrender to the American and British troops, rather than to the Soviets.

Many officers decided to escape, particularly those in the SS and those on the U-boats, and many of them would become part of the postwar cult of the Black Sun and Nazi survival. Following the

118

defeat of Nazi Germany, in 1946 the SS was declared a criminal organization by the Allied Tribunal in Nuremberg. Any member of the SS from that point on was an international criminal.

The Strange Death of Himmler

As for Himmler, in early 1945, the German war effort was on the verge of collapse and Himmler's relationship with Hitler had deteriorated considerably. Attempts had been made on Hitler's life and a number of high-ranking German officers had been arrested and executed. The SS had taken control of the entire security and intelligence apparatus when the Abwehr (army intelligence) was dissolved and the head of the Abwehr, Admiral Wilhelm Carnaris, was arrested. He was eventually executed on Hitler's orders on April 9, 1945, just weeks before Germany's surrender. Many officers and high-ranking officials began making plans to escape Germany or negotiate a surrender with the British and Americans.

In the final months of the war Himmler considered independently negotiating a peace settlement with the British and Americans. Himmler had a masseur, Felix Kersten, who had moved to Sweden and acted as an intermediary in negotiations with Count Folke Bernadotte, the head of the Swedish Red Cross.

Himmler and Hitler met for the last time on April 20, 1945—Hitler's birthday—in Berlin, and Himmler swore unswerving loyalty to Hitler. At a military briefing on that day, Hitler stated that he would not leave Berlin, in spite of Soviet advances. Along with Göring, Himmler quickly left the city after the briefing. On April 21, Himmler met with Norbert Masur, a Swedish representative of the World Jewish Congress, to discuss the release of Jewish concentration camp inmates. As a result of these negotiations, about 20,000 people were released in the White Buses operation.

On April 23, Himmler met directly with Count Bernadotte at the Swedish consulate in the Baltic German city of Lübeck. Representing himself as the provisional leader of Germany, Himmler claimed that Hitler would be dead within the next few days. Hoping that the British and Americans would fight the Soviets alongside what remained of the German Wehrmacht, Himmler asked Bernadotte to inform General Dwight Eisenhower that Germany wished to surrender to the Western Allies, but not to the Soviet Union. Himmler wanted the Germans to keep fighting on this front. Count Bernadotte asked Himmler to put his proposal in writing, and Himmler obliged.

As the last days of the war approached, on April 27, Himmler's SS representative at Hitler's HQ in Berlin, Hermann Fegelein, was caught in civilian clothes preparing to desert his position and sneak out of Berlin. He was arrested and brought back to the Führerbunker.

The next day, on the evening of April 28, the BBC broadcast a Reuters news report about Himmler's attempted negotiations with the western Allies through Swedish diplomats. Hitler had long considered Himmler to be second only to Joseph Goebbels in loyalty to him. Hitler called Himmler "der treue Heinrich" (the loyal Heinrich). Suddenly, everything changed.

Hitler flew into a rage at this apparent betrayal, and told those still with him in the Berlin bunker complex that Himmler's secret negotiations were the worst treachery he had ever known. Hitler ordered Himmler's arrest, and Fegelein was court-martialed and shot.

By this time, the Soviets had advanced to the Potsdamer Platz, only 300 meters (330 yards) from the Reich Chancellery, and were preparing to storm the Chancellery. This report, combined with Himmler's treachery, prompted Hitler to write his last will and testament. In the testament, completed on April 29—one day prior to his supposed suicide—Hitler declared both Himmler and Göring to be traitors. He stripped Himmler of all of his party and state offices and expelled him from the Nazi Party. Everyone knew that the Third Reich would soon be finished.

On April 30 Hitler was said to have committed suicide along with his wife Eva Braun at their bunker in Berlin. Whether this is what happened or not, Hitler had named Grand Admiral Karl Dönitz as his successor.

Starting on May 1, 1945 the northern German port city of Flensburg—on the border with Denmark—was the seat of the last government of Nazi Germany, the so-called Flensburg government led by Karl Dönitz. This government came into power with the announcement of Hitler's death and governed the Third Reich for one week, until German armies surrendered and the town was occupied by Allied troops in the days that followed the May 7 surrender. The regime was officially dissolved on May 23, 1945. It is interesting to note that Flensburg, with a large Danish population, was the site of the first shop devoted to sex toys, lingerie and contraception devices—a sex shop—to open as a business, which was in 1962.

Now that Hitler was no longer in charge of the Third Reich, Himmler met with Dönitz in Flensburg around May 2 and offered himself as second-in-command. He maintained that he was entitled to a position in Dönitz's interim government as Reichsführer-SS, believing the SS would be in a good position to restore and maintain order after the war. On May 4 Dönitz rejected Himmler's overtures and initiated his own peace negotiations with the Allies. He wrote a letter on May 6 formally dismissing Himmler from all his posts.

On May 7, 1945, the German High Command, in the person of General Alfred Jodl, signed the unconditional surrender of all German forces, East and West, at Reims, in northeastern France. At first, General Jodl hoped to limit the terms of German surrender to only those forces still fighting the Western Allies. But General Dwight Eisenhower demanded complete surrender of all German forces, those fighting in the East as well as in the West. If this demand was not met, Eisenhower was prepared to seal off the Western front, preventing Germans from fleeing to the West in order to surrender, thereby leaving them in the hands of the enveloping Soviet forces.

Jodl radioed Grand Admiral Dönitz with the terms. Dönitz ordered him to sign the document. So with Russian General Ivan Susloparov and French General Francois Sevez signing as witnesses, and General Walter Bedell Smith, Eisenhower's chief of staff, signing for the Allied Expeditionary Force, Germany was—at least on paper—defeated. The fighting would still go on in the East for another day or so, but the war in the West was over. General Jodl, who was wounded in the assassination attempt on Hitler on July 20, 1944, was later found guilty of war crimes (which included the shooting of hostages) at Nuremberg and hanged on October 16, 1946.

For Himmler, starting May 6, he was rejected by his former

comrades and hunted by the Allies. The German high command was in the northern cities of Kiel and Lübeck near the Danish border. While the Russians were already fighting in Berlin and the British/American forces were in southern Germany, the very north of Germany plus Denmark and Norway were still controlled by the Third Reich.

High-ranking officers trying to escape Germany in the last days of the war—including allegedly Hitler and his family—first flew from Berlin or other areas of Germany to airfields in the very north of Germany, near the Danish border. Airfields in Denmark and Norway could also be used. From these airfields the fleeing Nazis transferred to other aircraft and flew to Spain where they would be welcomed for a short time until they could transit to other destinations, typically Argentina. Apparently some SS officers escaped by flying to Norway and boarding a U-boat, long-range aircraft or flying disk to the secret bases in Greenland and the Canadian Arctic. In the fictional work we visited last chapter, Landig has his two SS heroes flying out of the Banak Airbase in northern Norway to a secret base.

Himmler attempted to go into hiding with a false name and false documents. He would probably have sought to get to Spain where he would be safe. Himmler carried a forged paybook under the name of Sergeant Heinrich Hitzinger that he hoped would give him the chance to escape. With a small band of SS companions, he headed south from near the border with Denmark on May 11 to Friedrichskoog, without a final destination in mind. They continued south to the town of Neuhaus, where the group split up.

On May 21, now two weeks after the end of the war, Himmler and two aides were stopped and detained at a checkpoint set up by former Soviet POWs in the town of Bremervörde, further south toward the Dutch border and west of Hamburg. Himmler was vaguely headed south in the direction of Wewelsburg Castle and this may have been his destination.

Now captured, over the following two days, Himmler was moved around to several camps and was brought to the British 31st Civilian Interrogation Camp near Lüneburg, southeast of Hamburg, on May 23. The officials noticed that Himmler's identity papers bore a curious stamp that British military intelligence had seen previously being used by fleeing members of the SS on their forged documents.

The duty officer, Captain Thomas Selvester, began a routine interrogation of the prisoner. But within minutes Himmler admitted who he was and Selvester had the prisoner searched. Himmler was then taken to the headquarters of the Second British Army in Lüneburg, where a doctor was to conduct a medical exam on him. The doctor attempted to examine the inside of Himmler's mouth, but the prisoner was reluctant to open it and jerked his head away. Himmler then bit into a hidden potassium cyanide pill and collapsed onto the floor. Within 15 minutes he was dead.

Shortly afterward, the British say that Himmler's body was buried in an unmarked grave near Lüneburg. The grave's location remains unknown; the British did not want it to become a cult pilgrimage site for former SS officers. It may have been that Himmler was cremated and his ashes thrown into a river as was

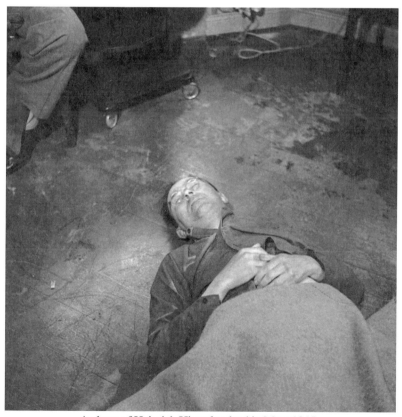

A photo of Heinrich Himmler dead in May, 1945..

123

the tradition within the SS. We simply do not know if Himmler was buried in an unmarked grave or cremated.

Wikipedia gives an interesting assessment of Himmler at the end of its page on him:

> Historian John Toland relates a story by Günter Syrup, a subordinate of [Rheinhard] Heydrich. Heydrich showed him a picture of Himmler and said: "The top half is the teacher, but the lower half is the sadist." Historian Adrian Weale comments that Himmler and the SS followed Hitler's policies without question or ethical considerations. Himmler accepted Hitler and Nazi ideology and saw the SS as a chivalric Teutonic order of new Germans. Himmler adopted the doctrine of Auftragstaktik ("mission command"), whereby orders were given as broad directives, with authority delegated downward to the appropriate level to carry them out in a timely and efficient manner. Weale states that the SS ideology gave the men a doctrinal framework, and the mission command tactics allowed the junior officers leeway to act on their own initiative to obtain the desired results.

Himmler's doctrine of "mission command" is important to the postwar activities of the SS. Hitler had effectively left the SS without a leader when he stripped Himmler of authority in April and Admiral Dönitz ordered him arrested on May 6, 1945. This order would have been broadcast throughout the armed forces of the Third Reich on that day and Himmler had to go into hiding immediately with a few loyal members.

But there were thousands of SS officers and troops that were still loyal to the SS and its goals—whatever they might be now that Germany had been overrun by the Allies and capitulated. Who were they loyal to now? It wasn't really to Hitler or Himmler, or to Admiral Dönitz.

It was to a secret society, a secret society today known as the Black Sun. And within that secret society—one possessing a staggering amount of materiel, including submarines, long-range aircraft, hidden bases and even flying saucers—the "mission command tactics allowed the junior officers leeway to act on their own initiative to obtain the desired results."

In other words, these SS commanders were now free to use their own initiative to proceed after the war to conduct whatever operations they saw fit "to obtain the desired results." But what were those desired results? What results could these postwar Nazis and SS officers hope to achieve after the war? Indeed, that is the focus of my previous books.

Aside from solidifying their territories in Antarctica and South America, they began a psychological warfare operation in the USA and around the whole world. This far-reaching operation involved flying saucers, Andromeda motherships, submarines and secret bases around the world. This operation may be continuing to this day.

Himmler's Wewelsburg Castle

Himmler was interested in mysticism and the occult from an early age. He tied this interest into his racist philosophy, looking for proof of Aryan and Nordic racial superiority from ancient times. He promoted a cult of ancestor worship, particularly among members of the SS, as a way to keep the race pure and provide morality to the nation. Viewing the SS as an "order" along the lines of the Teutonic Knights, he had them take over the Church of the Teutonic Order in Vienna in 1939. He began the process of replacing Christianity with a new moral code that rejected humanitarianism and challenged the Christian concept of marriage. The Ahnenerbe, a research society founded by Himmler in 1935, searched the globe for proof of the superiority and ancient origins of the Germanic race. It was the 1938 Ahnenerbe expedition to Tibet that paved the way for the secret air base in western Tibet that has been proposed.

At the center of Himmler's

A 1630 print of Wewelsburg castle.

125

occult world was Wewelsburg Castle in the northeast of North Rhine-Westphalia state. Himmler bought the castle in 1934 to be an academy for SS officers. Himmler's plans included making it the "center of the new world" ("Zentrum der neuen Welt") following the "final victory." This was presumably the creation of Greater Germany and the defeat of the Soviet Union. The monumental estate of Wewelsburg was never realized; only detailed plans and models exist. In 1941 the Black Sun insignia was placed in the floor of the main room at Wewelsburg Castle. Says Wikipedia about the castle:

The Black Sun mosaic at Wewelsburg.

> The castle crew consisted of members of all SS branches, the "General SS" ("Allgemeine SS"), the police and the "Armed SS" ("Waffen SS"). Also working at the castle were proponents of a kind of SS esotericism consisting of Germanic mysticism, an ancestor cult, worship of runes, and racial doctrines. Himmler, for example, adapted the idea of the Grail to create a heathen mystery for the SS.
>
> No proof exists that Himmler wanted a Grail castle, but redesign of the castle by the SS referred to certain characters in the legends of the Grail: for example, one of the arranged study rooms was named Gral ("Grail"), and others, König Artus ("King Arthur"), König Heinrich ("King Henry"), Heinrich der Löwe ("Henry the Lion"), Widukind, Christoph Kolumbus ("Christopher Columbus"), Arier ("Aryan"), Jahrlauf ("course of the seasons"), Runen ("runes"), Westfalen ("Westphalia"), Deutscher Orden ("Teutonic Order"), Reichsführerzimmer ("Room of the Empires Leader(s)"; "Reichsführer-SS", or "the Reich's Leader of the SS" was Himmler's title), Fridericus (probably in reference to Frederick II of

Prussia), Tolle Christian (probably referring to Christian the Younger of Brunswick, Bishop of Halberstadt), and Deutsche Sprache ("German language"). In addition to these study rooms, the SS created guest rooms, a dining room, an auditorium, a canteen kitchen, and a photographic laboratory with an archive.

Oak was used to panel and furnish these rooms, though (according to contemporary witnesses) only sparingly. All interior decoration was shaped by an SS sensibility in art and culture; the preferred elements of design were based on runes, swastikas, and Germanically interpreted Sinnzeichen (sense characters). Tableware, decorated with runes and Germanic symbols of salvation, was manufactured specifically for Wewelsburg castle, and Himmler's private collection of weapons was housed in the castle.

From 1939, the castle was also furnished with miscellaneous objects of art, including prehistoric objects (chiefly arranged by the teaching and research group Das Ahnenerbe), objects of past historical eras, and works of contemporary sculptors and painters…

All regalia and uniforms of Nazi Germany, particularly those of the SS, used symbolism in their designs. The stylized lightning bolt logo of the SS was chosen in 1932. Himmler modified a variety of existing customs to emphasize the elitism and central role of the SS: He established an SS naming ceremony to replace baptism, marriage ceremonies were to be altered, a separate SS funeral ceremony was to be held in addition to Christian ceremonies, and SS-centric celebrations of the summer and winter solstices were instituted.

Biographers have claimed that Himmler believed that the power of the old occult masters and Christian Celto-Germanic Nature religion would help the Nazis rule the world. Himmler claimed that the Catholic Church's Inquisition had purposefully attempted to repress an indigenous German pagan nature-based religion known as völkisch, in a conspiracy against the Aryan race. Some biographers of Himmler say that he claimed that one of his own ancestors had been burned as a witch. Himmler was also deeply involved in astrology. He officially approved pagan holidays and took rites from traditional pagan cults.

Himmler's Witch Library and Houska Castle

Some accounts claim that all of the Nazis, including Hitler, attended ceremonies of the new SS cult. Some of these ceremonies are thought to have taken place in Houska Castle located 47 kilometers north of Prague. Built in the 13th century to serve as an administration center, the castle is considered one of the best preserved in the world and still contains a Gothic chapel, a green chamber with Late-Gothic paintings, and a knights' drawing room.

Folklore stories tell that the castle covers one of the gateways to hell, having been built to prevent demons (trapped in lower levels) from reaching the world. The castle is said to have been constructed over a large hole in the ground that was said to be so deep no one could see the bottom. Animal-human hybrids were reported to have crawled out of it, and dark-winged, otherworldly creatures flew in its vicinity.

During World War II, the Wehrmacht occupied the castle until 1945. The Nazis were said to have conducted experiments into the occult, which would probably mean SS ceremonies and experiments. In some ways the castle is the model for the popular video game *Wolfenstein*, which concerns a castle where the SS are conducting experiments with Tesla-type devices.

The castle has been open to the public since 1999. Tourists may visit the chapel and see the fading frescoes and murals including pictures of demon-like figures and animal-like beings.

On March 18, 2016, the *Daily Mail* in London carried this story about a special witches library that Himmler had collected that was found in Prague. The article said that the books were to be sent to Wewelsburg Castle:

> A rare library of books on witches and the occult that was assembled by Nazi SS chief Heinrich Himmler in the war has been discovered in the Czech Republic. Himmler was obsessed with the occult and mysticism, believing the hocus-pocus books held the key to Ayran supremacy in the

world. The books—part of a 13,000-strong collection—were found in a depot of the National Library of Czech Republic near Prague which has not been accessed since the 1950s.

Norwegian Masonic researcher Bjørn Helge Horrisland told the Norwegian newspaper *Verdens Gang* that some of the books come from the library of the Norwegian order of Freemasons in Oslo, seized during the Nazi occupation of the country.

In 1935 Himmler founded the 'H Sonderkommando'—H standing for Hexe, the German word for witch—to collate as much material as possible on sorcery, the occult and the supernatural. The bulk of the collection was called the 'Witches Library' and concentrated on witches and their persecution in medieval Germany. One of Himmler's quack theories was that the Roman Catholic Church tried to destroy the German race through witchhunts. He also discovered that one of his own ancestors was burned as a witch.

Adolf Hitler never shared the enthusiasm for the occult held by his master butcher, but he gave him free reign to live out his fantasies.

The books were intended to be stored at Wewelsburg Castle in western Germany, the 'Black Camelot' of Nazism where Himmler created a court of SS 'knights' modeled on the legend of King Arthur and the Knights of the Round Table.

The castle [Wewelsburg] today is a museum and place of remembrance. The swastika-daubed ceiling of the room where he met with his evil knights forms the centerpiece of the exhibition. Historians are to analyze the Witches Library and a Norwegian TV company is to make a documentary about the find.

So we have two castles, one in Germany and one in Czech, that were associated with Himmler and the SS and their dark rites. Officers and other recruits into the SS were from Germany, Austria, Denmark, Czech Republic, Ukraine and the Baltic states.

We really don't know what went on at Houska Castle and probably never will. But one thing that we do know is that any SS officers in that castle would be wearing the Totenkopf ring, a very special piece of regalia.

The Death's Head Ring

The Totenkopf (death's head) symbol was used by German military units for hundreds of years. Use of the Totenkopf as a military emblem began under Frederick the Great (1740-1786), who formed a regiment of Hussar cavalry in the Prussian army commanded by Colonel von Ruesch. It adopted a black uniform with a Totenkopf emblazoned on the front of its battle hat. The Totenkopf continued to be used by the Prussian and Brunswick armed forces until 1918, and some of the storm troopers that led the last German offensives on the Western Front in 1918 wore Totenkopf badges.

In the early days of the Nazi Party, Julius Schreck, an early Nazi and the leader of the Stabswache (Adolf Hitler's bodyguard unit), resurrected the use of the Totenkopf as the unit's insignia. This unit grew into the Schutzstaffel (SS), which continued to use the Totenkopf as one of its insignias throughout its history. Himmler is reported to have written that the Totenkopf had the following meaning:

> The Skull is the reminder that you shall always be willing to put your self at stake for the life of the whole community.

The 3rd Panzer Division of the Waffen-SS had Totenkopf patches on their uniform collars instead of the SS runes. Both the 3rd Panzer Division of the Waffen-SS and the Luftwaffe's 54th Bomber Wing Kampfgeschwader were given the unit name "Totenkopf." This Luftwaffe unit used a similar graphic skull and crossbones insignia as the SS units with the same name.

The Totenkopf appeared on SS uniforms and was famously worn as the Totenkopf ring. Himmler placed particular importance on the death's-head rings; they were never to be sold, and were to be returned to him upon the death of the owner.

130

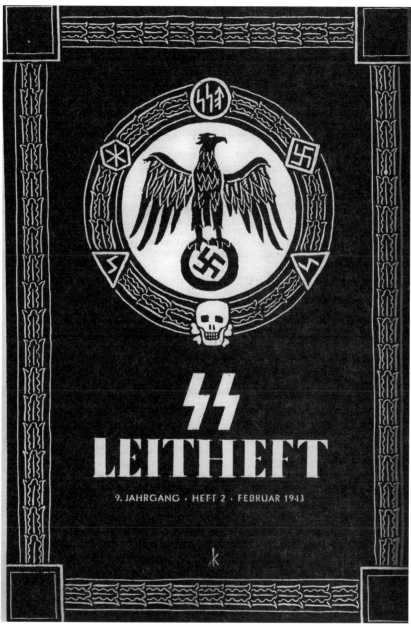

Front cover of the SS magazine *SS Leitheft* (*SS Leadership*) from February 1943
showing an artistic rendering of the Totenkopf ring.

We need to remember that the SS was a secret society. They had initiation ceremonies, secret passwords, ranks, insignias and special attire such as uniforms and rings. The SS Death's Head ring was a special ring of a secret society. It was to be worn on the third finger of the left hand. Each ring came in a special numbered box and was unique in some way. While thousands of these rings were made from 1935 to 1945 only a few are extant today, and they are valuable collectors items.

Says Wikipedia about the SS Death's Head ring:

> The SS-Ehrenring ("SS Honor Ring"), unofficially called Totenkopfring (i.e. "Skull Ring," literally "Death's Head Ring"), was an award of Heinrich Himmler's Schutzstaffel (SS). It was not a state decoration, but rather a personal gift bestowed by Himmler. The SS Honor Sword and SS Honor Dagger were similar awards.
>
> The ring was initially presented to senior officers of the Old Guard (of which there were fewer than 5,000). Each ring had the recipient's name, the award date, and Himmler's signature engraved on the interior. The ring came with a standard letter from Himmler and citation. It was to be worn only on the left hand, on the "ring finger." If an SS member was dismissed or retired from the service, his ring had to be returned.
>
> The name of the recipient and the conferment date was added on the letter. In the letter, according to Himmler, the ring was a "reminder at all times to be willing to risk the life of ourselves for the life of the whole."
>
> It became a highly sought-after award, one which could not be bought or sold. Some SS and police members had local jewelers make unofficial versions to wear. In 1938, Himmler ordered the return of all rings of dead SS men and officers to be stored in a chest in Wewelsburg Castle. This was to be a memorial to symbolize

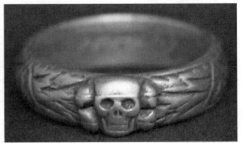

The Totenkopf (Death's Head) ring.

the ongoing membership of the deceased in the SS order. In October 1944, Himmler ordered that further manufacture and awards of the ring were to be halted. Himmler then ordered that all the remaining rings, approximately 11,500, be blast-sealed inside a hill near Wewelsburg. By January 1945, 64% of the 14,500 rings made had been returned to Himmler after the deaths of the "holders." In addition, 10% had been lost on the battlefield and 26% were either kept by the holder or their whereabouts were unknown.

'SIG' RUNE

The design of the ring reflects Himmler's interest in Germanic mysticism and includes the Totenkopf symbol and Armanen runes. Runes seen on the ring

•One Sig Rune left and right of the skull framed by a triangle represents the power of the sun and conquering energy.

'HAGAL' RUNE

•A Hagal rune (framed by a hexagon) which represents the faith and camaraderie that was idealized by the leaders of the organization. The esoteric meaning of the Hagal rune was, according to Guido von List, to: "…enclose the universe in you and you control the universe."

•A swastika (standing on the vertex) framed by a square. The SS liked to portray the swastika as another influential symbol of the power of the Aryan race.

'SWASTIKA' RUNE

•The double runes on the rear of the ring framed by a circle were to be Heilszeichen (literally: signs of salvation) of the past. They were a creation of the SS designers rather than

'DOUBLE' RUNE

133

historical runes. They are Wiligut's [Karl Maria Wiligut, designer of the ring] variation of the "gibor" rune plus a bind rune for "o" and "t." The bind rune was designed by Wiligut, and spells "Gott" the German word for God.

The ring is wreathed with oak leaves.

Most people would have trouble recognizing all the runes, particularly the "double" rune. Later the SS would add the Black Sun symbol to its insignias, a yantra-mandala meditation device created out of runes. What might be interesting for speculation here is whether these runic symbols, individually or together, might have appeared on the Haunebu, Vril and Andromeda craft or on the uniforms of the occupants of the craft. No matter what the occupants of any UFO may be wearing—overalls, metallic-like suits or whatever—we can call them uniforms.

So, were these symbols occasionally seen by UFO witnesses? Odd hieroglyphs and symbols have often been reported and these reports may well be of one or more of these SS runes. Particularly, the double rune would seem like hieroglyphs that were curious and hard to remember.

Also, we may suppose that after the war most Germanic symbols and numbers would have been painted over with black. Did the SS then put the Black Sun symbol on the Haunebu and Vril craft? Perhaps some of the SS runes were also painted on parts of the craft. Each craft, of which there must have been a dozen or more, would have needed some special marking, quite possibly a rune.

With the Andromeda craft, the mothership, it seems unlikely that it had any markings on the outside of the craft at all. There were few of these craft and it would seem any rune or Black Sun markings were on the inside of the craft and these could be seen by anyone inside the craft, including "abductees."

The Other SS: The SD

The intelligence agency of the SS was called the SD which was short for Sicherheitsdienst (Security Service). The full title of the SD is Sicherheitsdienst des Reichsführers-SS (Security Service of the Reichsführer-SS). The SD was the intelligence agency of the

SS and the Nazi Party in Nazi Germany. Established in 1931, the SD was the first Nazi intelligence organization and the Gestapo (formed in 1933) was considered its sister organization through the integration of SS members and operational procedures. The SD was administered as an independent SS office between 1933 and 1939. That year, the SD was transferred over to the Reich Security Main Office (Reichssicherheitshauptamt; RSHA), as one of its seven departments. Its first director, Reinhard Heydrich, intended for the SD to bring every single individual within the Third Reich's reach under "continuous supervision."

Emblem of the SD.

The SD was first formed as the Ic-Dienst (Intelligence Service) operating out of a single apartment and reporting directly to Heinrich Himmler. Himmler appointed a former junior naval officer, Heydrich, to organize the small agency. The office was renamed Sicherheitsdienst (SD) in the summer of 1932.

The SD became more powerful after the Nazi Party took control of Germany in 1933 and the SS started infiltrating all leading positions of the security apparatus of the Reich. Even before Hitler became Chancellor in January 1933, the SD was a veritable "watchdog" over the SS and over members of the Nazi Party and played a critical role in consolidating political-police powers into the hands of Himmler and Heydrich.

The SD became the official security organization of the Nazi Party in 1934. Consisting at first of paid agents and a few hundred unpaid informants scattered across Germany, the SD was quickly professionalized under Heydrich, who commissioned National Socialist academics and lawyers to ensure that the SS, and its Security Service in particular, operated "within the framework of National Socialist ideology."

Heydrich was given the power to select men for the SS Security Service from among any SS subdivisions since Himmler considered the organization of the SD to be important. In September 1939,

135

SD officers in uniform, Poland, 1939.

the SD was divided into two departments, the interior department (Inland-SD) and the foreign department (Ausland-SD), and placed under the authority of the Reich Security Main Office (RSHA).

Once Hitler was appointed Chancellor by German President Paul von Hindenburg, he quickly made efforts to manipulate the aging president. On February 28, 1933, Hitler convinced Hindenburg to declare a state of emergency which suspended all civil liberties throughout Germany, due at least in part to the Reichstag fire on the previous night. Hitler assured Hindenburg throughout that he was attempting to stabilize the tumultuous political scene in Germany by taking a "defensive measure against Communist acts of violence endangering the state."

Wasting no time, Himmler set the SD in motion as they began creating an extensive card-index of the Nazi regime's political opponents, arresting labor organizers, socialists, Jewish leaders, journalists, and communists in the process, sending them to the newly established prison facility near Munich, Dachau. Himmler's SS and SD made their presence felt at once by helping rid the regime of its known political enemies and its perceived ones, as well. As far as Heydrich and Himmler were concerned, the SD left their mission somewhat vaguely defined so as to "remain an instrument for all eventualities."

For a while, the SS competed with the Sturmabteilung (SA) for influence within Germany. Himmler distrusted the SA and came

136

to deplore the "rabble-rousing" brownshirts (despite once having been a member) and what he saw as indecent sexual deviants amid its leadership. At least one pretext to secure additional influence for Himmler's SS and Heydrich's SD in "protecting" Hitler and securing his absolute trust in their intelligence collection abilities, involved thwarting a plot from Ernst Roehm's SA using subversive means.

On 20 April 1934 Hermann Göring handed over control of the Geheime Staatspolizei (Gestapo) to Himmler. Heydrich, named chief of the Gestapo by Himmler on 22 April 1934, also continued as head of the SD. These events further extended Himmler's control of the security mechanism of the Reich, which by proxy also strengthened the surveillance power of Heydrich's SD, as both entities methodically infiltrated every police agency in Germany.

The SD was the overarching agency under which the Einsatzgruppen der Sicherheitspolizei und des SD, also known as the Einsatzgruppen, was subordinated; this was one of the principal reasons for the later war-crimes indictment against the organization by the Allies. The Einsatzgruppen's part in the Holocaust has been well documented. Its mobile killing units were active in the implementation of the Final Solution (the plan for genocide) in the territories overrun by the Nazi war machine. This SD subsidiary worked closely with the Wehrmacht in persecuting Jews, communists, partisans, and other groups, as well. Starting with the invasion of Poland throughout the campaign in the East, the Einsatzgruppen ruthlessly killed anyone suspected of being an opponent of the regime, either real or imagined. The men of the Einsatzgruppen were recruited from the SD, Gestapo, Kripo, Orpo, and Waffen-SS.

On July 31, 1941, Göring gave written authorization to SD Chief Heydrich to ensure a government-

Reinhard Heydrich in SS uniform.

wide cooperative effort in the implementation of the so-called Final Solution to the Jewish question in territories under German control. An SD headquarter's memorandum indicated that the SD was tasked to accompany military invasions and assist in pacification efforts. The memo explicitly stated:

> The SD will, where possible, follow up immediately behind the troops as they move in and, as in the Reich, will assume responsibility for the security of political life. Within the Reich, security measures are the responsibility of the Gestapo with SD cooperation. In occupied territory, measures will be under the direction of a senior SD commander; Gestapo officials will be allotted to individual Einsatzstäbe. It will be necessary to make available for special deployment a unit of Verfügungstruppe or Totenkopf [Death Head] formations.

Correspondingly, SD affiliated units, including the Einsatzgruppen followed German troops into Austria, the Sudetenland, Bohemia, Moravia, Poland, Lithuania, as well as Russia. Since their task included cooperating with military leadership and vice versa, suppression of opposition in the occupied territories was a joint venture. There were territorial disputes and disagreement about how some of these policies were to be implemented. Nonetheless, by June 1941, the SS and the SD task forces were systematically shooting Jewish men of military age, which soon turned to "gunning down" old people, women, and children in the occupied areas.

The SD was tasked with the detection of actual or potential enemies of the Nazi leadership and the neutralization of such opposition, whether internal or external. To fulfill this task, the SD developed an organization of agents and informants throughout the Reich and later throughout the occupied territories, all part of the development of an extensive SS state and a totalitarian regime without parallel.

The SD was mainly an information-gathering agency, while the Gestapo—and to a degree the Criminal Police (Kriminalpolizei or Kripo)—was the executive agency of the political-police system.

138

The SD and Gestapo did have integration through SS members holding dual positions in each branch. Nevertheless, there was some jurisdictional overlap and operational conflict between the SD and Gestapo.

As part and parcel of its intelligence operations, the SD carefully tracked foreign opinion and criticism of Nazi policies, censoring when necessary and likewise publishing hostile political cartoons in the SS weekly magazine, *Das Schwarze Korps* ("*The Black Corps*"). An additional task assigned to the SD and the Gestapo involved keeping tabs on the morale of the German population at large, which meant they were charged to "carefully supervise the political health of the German ethnic body" and once any symptoms of "disease and germs" appeared, it was their job to "remove them by every appropriate means."

Following Germany's defeat in World War II, the tribunal at the Nuremberg trials officially declared that the SD was a criminal organization, along with the rest of Heydrich's RSHA (including the Gestapo) both individually and as branches of the SS in the collective. Heydrich was assassinated in 1942; his successor, Ernst Kaltenbrunner, was convicted of war crimes and crimes against humanity at the Nuremberg trials, sentenced to death and hanged in 1946.

Salon Kitty and SS Orgies

In the 1930s, "Salon Kitty" was a high-class brothel at 11 Giesebrechtstrasse in Charlottenburg, a wealthy district of Berlin. Its usual clientele included German dignitaries, foreign diplomats, top industrialists, high-ranking civil servants and senior Nazi Party members. Its madame was Katharina Zammit, better known as Kitty Schmidt, who ran the brothel from its inception. Schmidt had secretly been sending money to British banks with fleeing refugees ever since the Nazis took power in Germany in January 1933.

When she eventually tried to leave the country on June 28, 1939, Sicherheitsdienst (SD) agents arrested her at the Dutch border and took her to Gestapo headquarters. Once there she was seen by Walter Schellenberg, who at that time worked in the counter-intelligence department of the SD. He gave her an ultimatum: cooperate with the Nazis or be sent to a concentration camp.

Using Salon Kitty for espionage purposes was an idea of the SS general Reinhard Heydrich, in many ways the chief police chief within Nazi Germany. Instead of infiltrating the brothel, Schellenberg took it over altogether. The idea was to entertain prominent guests with wine and women, so they would disclose secrets or talk about their real opinions to ensure their support could be relied upon. The nine rooms of the salon were lavishly expanded and renovated to the highest standards of the 1930s. Schellenberg installed covert listening devices in the rooms and converted the basement into a "workshop" where five operators could make transcriptions of conversations from the bedrooms.

Wikipedia reports that for the purpose of espionage, the SS started looking for young women to work in the brothel. In a circular deemed "top secret," Schellenberg asked administrative offices in Berlin for assistance. The requirement profile read: "Wanted are women and girls, who are intelligent, multilingual, nationalistically minded and furthermore man-crazy." (Gesucht werden Frauen und Mädchen, die intelligent, mehrsprachig, nationalistisch gesinnt und ferner mannstoll sind.)

Berlin's Sittenpolizei ("vice squad") arrested dozens of Berlin prostitutes and selected the most attractive as potential agents to work at Salon Kitty. Among other things, they were trained to recognize military uniforms, and to glean secrets from innocuous conversation. They were not told about the microphones, but had to make a report after every encounter.

In March 1940, Schmidt was told to continue business as if nothing had happened, except now she had a special book of twenty additional girls she should only show to certain clients. If a customer used the phrase "I come from Rothenburg," she was instructed to show him the book, allow him to make his decision and call for the girl he had selected. The girl would then spend the night with the guest and depart later.

Salon Kitty became even more popular when selected guests in the military and diplomatic corps were told the "secret codeword" and monitors made thousands of recordings during their visits. One of the customers was Galeazzo Ciano, son-in-law of Italian dictator Benito Mussolini and Foreign Minister of Fascist Italy, whose forthright opinions about the Führer were not particularly positive. Another visitor, SS General Sepp Dietrich, wanted all the 20 special girls for an all-night orgy, but he revealed no secrets.

Additionally, propaganda minister Joseph Goebbels had been marked as a client; he enjoyed "lesbian displays" that were otherwise considered anti-social acts outside of that context. Heydrich also made a number of "inspection tours," although the microphones were turned off on those occasions.

As the war progressed, the clientele of Salon Kitty decreased. In July 1942, the building was demolished during a British air attack and the brothel had to be relocated. Within the year the SD decided to abandon the project and handed the salon back to Schmidt, with the threat that she should keep silent or face retaliation.

Madame Schmidt did not talk about the matter even after the war. She died in 1954, at the age of 71, without revealing the identity of any of her former employees. The number of Gestapo recordings from the brothel was estimated by the Stasi (East German Security Service) to be about 25,000. Virtually all of the recordings have since been lost or destroyed due to their post-war unimportance.

The story of what happened at Salon Kitty first came to light in Walter Schellenberg's memoirs, published in Germany in 1956 under the title *The Labyrinth*. Peter Norden later expanded the story in his 1973 book *Madam Kitty*. This book became the basis for the controversial 1976 film *Salon Kitty*, directed by Tinto Brass and starring Helmut Berger as Walter Schellenberg (renamed Helmut Wallenberg) and Ingrid Thulin as Kitty Schmidt (renamed Kitty Kellermann). This became the first of the Nazi exploitation films to follow hyping SS orgies at Salon Kitty during the war.

Wikipedia tells us that the 1981 BBC comedy drama *Private Schulz*,

The 1976 film Salon Kitty..

141

about a German fraudster and petty criminal's unwilling World War II service in the SS, prominently features the Salon Kitty. In the first episode, Schultz has been given the job of manning a listening post in the brothel's basement and recording the conversations picked up by the hidden microphones.

The concept of the Gestapo using a brothel full of spies to find traitors within the Nazi regime has been recycled several times in various European Nazi exploitation films such as *Salon Kitty, L'ultima orgia del III Reich, Ilsa:She Wolf of the SS, Love Camp 7,* and others.

Meanwhile, back in London, the Czechoslovak government-in-exile resolved to kill the SS general Reinhard Heydrich. Jan Kubiš and Jozef Gabčík headed the team chosen for the mission, trained by the British Special Operations Executive (SOE). On December 28, 1941 they parachuted into Czechoslovakia where they lived in hiding, preparing for the mission. On May 27, 1942, Heydrich planned to meet Hitler in Berlin. German documents suggest that Hitler intended to transfer him to German-occupied France where the French resistance was gaining ground. To get from his home to the airport, Heydrich would have to pass a section where the Dresden-Prague road merges with a road to the Troja Bridge.

The junction in the Prague suburb of Libeň was well suited for the attack because motorists have to slow for a hairpin bend. As Heydrich's car slowed, Gabčík took aim with a Sten submachine gun, but it jammed and failed to fire.

Other SS orgy movies of the 70s.

142

Heydrich ordered his driver, Klein, to halt and attempted to confront Gabčík rather than speed away. Kubiš, who had not been spotted by Heydrich, threw a converted anti-tank mine at the car as it stopped, which landed against the rear wheel. The explosion ripped through the right rear fender and wounded Heydrich, with metal fragments and caused serious damage to his left side; he suffered major injuries to his diaphragm, spleen, and one lung, as well as a broken rib.

A Czech woman went to Heydrich's aid and flagged down a delivery van. He was placed on his stomach in the back of the van and taken to the emergency room at Bulovka Hospital. He died of his wounds a few days later.

The Decline of the Abwehr and the Rise of the SS

The SS consolidated their power again when the German Military Intelligence agency known as the Abwehr was dissolved and taken over by the SS in 1945. As I describe in my book *Haunebu: The Secret Files,* the Abwehr operated from 1920 to 1945. Under General Kurt von Schleicher the individual military services' intelligence units were combined and were centralized under his Ministry of Defense in 1929, forming the foundation for the more commonly understood manifestation of the Abwehr. Each Abwehr station throughout Germany was based on army district, and more offices were opened in amenable neutral countries and in the occupied territories as the greater Reich expanded.

The Ministry of Defense was renamed the Ministry of War in 1935. In that year Vice-Admiral Wilhelm Canaris became the director of the Abwehr with its headquarters located in Berlin. Says Wikipedia:

> Before he took over the Abwehr on January 1, 1935, the soon-to-be Admiral Canaris was warned by Patzig of attempts by Himmler and Reinhard Heydrich to take over all German intelligence organizations. Heydrich, who headed the Sicherheitsdienst (SD) from 1931, had a negative attitude towards the Abwehr—shaped in part by his belief that Germany's defeat in the First World War was primarily attributable to failures of military intelligence,

The elaborate funeral held for Reinhard Heydrich complete with a large SS banner.

A photograph of an early Vril craft hovering in front of a car. Date unknown.

A photograph of a Haunebu I with a truck in the background. Date unknown.

A photo of a Haunebu II on the ground with troops in the background. Date unknown.

This color photo was taken in the afternoon of March 21, 1974 in Varnamo, Sweden. A famous UFO photo, it seems to show a small Vril craft hovering near a house.

An early test of the Haunebu in this undated photo.

A rare color photo of a Haunebu in flight. Unknown date.

Left: A Vril saucer photographed in flight, date unknown.

A photo of a Haunebu with officers standing in front. Unknown date.

A fully-armed Haunebu III from the Ettl document dump.

Balcarce, Argentina, July 19, 1974. This disc-shaped object approached an automobile driven by Sr. Antonio Le Pere. It was approximately 6pm when Le Pere noticed the object keeping pace with him from a position only a few hundred meters to his left, and barely 10 meters above the ground. He slowed his vehicle as he readied his camera to take a picture, which he did before it started climbing and flew away. Le Pere took the picture through the rolled down window on the driver's side of the car, shooting over his left arm holding the steering wheel. The object was of a coppery-brownish, smooth-finished reflective material like metal, or something between a metal and ceramic. It had a raised dome on its top surface and seemed to have a reddish glow either on the rim edge or surrounding the rim closely.

Above: A December 2021 photograph that is also from Balcarce, Argentina, a small city south of Buenos Aires. Does this area have a secret Black Sun base? *Right*: A screen shot of a Haunebu at Cerro Uritorco in Argentina from a television newscast.

A Vril saucer photographed over Obihiro-Hokkaido, Japan on November 12, 1974.

Left: Two glowing discs photographed flying above the Zurich, Switzerland airport in the summer of 1966.

A photo of a Vril craft at Scheibe, Rheinland, Germany, 1979.

Former emblem of the Ukrainian Azov Battlion with the Black Sun logo.

An illustration of a Haunebu II from the Squadron model kit.

This selfie by Dmitry Utkin shows that he has an "SS" tattoo on each shoulder. Why is this?

Zelensky guard appears to wear Nazi insignia

Published: 14 Sep 2022 | 14:04 GMT

This photo of Ukrainian president Volodymyr Zelensky shows him with a bodyguard who has a large SS Totenkopf badge on the back of his bulletproof vest.

and by his ambitions to control all political intelligence-gathering for Germany.

Canaris was said to be a master of backroom dealings and he thought he knew how to deal with Himmler and Heydrich. Though Canaris tried to maintain a cordial relationship with the two men, the antagonism between the SS and the Abwehr continued.

Matters came to a head in 1937 when Hitler decided to help Joseph Stalin in the latter's purge of the Soviet military. Hitler ordered that the German Army staff should be kept in the dark about Stalin's intentions because they might warn their Soviet counterparts due to their long-standing relations.

At this point special SS teams, accompanied by burglary experts from the criminal police, broke into the secret files of the General Staff and the Abwehr and removed documents related to German-Soviet collaboration. In order to conceal the thefts, the burglars started fires where they had broken in, including at the Abwehr headquarters in Berlin.

On September 10 1943, an incident occurred which came to be known as the "Frau Solf Tea Party." This tea party resulted in the dissolution of the Abwehr. Hanna Solf was the widow of Dr. Wilhelm Solf, a former Colonial Minister under Kaiser Wilhelm II and the ex-Ambassador to Japan. Frau Solf was known to be involved in the anti-Nazi intellectual movement in Berlin. Members of her group were known as members of the "Solf Circle." At a tea party hosted by her on September 10, a new member was brought into the circle, a young Swiss doctor named Paul Reckzeh. Dr. Reckzeh was an agent of the Gestapo and he reported on the meeting, providing the Gestapo with several incriminating documents. The members of the Solf Circle were all rounded up on January 12, 1944. Eventually everyone who was involved in the Solf Circle was executed, except for Frau Solf and her daughter.

One of the persons executed was Otto Kiep, an official in the Foreign Office. Kiep had friends in the Abwehr, among whom were Erich Vermehren and his wife, the former Countess Elizabeth von Plettenberg, who were stationed as Abwehr agents in Istanbul. Both of them were summoned to Berlin by the Gestapo in connection with the Kiep case but in fear of their lives, they contacted the British Embassy and defected. Hitler had long suspected that the Abwehr had been infiltrated by anti-Nazi defectors and Allied agents, and the defection of Vermehren now confirmed it. Hitler and the SS also mistakenly believed that Erich and his wife absconded with the secret codes used by the Abwehr and gave them over to the British.

Wilhelm Canaris in uniform.

Hitler summoned Canaris for a final interview and accused him of allowing the Abwehr to "fall to bits." Canaris quietly agreed that it was "not surprising," as Germany was losing the war. Hitler fired Canaris on the spot and on February 18, 1944, Hitler signed a decree that abolished the Abwehr. Its functions were taken over by the RSHA and overseen by Walter Schellenberg. With this action the SS took over all military intelligence and this strengthened Himmler's control over the military. Schellenberg was captured by the British at the end of the war, was sentenced to six years in prison at the Nuremberg trials, but got out early because of a liver condition and died in Switzerland in 1952.

Canaris was given the empty title of Chief of the Office of Commercial and Economic Warfare. He was arrested on July 23, 1944, in the aftermath of the "July 20 Plot" against Hitler and executed in the spring of 1945, shortly before the end of the war.

English historian Hugh Trevor-Roper in his book *The Last Days of Hitler* (University of Chicago Press, 1992) says the Abwehr was "rotten with corruption, notoriously inefficient, [and] politically suspect." He adds that it was under the "negligent rule" of Admiral Canaris, who was "more interested in anti-Nazi intrigue than in his official duties." According to Trevor-Roper, for the first two years of the war it was a "happy parasite" that was "borne along... on the success of the German Army."

As for German intelligence operations in South America—and elsewhere—that had been under the Abwehr, they were now under

Wilhelm Canaris at the Eastern Front in 1941.

the SS. As of 1944, the SS controlled all military intelligence and this would include the missions that the Haunebu and other craft were to fly.

The SS Takes Control of the Black Reich

As the Third Reich dissolved and territory continued to be lost the SS was now in control of all of the intelligence and security apparatus of what was left of the Nazi war machine. This was an astonishing array of: submarines; submarine bases; long-range aircraft; secret airbases in far-flung parts of the world; Vril and other special craft; plus electromagnetic pulse-type weapons that could disable or confuse trucks and aircraft (but not submarines, I theorize).

The SS had immense power at the end of the war and Hitler had demanded that the Third Reich fight to the last man, precipitating a bloodbath on his own country. But while the SS commanded these many airbases and submarine bases—some of them secret, some not—plus the military hardware associated with them, they had lost virtually all of the territory in their homeland and had no army left to fight for them. All they could do was escape to the various safety zones that they had carefully invested in during the years leading up to the war.

And so we can see how the Haunebu and the Vril were

The peaked visor cap with the Totenkopf symbol worn by SS officers.

important in the last months of the war and the years afterward in moving people, passports and financial documents out of Germany to Spain, Spanish possessions and South America. Others traveled by submarine to the Canary Islands, Antarctica and ultimately on to South America. The SS could only take a small elite from their ranks with them as they vacated the Reich. The big enemy, the Soviet Union, had vanquished the Germans and the elite within the SS would carry on with their high tech toys.

But what did they really have? The idea of fighting the world powers from Antarctica and Argentina was not going to work and therefore the weapons that all of their machines had were largely unnecessary. The submarines used by the Black Fleet after the war were probably the most heavily armed, but even they knew that they needed only defensive armaments, which would include some torpedoes. It seems that all of the dark U-boats after the war removed the deck guns that were clearly signs of a warship. When U-boats surrendered in Argentina, they were all missing their deck guns—they were no longer necessary.

148

The long-range aircraft, though originally designed as bombers, would not be going on any bombing missions. Any such mission would have been a one-way suicide mission with the complete loss of a very valuable plane, one of their few assets. Therefore, they were probably used on only a few long-range flights at the end of the war. Destinations such as Tibet, northern Norway, Greenland, Spanish Sahara and Argentina have been suggested.

Operation Bolivar had been the German Abwehr secret infiltration of Latin America. The setup of Operation Bolivar began with a network of radio stations in Argentina, Brazil, Paraguay and Chile. Some of the Abwehr spies involved with Operation Bolivar were the German naval and air attaché in Chile, Ludwig von Bohlen (Bach); the naval attaché in Rio de Janeiro, Hermann Bohny (Uncle Ernest); the military attaché in Buenos Aires, General Niedefuhr; and the naval attaché in Buenos Aires, Captain Dietrich Niebuhr (Diego), who headed the espionage organization in Argentina. In mid-1941, Herbert von Heyer (Humberto) joined the organization to provide maritime intelligence.

Significant German espionage activity in Brazil ended in March 1942, when Brazilian authorities rounded up all suspected enemy agents. At this time all German espionage activities in South America, mainly radio communications, was to be centered on the Buenos Aires control station for communicating directly with Berlin. Ultimately secret radio control stations were set up in Paraguay and Chile. This network of spies was controlled by the SS starting in 1944. Not only that, but it became larger and more powerful after the war.

The Nazis had always had a great interest in South America and its resources. South America had large pockets of German immigrants most of whom supported Germany in all of its efforts, including the colonization of South America. South America has tremendous resources in the mining and farming industries but was lacking in industrial manufacturing. This would change after the war, with the help of German companies who invested heavily in Argentina and Chile. What remained of the Third Reich could resettle in this southern third of South America where there was plenty of land, forests, mountains and lakes plus a growing manufacturing sector.

The final note on Operation Bolivar is that information gained by US Naval Intelligence during the war was used by the State Department in preparing a case against the Peronista government of Argentina regarding its wartime support of the Axis in early 1946. At this time it was largely thought that the German intelligence operations had come to a halt in South America. But we now know that this was not the case. The SS continued to have intelligence operations throughout South America after the war and parts of Argentina, Paraguay and Chile became what we could call de facto colonies of the SS and the remnants of the Third Reich.

Combined with the secret U-boat bases in Antarctica and elsewhere, the remnant of the Third Reich under the control of the SS became a third power—a power that spanned the Atlantic and would become a secret society of gold ingots, fake passports, black submarines, secret bases and flying saucers.

The Revell model for the Haunebu II. Note the weapons.

Chapter 4

The SS Never Surrendered

Do you want to ride
See yourself going by
The other side of the sky
I've got a silver machine
—*Silver Machine*, Hawkwind

What is important when looking at all of these post-war activities in Antarctica, South America and elsewhere is to remember that the SS never surrendered, though the German Navy, Army and Air Force did surrender. But since the SS had taken over all military intelligence functions from the Abwehr in late 1944 they now controlled all of the secret projects and bases that the Germans had been preparing since the 1930s. Canaris, the former head of the Abwehr, was sentenced to death by an SS court and hung at the Flossenburg concentration camp on April 9, 1945, only a few weeks before the end of the war.

Himmler was fired from his job as head of the SS about a week before the end of the war. Therefore, there was no head of the SS at the time of the surrender of the Third Reich on May 7, 1945. The SS did not surrender to either the Soviets or to the British and Americans. Instead, they went underground and underwater— literally diving into the ocean in their many U-boats and leaving via various long-range airplanes to Spain, northern Finland and Norway, and even to Tibet. While we know that certain SS officers fled Europe at the end of the war—never surrendering to the Allied forces—it is less clear how many submarines and their crews fled to secret locations after the end of the war.

The researcher Henry Stevens concludes in his book *Dark Star*[46] that a small fleet of German submarines continued to move after the war between Europe, Greenland, a secret Nazi submarine base in the Canary Islands and ports in the southern Atlantic including Antarctica, Chile and Argentina.

Stevens also concludes that the bases used by the Germans in Antarctica were supplied from Europe initially and then later by German colonies in Argentina and Chile. He also concludes that these colonies were part of a secret manufacturing process that built flying saucers from parts that were specially imported from countries around the world, including Germany and the United States. Says Stevens:

> There is the idea that near the very end of the war in Europe, the German Navy refitted some damaged U-boats with non-conventional propulsion systems. This was unlike other developments by the German Navy, which involved extensive testing and prototypes and perhaps a whole line of test U-boats. These strange U-boats seemed to have been one-off and done on an individual and perhaps opportunistic basis. After the war, these U-boats may have continued to function as sort of a phantom navy for the post-war SS.[46]

It is said that there were 35 U-boats participating in the still-secret final battle with portions of the British fleet somewhere near Iceland, on May 6, 1945 (approximately) in which the renegade U-boats sank all of the British ships, victims of the fury, during a daylong battle. But this was not the final battle of WWII; that battle was apparently fought in Antarctica during Operation Highjump as discussed in my book *Antarctica and the Secret Space Program*.[10]

Submarines of the Black Fleet

For years after WWII there were a number of strange incidents that involved submarines of unknown nationality and origin. Some of these submarines were undoubtedly German U-boats that had not surrendered at the end of the war. These "mystery submarines" were part of what has been called the Black Fleet or the Ghost Fleet.

Stevens says that submarines of unknown nationality were seen immediately following World War II. He says that submarines of unknown nationality were especially prominent in reports from Norwegian fjords. This was the area of operation for the German U-boat fleet and waters they knew very well.

There is considerable evidence for German U-boat activity after the war, such as the story of a whaler called the *Juliana* (probably not the real name of the ship). A curious French newspaper article from *France Soir*, dated September 25, 1946 said (in French):

> One and one half years after the end of the fighting in Europe, an Icelandic whaleboat was stopped by a German U-boat. The whaleboat has been identified as the "Juliana" which was located in the waters near the island of Malvinas and the Antarctic zone, when it was stopped by a German U-Boat of magnificent size, bearing the German mourning flag (red with black borders).
>
> The commander of the U-Boat approached the whaleboat with a raft and gave orders to captain Hekla to surrender a part of the ship's provisions. The captain of the whaleboat had no other choice than to comply with the orders given by the German Navy officer. This officer spoke accurate English and paid for the provisions with U.S. dollars. In addition, he also paid a premium of $10.00 to each crewmember. The officer gave the captain of the whaler information pertaining to the location of whales. The ship later went to this described location and harpooned two whales. The rumors concerning U-Boats of the German Navy in the waters of "Fireland" and the Antarctic zone are now a fact (Telegram from AFP, dated Paris, September 25, 1946).[46]

It should be noted that while this story has the appearance of being true it seems likely that the names have been changed; there does not seem to be any Icelandic vessel that was ever named "Juliana" or an Icelandic captain named Hekla. Hekla is actually an active volcano in southern Iceland and most males in Iceland have a name that ends in "son." It would seem to be a "nom de guerre" for the captain to call himself "Hekla."

Henry Stevens tells another curious story that happened at the very end of the war when the submarine U-534 refused to surrender as ordered to by Admiral Dönitz. Instead, she headed north from Denmark en route to Norway with two other U-boats that were unidentified. Says Stevens about the U-534:

> May 5th, 1945: U-534 was sailing in the Kattegat, North-West of Helsingor. Although Admiral Dönitz had ordered all his U-boats to surrender as from 08:00 May 5th, U-534 refused to surrender. U-534—with two other U-boats in company—was heading north towards Norway, without flying the flag of surrender. Their departure was noted by Danish fishermen and passed on to RAF Coastal Command that in turn sent out an air-patrol.
>
> A Liberator from 547 squadron attacked U-534. With all three U-boats firing at her she was shot down and crashed in to the sea. One survivor was rescued by a boat from the nearby lightship. By that time the two other U-boats dived, leaving U-534 alone on the surface.

At that point, says Stevens, a British surface ship attacked and sank the U-534 leaving three dead and 49 survivors. But the big story is that the other two U-boats got away! The only possible conclusion is these U-boats did not want to surrender and were going to join the Black Fleet in Norway.

Many of the German submarines had extremely long ranges without ever having to refuel, and even those submarines that could not go for extreme distances without refueling would have been able to stop at secret submarine bases to refuel and resupply. These bases were located in Norway, Greenland, the Spanish Sahara, the Canary Islands, and even Antarctica. It seems that there might have been a secret submarine base in a fjord in the south of Chile as well.

The Secret Submarine Base in the Canary Islands

It is thought the Germans had a number of secret submarine bases outside of their regular bases in Germany, Poland, France and Norway (Italy had submarine bases as well). It is now known that there were secret bases in Greenland, the Canary Islands isle of Fuerteventura, and Antarctica. It is also thought that the Germans might have had secret bases in southern Argentina and Chile that were built during the war.

The secret base at Fuerteventura was key to secret submarine operations in the Atlantic, including voyages to Argentina and Antarctica. The island of Fuerteventura is a large, sparsely populated, rocky island in the eastern part of the Canary Islands, closest to the African coast. This part of the African coast was the Spanish Sahara, an area that welcomed many ex-Nazis after the war. It was even rumored that Adolf Hitler was living in the Spanish Sahara (when it was still a colony of Spain).

According to Henry Stevens:

> There is no longer any doubt that a secret German [submarine] base existed on Fuerteventura during the Second World War. One is reminded of the statement by Admiral Karl Dönitz about how the German Navy knew all the ocean's hiding places. Well, this is certainly one of them—a secret base in plain sight.
>
> This base has been mentioned by me in both my earlier books. Others have discussed this base, writing in the German language. For some reason general knowledge of this base has not penetrated the consciousness of the English-speaking world, probably because of the language barrier. I say this because the real description of the base is in German that has never been translated into English.
>
> Fuerteventura is a resort spot but an out-of-the-way one. From discussions I have heard there is a small tourist town there that includes a bar. Rumors of the secret German base have always been discussed and questions asked about it, mostly by tourists.

Evidently, everyone or most everyone on the island denies these rumors in public but affirm them in private. This base was made famous as the secret U-boat bunker on an unnamed island featured in the George Lucas/Steven Spielberg film *Raiders of the Lost Ark.* In that film a U-boat sailed right inside the island, using a tunnel, into a huge cavern that was perhaps an ancient volcanic blister. There, the Nazi bad guys had erected submarine support equipment, turntables for U-boats, along with supporting manpower. This secret U-boat base as depicted by Lucas is the one in the Canary Islands.

In 1971 *Stern* magazine published an article about the father of this base and the base itself in an article titled "The Fantastic History of Don Gustavos, His Secret House and the U-Boat Base." According to the rumors and the facts on the ground, the father of this secret base was a German General, Gustav Winter. General Winter built a large, white villa on the high point of this island. The rumor was that a staircase descended down into the bowels of the island, connecting to this secret base.[46]

Stevens says that the German researchers Heiner Gehring and Karl Heinz-Zunneck did some research on General Winter, which revealed a few things about this secret U-boat base. Winter was born in 1893 in the Black Forest and was trained as an engineer. He died in 1971, a few months before the *Stern* article was published.

General Winter performed some outstanding service for the Germans, and for that service he was granted land on the southern peninsula of Fuerteventura. During World War II, General Winter was the driving force behind a project to build a secret U-boat bunker on the island. He was also an agent for the Abwehr, the military spy service. The major feature of this bunker was a huge natural cavity that was connected to the sea by tunnels bored into the solid rock.

Ventilation shafts were dug upward towards what was now the large Villa Winter. This large villa also included an airport which could land even large aircraft. This facility functioned as a military base during the war and was heavily armed and guarded.

After the war parts of the facility, with the exception of the airport, were destroyed with explosives. Today part of this large site belongs to a nature park but part of the property is still privately owned.

Stevens says that the submarine bunker was still active until about 1950 Heiner Gehring and Karl Heinz-Zunneck were told, though only accessible from the ocean. The researchers were told by an informant that the base was known to the Americans, who allowed it to be used to bring Project Paperclip Nazi scientists and officers secretly to the United States.

The German journalists were told that there were originally three subs that came and went from the base but one of them was sunk near Florida. These submarines, and the base, were being operated by the SS, with U-boat officers from the Abwehr during and after the war. The crews of the submarines were still living in the Canary Islands in many cases, though some had gone back to Germany.

Says Stevens:

> Here in the Canary Islands was an SS base that operated after World War Two. In fact, two U-boats were on-call and continued to be on-call for some time even after their last mission. We know this because the informant, "Charlie," includes the detail that the crew lived in the Canary Islands.
>
> This base functioned at least up until 1950 and with the knowledge and consent of the Americans. This would be the intelligence services of the USA, probably the CIA. We will get into this relationship later but we begin to see that this relationship between the surviving SS organizations, which became the "Nazi International" or The Third Power, was not always adversarial.
>
> Knowledge of this base and its continued existence after the war brings up claims of other facilities, laboratories, being operated by the SS after the war. Yes, there are those that say this is so and was done, not over the horizon in some never-never land, but right in Europe itself![46]

Stevens goes on to tell the story of a "Mrs. Maria W." who was aware of secret facilities in Western Germany after the war, including a secret SS research facility in the Jonas Valley. She went on to describe a small train track running to Bienstein (presumably also from the area of the Jonas Valley) that ran into a mountain. The Russians found the train track but did not ever follow the track fully into the mountain. This was the entrance to a German underground laboratory. For whatever reason, the Russians did not investigate the German facility there. "Mrs. W" says this was a "Fusionsanlage" an atomic fusion facility. Not fission but fusion, as in a hydrogen bomb! And importantly, the woman says this facility operated until 1952! At that time it was supposedly shut down but remains ready to fully resume operation.

So here we have evidence that the SS continued to operate in Germany and Europe after the war and had laboratories in West Germany and probably Austria and elsewhere that were still functioning on a limited basis.

The Final Battle and the Move to Argentina

Writers like Wilhelm Landig who are quoted in Henry Stevens' book *Dark Star*[46] claim that at the end of the war a number of submarines refused to surrender to the Allies and became part of the Black Fleet. This fleet left from ports in northern Germany, Denmark, and Norway or were already at sea in the final days before Germany surrendered. Many of these submarines congregated

A map of Argentina showing the major cities in Patagonia.

in the North Sea off the east coast of Iceland. Here a portion of the British fleet gathered in search of these wayward craft and a battle was had on May 6, 1945, one day before the Germans began signing surrender documents on May 7. Hitler was said to have committed suicide on April 30.

So, only a few days before Germany's surrender a battle took place in the North Sea and all of the British ships were sunk. Landig claimed that a Haunebu was launched from the secret base in Greenland called "Beaver Dam" to locate the British fleet. After the battle the U-boats went their separate ways to various secret submarine bases that the Third Reich had started developing in the 1930s. These included secret submarine bases in Greenland, the Canadian Arctic (a base known as Point 103), the Russian Arctic, the Canary Islands, Antarctica and South America.

As the Allies took control of what was left of the Third Reich on May 8 and 9 a Black Fleet of U-boats were heading for various destinations while long-range aircraft—and flying saucers—left from airfields in northern Italy, Austria, Czech areas, northern Germany, Denmark and even Norway. Apparently some of these long-range aircraft flew to northern Finland and Tibet. Other aircraft flew to Spain, the Canary Islands and the Spanish Sahara. This exodus of craft and personnel had begun in late April 1945.

The Secret U-Boat Base in Chilean Tierra del Fuego

Ultimately, the secret base at New Schwabenland in Antarctica would be used by many of the U-boats as well as some of the Haunebu and Vril craft. While long-range aircraft may not have been able to land at the base in Antarctica it certainly would have been possible for an Andromeda mothership to land there. The secret bases in Patagonia and other areas of Argentina, Chile and Paraguay were key to ex-Nazis and SS officers to infiltrate South America and attempt to reconstitute the Reich in the resource-rich and under-populated areas of these countries.

In his book *Hitler in Argentina*,[8] famous "sharkhunter" (submarine hunter) Harry Cooper discusses on page 209 that the German Navy had established a secret Abwehr base inside a fjord on the Chilean western side of Tierra del Fuego on the southern tip of South America. Says Cooper:

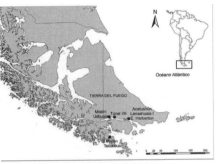

A map of Tierra del Fuego.

From what we know today, the German Abwehr base could have existed in Tierra del Fuego—on Chilean territory—south of the Admiralty Fjord, south-easterly of the Parry Fjord, and near a narrow, small but long secondary fjord, which is still today an extremely isolated and hard-to-access nature preserve.

The base could have been activated on orders of Abwehr boss Canaris as early as 1935 or 1936. ...a German Navy (VM-BE) was designated by Abwehr IV in the secret files of operations orders/commando missions for May 1940 in relation to the V-ship for Tierra del Fuego for the U-boat locations in the environs of Tierra del Fuego.

The inference was that one could depart from a secret base, in which a pilot from the V-ship (a VM [type of sub]) waits in order to bring the V-Ship to a safe holding point, noted on extant land maps as land. The U-boat locations in Tierra del Fuego, especially Claerence, only makes sense if they had logistics, supplies, pilotage, etc.

According to Cooper this secret Abwehr submarine base in the Chilean section of Tierra del Fuego was still operational up until 1952. He claims that this U-boat base is still a secret to this day. Discussing a 12-page document given to them by agent "Pizzaro" Cooper says:

Only Chile had kept itself neutral or rather silent for the most part. Brasil-Mexico, 1945, even Argentina, declared a state of war on Germany. As early as 1941 Peru interned German freighters and other states like Uruguay refused to help as early as 1939. Only Chile played fair, and from the many KTB notes of the Abwehr, there are references to this fair, helpful or neutral, silent behavior.

Therein lies the supposition that the secret base is on Chilean territory.

The development of U-boat places—hideouts, shelters, secret berths—well before the war in Tierra del Fuego, intensifies this supposition.

The altogether established six secret U-boat places in Tierra del Fuego, in addition to four further emergency shelters, isolated anchoring spots in the tangle of islands with thousands of canals and hundreds of large fjords, intensifies this hypothesis.

Cooper then muses on some of the material taken from a quotation from a source:

...a secret base—the base is not some sort of empty hiding place, by base we mean equipment, personnel on location, supplies, fuel, provisions for a long time, logistics. Bases in comparison were always with crews with a [radio] signal.

—putting in also means to be somewhere, at the end of

A map of Tierra del Fuego showing some of the many fjords.

a distance of travel, the end of a sea canal. Putting in must mean here to be able to put into a bay, canal (channel), shed, small safe anchorage, etc.

—which is only reachable through a narrow channel— this is the clearest indication. The word only, that is, no other possibility, a channel that is narrow, a channel can also be the Tierra del Fuego channel.

The sentence is clear: to put into a secret base, presumably of the German Abwehr… only through a narrow channel, can the base be reached, and the base is a great distance overseas. It can't be clearer, to be sure its in South America.[8]

So we are dealing with a German Navy document that states that there is a secret base up a narrow channel like a fjord in a distant part of the world which has been determined to be the Chilean section of Tierra del Fuego, an area of countless fjords and narrow channels.

It is just like the German Navy to choose such an area for not just one base but a series of U-boat bases, perhaps up to six different bases in addition to four other special anchoring sites, all of which are in this area of the Chilean fjords of Tierra del Fuego.

What this creates is a network of six full-blown U-boat bases in an area of the world that is isolated—but accessible to U-boats. This secret series of U-boat bases could be used to hide submarines and to do repair work on them.

It is suggested in Cooper's book that the Antarctic base in Neuschwbenland, although it existed during and after the war, was exposed as a cover to protect the more important secret U-boat bases in Tierra del Fuego that were more useful to their efforts in South America to create a Fourth Reich on that continent.

Cooper says on page 213 of his book[8] that:

Since the Kaltenbrunner/Garbers meeting in November 1944 in Berlin-Fuerstenwalde took place, that is after the meeting in the Hotel "Maison Rouge" in Strassburg on 10 August 1944, the heads of the German armaments and supply industries met to secure the existence of a new

Fourth Reich after the end of the war. Everyone knew it was no longer possible to win the war. It is highly probable that the leaders of the Abwehr, perhaps Kaltenbrunner himself, took part in this meeting.

The transfer of assets, licenses, and investments to safe countries was agreed and was, according to the OSS/CIA, set immediately into motion. The countries of refuge for the revival of a Fourth Reich were: Switzerland, Portugal, Spain, Turkey—and South American countries with an emphasis on Argentina.[8]

On the next page Cooper quotes from a June 1995 German-language article that was titled "Only Little Fish Get into the Nazi Hunter's Nests." According to Cooper:

This article reports on the transfer of money to South America and the discovery of files which were found in the archives of the Argentinian Foreign Ministry, which attest to the fact that the former military governments and Peron protected top Nazi refugees. Around 1,000 new names of Nazis who after 1945 were transferred to Argentina could be found in these files. Even German television briefly reported about the discovery of the files, but said no more.

The refugees were German, Flemish collaborators and Croatian personalities, who were working for the Third Reich. Peron was supposed to have received 60 million dollars in currency. A further 40 million was to be distributed to the refugees to facilitate their new lives in South America. The capital, so it was noted (journalist Gaby Weber), originated from Swiss-Lichtenstein Nazi bank accounts. A great deal has already been written about this.

Suffice to say that it was widely known that this was a refugee movement—and a well-organized one at that. However, the coordination points were never clearly described, and their headquarters is unknown. There are exceptions for Spain or Portugal and for South American residences. The coordinator for the refugee organization was to have been as of April 1945—when the first refugee movement began—a General/Obergruppenfuehrer Wagner. He wasn't a General in the Waffen SS, there were Obergruppenfuehrer(s) without this rank.

For the Middle East (Egypt/Syria), the coordinator was Obersturmbannfuehrer (Oberstleutnant) Franz Roestel. Cover name: Haddad Said.

…It is well known that the refugee organizations ran from Germany through Austria into Italy …and with further shelters of places, where there were convents.

…A total of over 750 ventures were established after the "Maison Rouge" meeting, through front men in South America.

So, here we have confirmation of the planning in 1944 to move certain manufacturing and assets to South America through Swiss-Lichtenstein banks and that over 750 business entities had been created in South America, mainly in Argentina but in other countries as well.

We get the whole idea that thousands of Nazis, most of them SS officers, were taken through Italy and Spain to Argentina where they were given money and a new identity in the form of an Argentine passport. This seems to be standard history at this point. What is missing from this is the flying saucers and secret U-boat bases in Chile and Argentina.

Colonia Dignidad in Chile

Cooper also discusses Colonia Dignidad (Noble Colony), a maximum security village that existed in the mountains south of Santiago near the town of Parral. Cooper says that the "colony" was created by some 300 former SS men in 1961. Says Cooper:

…The village was heavily armed and guarded—nobody was allowed inside. The honor, ethics and education of old Germany were strictly maintained inside.

In file photos we see the neatly maintained grounds—typical German lifestyle as we have seen throughout our travels in Germany and Austria. Everything is in order and well maintained.

However, some years ago, during the Chilean coup in which Salvador Allende was overthrown by the military under Augusto Pinochet, a dark cloud of suspicion came over Colonia Dignidad.

It was rumored that a great many outspoken supporters of Allende were brought into Colonia Dignidad by Pinochet followers—but they never came out... at least not alive.

Towards the end of the 20th Century, the leader of the Colonia Dignidad, Paul Schafer, was accused of child abuse on about two dozen children the complex. Some think the charges were accurate while others think they were a convenient way to make him disappear and break up the tightly held community. He was jailed [in Chile] and died in prison at age 89.

Colonia Dignidad was renamed Villa Baviera some time thereafter [Schafer's arrest].

Indeed, Colonia Dignidad has now created something of a storm in Chile with revelations that there were secret tunnels beneath the village that were used for torturing and killing Pinochet's enemies. Colonia Dignidad had barbed wire fences, guard towers, bunkers, and tunnels. From the Wikipedia entry for Colonia Dignidad we learn an assortment of facts:

> Colonia Dignidad ("Dignity Colony") was an isolated colony of Germans established in post-World War II Chile by emigrant Germans which became notorious for the internment, torture, and murder of dissidents during the military dictatorship of General Augusto Pinochet in the 1970s while under the leadership of German emigrant preacher Paul Schafer. Colonia Dignidad has been described as a "state within a state."
>
> ...The first inhabitants of Colonia Dignidad arrived in 1961, brought by German citizen Paul Schafer, who was born in 1921, in the town of Troisdorf. Schafer's first employment in Germany was as a welfare worker for children in an institution of the local church, a post from

which he was fired at the end of the 1940s; he then faced accusations of sexual abuse against children in his care.

...To the outside world, the colony portrayed itself as a prime example of German efficiency, cleanliness and communal work. The profitable agricultural production and an attached charity hospital helped in preserving this image for a long time. The colony had its own press operations who recorded and broadcast videos showing their happy residents amid celebrations and commemorations: men dedicated to farm work, women and girls embroidering or preparing butter. Diplomats at the German embassy ignored reports of the violence and crime and praised it as a "model colony."

However, Schafer's propaganda efforts were again and again overshadowed by allegations of people escaping from the colony and obtaining asylum in Germany. The first, Wolfgang Müller, fled in 1966 and first exposed the atrocities that occurred within the colony. Müller obtained German citizenship and worked for a newspaper, soon becoming an activist in Germany against the leaders of Colonia Dignidad, and finally became the president of the foundation dedicated to the support of victims in Chile.

...Journalist John Dinges has suggested that there was some degree of cooperation between the German Intelligence Service, German arms dealer Gerhard Mertins, and Colonia Dignidad, including creation of bunkers, tunnels, a hospital, and runways for the decentralized production of armaments in modules (parts produced in one place, other parts in another).

Because of Colonia Dignidad's close association with the Chilean military and strategic proximity to the Argentina–Chile border, the Colonia served as a base for the Chilean military during the 1978 Beagle conflict between Chile and Argentina. The hospital at Colonia Dignidad also served as a laboratory for the manufacture of weaponized sarin as part of the Pinochet government's Project Andrea.

... During the military dictatorship of Augusto

Pinochet, from 1973 to 1990, Colonia Dignidad served as a special torture center. In 1991, Chile's National Commission for Truth and Reconciliation concluded that a number of people apprehended by the DINA [Chilean secret police] were held at Colonia Dignidad, and that some of the colony's residents actively helped the DINA torture some of the captives.

...Prisoners being tortured in the tunnels under Colonia Dignidad were each interrogated to gain an understanding of their personality in order to gauge the appropriate torture technique. These techniques led to a number of afflictions lasting indeterminate periods of time. As many as 100 of the citizens taken to Colonia Dignidad by the DINA were murdered at the colony.

There are more than 1,100 desaparecidos (disappeared people) in Chile, some taken to the Colony where they were tortured and killed. One of them is a U.S. citizen, Boris Weisfeiler, a Soviet-born mathematics professor at Pennsylvania State University. Weisfeiler, then 43 years old, vanished while on a hiking trip near the border between Chile and Argentina in the early part of January 1985. It is presumed that Weisfeiler had been kidnapped and taken to the Colony where he was tortured and killed.

...The Central Intelligence Agency and Simon Wiesenthal claim that Josef Mengele, the infamous Nazi concentration camp doctor, known as the "Angel of Death" for his lethal experiments on human subjects, was present at the colony. The colony itself rejected the accusation when Wiesenthal published it in 1997 in the Chilean press. The German government states that to this date, there is "no evidence to support or invalidate Wiesenthal's claim or the more general allegation that the Colonia Dignidad or its legal successors was a place of refuge for Nazi criminals."

The Nazi underground in South America was established some time before World War II. Juan Perón provided shelter to some escaped Nazi criminals. Nazi sympathy in South America decreased until Pinochet took power. It was suggested that part of the intense racism, anti-Semitism, and classism in Chile can be attributed to Nazi presence.

...Colonia Dignidad was a "Nazi stronghold protected by the Chilean government" [Infield, Glenn, *Secrets of the SS*, 1981, p. 206]. Former members of the SS and Gestapo had the job of demonstrating Nazi torture methods to the secret police of Chile. Many of Schafer's followers who had Nazi pasts joined him to escape post-World War II war crime investigations. The presence of Colonia Dignidad had an effect on the general political opinion of the surrounding areas, and the government as well because of this, considering the political ties between Colonia Dignidad and the Chilean government.

There is plenty more to know about Colonia Dignidad than we shall go into here. Let us just say that this "SS Colony" in Chile is something out a James Bond or *Man From Uncle* movie. It's got it all, folks: an armed compound with tunnels, barracks, and even a weapons manufacturing plant! Yes, that's right, they didn't just have sophisticated weapons—but they made them right there in the various machine shops and such. These SS Nazis had two airfields, at least one airplane, and even had a sarin nerve gas factory on the site at one point. What were they up to—trying to promote and set up the Fourth Reich? Uh, yeah. More on 007 and the *Man From Uncle* in a future chapter.

Cooper discusses a number of Nazis who escaped to South America. One of them is the little-known Croatian Nazi Ante Pavelić. Pavelić was a Croatian politician who founded and headed the fascist ultranationalist organization known as the Ustaše in 1929 and served as dictator of the Independent State of Croatia, a fascist puppet state built out of parts of occupied Yugoslavia by the authorities of Nazi Germany and Fascist Italy, from 1941 to 1945. Pavelić and the Ustaše persecuted many racial minorities and political opponents during the war, including Serbs, Jews, Romani, anti-fascists, and others. With the fall of Germany Pavelić needed to escape Europe.

Cooper says it is known that Pavelić entered Italy in the spring of 1946 disguised as a priest with a Peruvian passport. Passing through Venice and Florence, he arrived in Rome disguised as a Catholic priest and using the name Don Pedro Gonner. In Rome he was given shelter by the Vatican and stayed at a number of residences that belonged to the Vatican. There he started to gather his associates.

Tito and his new Communist government accused the Catholic Church of harboring Pavelić who they stated, along with the Western "imperialists," wanted to "revive Nazism" and take over communist Eastern Europe. The Yugoslav press claimed that Pavelić had

Ante Pavelić in uniform.

stayed at the papal summer residence at Castel Gandolfo, while CIA information states that he stayed at a monastery near the papal residence in the summer and autumn of 1948. Anglo-American intelligence agencies had employed former fascists and Nazis as agents against communist powers.

Pavelić arrived in Buenos Aires on November 6, 1948 on the Italian merchant ship *Sestriere*, where he initially lived with the former Ustaše and writer Vinko Nikolić. In Buenos Aires Pavelić was joined by his wife and three children. Pavelić took up employment as a security advisor to Argentinian president Juan Perón. Pavelić's arrival documents show the assumed name of Pablo Aranjos, which he continued to use. In 1950 Pavelić was given amnesty and allowed to stay in Argentina along with 34,000 other Croats, including former Nazi collaborators and those who had fled from the Allied advance. Following this, Pavelić reverted to his earlier pseudonym Antonio Serdar and continued to live in Buenos Aires.

On April 10, 1951, on the 10th anniversary of the Independent State of Croatia, Pavelić announced the Croatia State Government. This new government considered itself to be a government in exile. Other Ustaše emigrants continued to arrive in Argentina, and they united under Pavelić's leadership, increasing their political activities. Pavelić himself remained politically active. Ultimately over 34,000 Croats came to Argentina and were given national

169

Adolf Hitler meets Ante Pavelić, 1941.

identity cards.

On April 10, 1957, the 16th anniversary of the founding of the Independent State of Croatia, Pavelić was grievously wounded in an assassination attempt by the Serbian Blagoje Jovović, a hotel owner and former Royal Yugoslav officer who had tried to assassinate Pavelić multiple times. Jovović shot Pavelić in the back and collar bone as he exited a bus near his home in El Palomar, a Buenos Aires suburb. Pavelić was transferred to the Syrian-Lebanese hospital, where his true identity was established.

Cooper, quoting from Wikipedia, says that after Perón's fall from power, Pavelić fell out of favor with the Argentine government; Yugoslavia again requested his extradition. Pavelić refused to stay in the hospital, even though a bullet was lodged in his spine. Two weeks after the shooting, as the Argentine authorities agreed to grant the Yugoslav government's extradition request, he moved to Chile. He spent four months in Santiago, and then moved to Spain. Reports circulated that Pavelić had fled to Paraguay to work for the Stroessner Nazi regime; however he was already in Spain by this time. His Spanish asylum became known only in late 1959.

Pavelić arrived in Madrid on November 29, 1957. He continued contacts with members of the Croatian Liberation Movement and

170

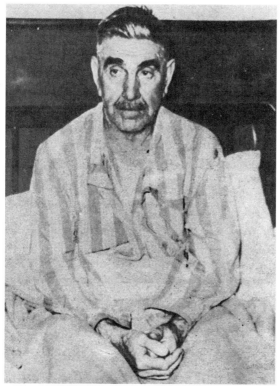

Ante Pavelić recovering at the hospital in Buenos Aires.

received visitors from around the world. Pavelić lived secretly with his family, probably by agreement with the Spanish authorities. Though he was granted asylum, the Spanish authorities did not allow him public appearances. He died two years later on December 28, 1959 at the Hospital Alemán in Madrid at the age of 70 from the gunshot wounds and was buried in Madrid's San Isidro Cemetery.

Cooper says that he visited Buenos Aires in January 2014 and says:

> I spoke with the lady who, with her attorney husband, now owned Pavelić's house and told her I was gathering evidence that Adolf Hitler lived out his life in Argentina. She was surprised. She said she thought everyone knew that; they knew it in Argentina. She pointed out the little monument on the corner where Pavelić was shot.[8]

171

What interests me here is the 34,000 Croats who came to Argentina during the late 1940s and early 1950s. Did some of these immigrants make it to the secret Black Sun bases that had been established in Chile, Paraguay, Bolivia, Peru, Argentina and elsewhere?

It may be that some of these Croats became part of the Black Sun secret society and even became complete Croat crews of the Vril and Haunebu saucers. It is interesting to consider that some of such crews would

A 1947 Argentine book.

speak with each other in Croat. This language is little-known outside of Croatia and to most people it would definitely sound like an alien foreign language. Many of the Croats would have made it to the ranches and farms of Patagonia and would have found a place to work, much like the settling of the frontier of the United States. It was a perfect time and place for the Fourth Reich to rebuild itself—yet it was not to happen.

Incredibly, flying saucers and cylindrical craft would be part of their resurgence.

The Fourth Reich of Black Sun devotees needed new blood to work in their secret bases and pilot their saucer craft and remaining submarines. Cooper mentions the small of town of San Antonio Oeste inside the little bay called Calete de los Loros or Parrot Cove in the Golfo San Matias near the Peninsula Valdes in Patagonia. Cooper says, "In this village was a large building for the Lahausen Wool Company, a cover for the German spy network through South America. The sailing ships and *Black Boats* came and went unhindered for years."[8]

This town is on the main highway and the railroad line that go directly west to Bariloche. Both San Antonio Oeste and Bariloche are in the Patagonian province of Rio Negro. South of this province is the heavily German Patagonian province of Chubut, where all kinds of UFO activity has occurred starting the in 1940s.

Hitler's Villa Near Bariloche

For many years, starting in the late 1940s, it has been believed that Adolf Hitler and Eva Braun escaped to Argentina at the end of WWII along with other Nazis and lived in the surroundings of San Carlos de Bariloche, a major resort town in the Andes of northern Patagonia. Hitler and Braun allegedly resided at the Inalco House, located at the northwest end of the large Nahuel Huapi lake, in part due to the estate's remoteness and lack of accessibility. This was alleged in the American crime magazine the *National Police Gazette* (circa 1950–1970) in a number of their issues. A number of books have been written on the subject as well, such as *Hitler: The Survival Myth*[33] (1983), the 2011 book *Grey Wolf*[4] as well as books by the Argentine writer Abel Basti.[62] These books have made the claim of Hitler living near Bariloche as well. *Grey Wolf* claims that Hitler and Eva Braun first flew out to Berlin to Denmark and then to Spain. From Spain they flew to the Canary Islands where they boarded one of the dark U-boats to make a voyage to Argentina, arriving in the summer of 1945.

Hitler allegedly arrived in Argentina, first staying at Hacienda San Ramón, east of San Carlos de Bariloche. Hitler then moved to a Bavarian-style mansion at Inalco. An Argentine businessman, Primo Capraro, sold the property to architect Alejandro Bustillo, who designed the house in early 1943. The plan includes bedrooms connected by bathrooms (and closets), similar to Hitler's Berghof residence.

Bustillo sold the estate to Enrique García Merou, a Buenos Aires lawyer linked to several German businesses; Merou is alleged

The house where Adolf Hitler allegedly lived: Casa Inalco.

to have assisted the Nazi ratlines. The residence was later sold to businessman Jorge Antonio, an associate of Argentine president Juan Perón. In 1970, the house was sold to José Rafael Trozzo, who also bought properties owned by escaped SS officer Reinhard Kopps, who—along with Capraro—had ties to SS commander Erich Priebke. The Trozzo family put the house up for sale in 2011 (the year *Grey Wolf* was released).

Purportedly, Eva Braun left Hitler around 1954 and moved to Neuquén with their daughter, Ursula ('Uschi'), and Hitler died in February 1962. Eva von Braun is thought to have still been alive in 2014 and in a hospital in Buenos Aires.

About the property, Wikipedia says:

> Citing a former Nazi presence in Bariloche, the investigative series *Hunting Hitler* (2015–2018) reveals a guard tower—reportedly built by the same architect as the Inalco House—looking over the lake (situated closer to Bariloche than the house), as well as a destroyed bunker on the other side of the lake; together the two sites (in addition to other possible lookouts such as a wooden building resembling a guard shack) may have provided a panoramic view used to safeguard the mansion, accessible from only the lake due to heavy forestation and long rumored to have

The SS-affilated Hotel Llao Llao near Bariloche, Argentina.

housed Hitler. Additionally, the *Hunting Hitler* team cited the proximity of German scientist Ronald Richter's Perón-backed nuclear fusion project on Huemul Island.

In a 2018 episode of *Expedition Unknown*, Abel Basti secured a rare excursion into the Inalco House, revealing little except for some old kitchen utensils in the basement. Using a metal detector on the grounds, host Josh Gates located a Nazi coin, leading him to conclude that Nazis (but not necessarily Hitler) could have used the house.

Near the Inalco House that Hitler lived in was the luxury SS hotel called Villa Llao-Llao. Located on the same lake as Hitler's villa Inalco, the Villa Llao-Llao was conceived in 1934 and completed with German financing at the end of 1937.

Architect Alejandro Bustillo chose the Puerto Pañuelo area in which to build the hotel because, besides the magnificent and beautiful scenery, it had a port. Built with cypress logs and larch tiles in the Canadian home style, it was opened to the public on January 9, 1938. On October 26th, 1939 a fire destroyed the building completely, but it was reopened on December 15th, 1940. Since then, members of the aristocracy, officials, diplomats and famous guests have stayed at the hotel. It closed in 1978 and eventually was resold.

Harry Cooper says in *Hitler in Argentina* that hundreds of former SS officers lived in and around the Villa Llao-Lloa and Bariloche. He says that the villa was famous for Nazi celebrations attended by hundreds of people, especially April 20, which is Hitler's birthday. Cooper notes that Dwight Eisenhower visited Villa Llao-Llao in 1960 while President of the United States.

A 1944 release of possible Hitler disguises.

175

Cooper wonders why Eisenhower would visit this hotel. It would seem that he knew about the Nazi-SS presence there.

Here we can also see how the CIA and probably Naval Intelligence knew about the Nazi activity around Argentina and especially Bariloche. They probably also had reports of Hitler living at his Inalco villa. But they didn't really care. They were happy to leave them be. Did they suspect that the flying saucers seen over the USA were coming from South America? It would seem that they surmised this as well.

A photo from Shark Hunters that purports to show the location of the New Schwabenland military base on the coast of Antarctica.

Chapter 5

Secret Submarines, ODESSA and SPECTRE

There's this place you can go called Tierra del Fuego
Down in the Southern Hemisphere
It's kinda Troy without Helen, past the Straits of Magellan
And things are always looking up down here
—*Party at the End of the World*, Jimmy Buffet

When it comes to a discussion about secret submarines, USOs and UFOs, Tierra del Fuego and Argentina come in at the top of the list. We reported earlier on the secret SS submarine bases now thought to have been built in the fjords of the Chilean section of Terra del Fuego.

Several reports of USOs in Argentina are given in the 1999 book *UFO Odyssey*.[11] The first concerned the Argentine navy searching for mystery submarines:

> Early in February 1960, the Argentine navy, with the assistance of United States advisers, alternately depth-bombed and demanded the surrender of submarines thought to be lurking at the bottom of Golio Nuevo, a 40x20-mile bay separated from the South Atlantic by a narrow entrance On a number of occasions, the Argentines declared that they had the mystery submarines trapped. Once, they even announced that they had crippled one of the unidentified subs.
>
> There were at least two mystery submarines, and they both had peculiar characteristics. They were able to function

177

and maneuver in the narrow gulfs for many days without surfacing. They easily outran and hid from surface vessels. And in spite of the combined forces of the Argentine fleet and the most modern US sub-hunting technology, they were able to escape capture and destruction.[11]

The second concerned the Argentine steamer *Naviero* off the coast of Brazil in 1967:

> Captain Julian Lucas Ardanza of the Argentine steamer *Naviero* was some 129 miles off the coast of Brazil on the night of July 3, 1967. The time was about 6:15 pm, and the *Naviero* was running at 17 knots. Captain Ardanza was enjoying his evening meal when one of his officers, Jorge Montoya, called him on the intercom to report something strange near the ship.
>
> According to reports in the Argentine newspapers, Captain Ardanza emerged on deck to view a cigar-shaped shining object in the sea, not more than 50 feet off the *Naviero*'s starboard side. The submarine craft was an estimated 105 to 110 feet long and emitted a powerful blue and white glow. Captain Ardanza and the other officers could see no sign of periscope, railing, tower, or superstructure on the noiseless craft. In his 20 years at sea, Captain Ardanza said that he had never seen anything like it.
>
> Chief Officer Carlos Lasca ventured that the object was a submersible UFO with a brilliant source of illumination. The seamen estimated the craft's speed at 25 knots, as opposed to the *Naviero*'s seventeen.
>
> After pacing the Argentine steamer for 15 minutes, the unidentified submarine object suddenly submerged, passed directly under the *Naviero*, and disappeared into the depths of the ocean, glowing all the while it dove deeper and deeper.[11]

Regarding this cigar-shaped craft in the South Atlantic, we can only surmise that its glow was part of the propulsion of the craft.

It is in essence the "Vril power" glow—electric-plasma fields being created by the "engines" of the craft. As long as the electric circuit is on the craft will generate the anti-gravity electric field that propels it through water, air and space.

An even earlier tale, occurring in 1942 during WWII, is told in *UFO Odyssey* and comes from the 1955 book *Flying Saucers Uncensored* by the British author Harold T. Wilkins.[32] This tale occurs in the Bass Strait south of Melbourne, Australia. This may seem a long way from the fighting of WWII but it is not very far from a German base in Antarctica or Tierra del Fuego. Says *UFO Odyssey*:

> In mid-February 1942, Lieutenant William Brennan of the Royal Australian Air Force (RAAF) was on patrol over the Bass Strait south of Melbourne, Australia, on the look-out for Japanese submarines or long-range German U-boats Fishermen in the area had reported mysterious lights bobbing on the sea at night, and after the Japanese attack on Darwin on February 19, the allied High Command was urging the strictest vigilance.
>
> About 5:50 pm on a sunny afternoon the air patrol was flying a few miles east of the Tasman Peninsula when a strange aircraft of a glistening bronze color suddenly emerged from a cloud bank near them. The object was about 150 feet long and approximately 50 feet in diameter. Lieutenant Brennan saw that the peculiar craft had a dome or cupola on its upper surface, and he thought he saw someone inside wearing a helmet.
>
> There were occasional greenish blue flashes emanating from its keel, and Lieutenant Brennan was astonished to see, "framed in a white circle on the front of the dome, an image of a large, grinning Cheshire cat."
>
> The unidentified aerial craft flew parallel to the RAAF patrol for several minutes, then it abruptly turned away and dived straight down into the Pacific. Lieutenant Brennan emphasized that the USO made a dive, not a crash, into the ocean, and he added that before the craft left them, he noticed what appeared to be four finlike appendages on its underside.[11]

This fascinating early UFO/USO encounter would appear to be the sighting of an early cigar-shaped craft created by the SS and flown out of Antarctica or Tierra del Fuego. It would seem to be an experimental craft with a dome on the upper surface and someone inside with a helmet on, as one would expect on a military craft. The Cheshire cat in a white circle is curious, and may be just the strange mascot for this particular craft but is even more likely to be the mistaken identification of a grinning totenkopf symbol used by the SS frequently on its airplanes and vehicles. Certain totenkopf badges accent this grinning aspect of the death's head.

The Cheshire Cat and the Totenkopf.

An encounter with a similar smallish cigar-shaped object was made at Kaipara Harbor on the west coast of the North Island of New Zealand in 1965. Says *UFO Odyssey*:

> On January 12, 1965, Captain K., an airline pilot on a flight between Whenuapai and Kaitaia, New Zealand, spotted a USO when he was about one-third of the way across Kaipara Harbor. As he veered his DC-3 for a closer look at what he had at first guessed to be a stranded gray-white whale in an estuary, it became evident to him that was a metallic structure of some sort.
>
> Captain K. saw that the object was perfectly streamlined and symmetrical in shape. He could detect no external control surfaces or protrusions, but there did appear to be a hatch on top. Harbored in no more than 30 feet of water, the USO was not shaped like an ordinary submarine. Captain K. estimated length to be approximately 100 feet with a

diameter of 15 feet at its widest part.

Later, the New Zealand Navy stated that it was impossible for any known model of submarine to have been in that particular area due to the configuration of the harbor and coastline. The surrounding mudflats and mangrove swamps would make the spot in which Captain K. saw his USO inaccessible to conventional undersea craft.

This means that this 100-foot-long craft had to land there from the air. It would also depart the swampy estuary by air. Glowing with its electric field it would eventually depart from its watery nest—where it did not think it would be discovered—and take off into the skies. Because of the polar route, New Zealand and Tasmania are not that far from Tierra del Fuego and Antarctica,

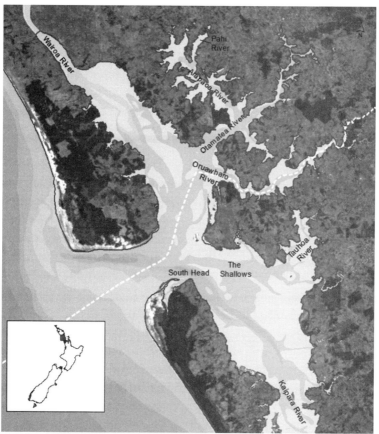

The location of Kaipara Harbor in the North Island of New Zealand.

especially the Palmer Peninsula that comes up from Antarctica near Tierra del Fuego.

A similar incident happened of Shag Harbor in Nova Scotia in 1967. This is one of Canada's most famous UFO incidents and actually is a UFO/USO incident involving a craft with a row of lit windows, like an airplane. On October 3, 1967, an elongated craft, with lit windows along its side, was seen gliding into the dark waters Shag Harbor and disappearing from view. Within 20 minutes, Canadian police were searching for the USO, thinking it might have been an aircraft that had crashed into the harbor. Two days of searching came up with nothing. The craft had gone into the water—and since it was a submarine it moved out of the harbor into the deep ocean and eventually flew away. Was it going to the secret base at Peary Land in northern Greenland?

The Humanoids

In the 1969 book *The Humanoids*,[33] a collection of papers on UFOs and their occupants, French investigator Jacques Vallee recounts a number of curious UFO encounters in France and elsewhere during 1954, a year of numerous reported encounters.

Vallee says that on September 17, 1954 near Cenon, France, a farmer meets a being in a diving suit who mades friendly gestures. The being entered an object which was sitting on the road and took off like lightening, throwing a greenish light.

On September 20, a guard at Santa Maria Airport in the Azores witnessed the landing of a craft from which emerged an individual who talked to him, but was not understood. The object then took off very fast.

On September 24 two women made independent reports of a dark grey disc seen in a clearing in the woods near Becar, France. A man of normal height was standing close to the object, which took off without noise.

On September 27 in Figeac, France, children saw "a box" with "an unknown man" standing close by. The object took off. Also on that day, on Lassus Road in Perpignan, France, a college student saw a circular object on the ground. Two beings came out, then re-entered the craft, which took off.

On September 28 in Buzais, France, a "mass of light" suddenly fell from the sky in front of the witness, who found himself unable to move. He saw three figures moving around the light.

On September 30 near Marcilly-sur-Vienne, France, eight construction workers saw a disc on the ground, with a small humanoid wearing a helmet nearby. (Yes, wearing a helmet...)

On October 1, two young men saw a luminous white disc moving about the sky near Jussey, France. The disc dove to the ground and two men described as very tall and dressed in white emerged from the craft and made gestures. The witnesses ran away in fear. Were they wearing white coveralls or uniforms of some sort?

On October 3 three men riding bicycles near Vron, France, saw an orange object on the road in front of them A man wearing a diving suit was standing close to it. The object took off as they came within 70 meters of it

On October 4 a farmer named Garreau saw an object about the size of a carriage land in his field in Chaleix, France. Two individuals of human type and normal height, wearing coveralls, emerged from the craft and spoke to the witness in a language he could not understand. Was it Croatian? Also on that day about 20 persons saw a circular, luminous object rise from the vicinity of the railroad tracks near Montceau-les-Mines. It took off vertically and disappeared.[33]

Vallee lists a number of incidents that take place on or near railroad tracks. I noted in my book *Haunebu: The Secret Files* that bomber pilots during WWII would frequently follow railway lines to find the city or industrial site such as oil wells to bomb. Is something like that going on here?

Vallee says that on October 6 near the military barracks at La Fere, France, soldiers saw a strange object which had landed 300 meters away. As one of them neared the site, he was mysteriously prevented from approaching. The object was luminous.

Also on October 6 two women saw a whitish light in the western sky. It seemed slowly to come towards the ground, and was later seen between the railroad station and the bridge, as it landed about 100 meters away from their home in Villiers-le-Lac. When the object moved, a very bright light was seen under its dark mass. It gave off a flow of sparks and rose, remained motionless in mid-air for a moment, then flew away very rapidly.

On October 7 some children at Hennezis, Eure, France, witnessed a luminous red object land near them. Two pilots of normal stature were seen. Also on this day a railroad employee in Jettingen, France, saw an object in a field, three meters away from the road, hovering about a meter above the ground. It was a circular craft about three meters in diameter and had a luminous rectangle, like the opening of a door on the side that could be seen. It took off and followed the witness in his car to the next town. Also on October 7 a truck driver near Saint-Jean-d'Asse, France, saw an intense blue light coming toward him. He said the object was cigar-shaped with red and blue lights. His car immediately died and his headlights went out.[33]

Also on October 7, 1954, Vallee tells us that in the evening a Mr. Marcel Guyot was coming from work near Saint-Etienne-siys-Barbuise with his son, Jacques, following ten minutes behind when he saw at a railway crossing three objects that gave off a bright white light. His son Jacques confirmed that he saw the same thing ten minutes later as the objects were still on the railway tracks. He said that one of objects was circular while the other two were cigar-shaped.

On October 9 near Huy, Belgium, a mailman saw a cigar-shaped object which landed near him. Two silhouettes, "approximately human," were seen aboard the craft. Then in the evening of October 9 a German cinema projectionist named Herr Hoge saw what he thought was a downed aircraft which had made an emergency landing about 70 meters from a road near Rinkerode in the Munster area of Germany. The object turned out to be a cigar-shaped craft and four men who appeared to be wearing rubber coveralls, were working under the craft. Also on October 9 a Mr. Jean Bertrand was driving on a road near Carcassonne, France when he saw on the road ahead of him a bright metallic craft. The top half seemed to be made of transparent plastic and he could easily see two human-like figures standing inside the small craft. The object then took off rapidly, flying to the east.

Also on October 9 a farmer in Lavoux, France, was riding his bicycle in the evening and suddenly stopped when he saw a human figure dressed in a diving suit, aiming a double light beam at him.

184

The individual seemed to have "boots without heels" and very bright eyes—possibly goggles. The individual walked into the forest and disappeared.

On October 10 near Charmes-la-Cote, France, a man who was riding a motorcycle suddenly saw in his headlight an aluminum-colored object shaped like a plate, with a dome and two "portholes" in it. On that same day a mathematics professor saw in the early afternoon, in the vicinity of Saint-Germain-de-Livet, about 200 or 300 meters from the road, a silvery disc, about 7 or 8 meters in diameter. It suddenly rose up into the sky without making any noise. It then dived at the ground and flew off at "a dizzying speed."

On October 11 two men were riding motorcycles at 3 am in the morning near Acquigny, France, and saw a strange object on the tracks of the Evreux-Louviers railway line. The object was apparently a machine that was shaped like a bell about two and a half meters high and hovering about one meter above the ground. The lower side of it was like a ring and it gave off reddish and greenish sparks. It then jumped up to hover about 10 meters above the ground with a burst of orange light. It then remained motionless for about one hour, during which time a third witness joined the first two. It finally turned brighter and flew away in an easterly direction.[33]

The curious encounter seems to be an encounter with the famous "SS Bell" that has been discussed in a number of Polish and English books, including Joseph Farrell's *SS Brotherhood of the Bell*.[27] One would think that from the description of the size of this bell it could only hold one or two, or possibly three, pilots inside of the cramped space, if this was indeed a bell craft designed by the SS.

But there is more from Vallee[33] who says that on October 11 two truck drivers in a petrol truck on the road in Lavarande, near Oran, Algeria, were frightened by a large flying saucer flying low over the road in front of them. They stopped their vehicle and ran away into the fields while the object flew toward Medea, Algeria.

A 1954 photo taken in Australia.

185

Then on October 12 in Tehran, Iran, a large disc came very close to the ground in a densely populated area. One of the witnesses, Chasim Faili, screamed when he thought he was going to be "kidnapped." A crowd gathered and the craft took off. The report, says Vallee, continues with a description of the operator of the craft, a man said to be "small and dressed in black." He was probably seated so it would be hard to tell how tall he was. Also on October 12 in the afternoon in the Mamora forest in Morocco on the road to Port Lyautey, a French engineer in his car saw a small being wearing silver coveralls running into a flying saucer and taking off.

On October 14 in Meral, France, a farmer observed an orange sphere that had landed. Upon approaching it, he found it was shaped like a flattened dome, five meters in diameter, which gave off a blinding light, illuminating the countryside over about 200 meters. The machine was transparent and a dark figure could be seen inside. It remained close to the ground, motionless, for about ten minutes, then flew off to the north. The witness went to the site and observed a sort of bright cloud, slowly falling on the ground. Upon arriving home he noticed that his clothes were covered with a white film of an adhesive substance, not unlike paraffin wax.

On October 15 in Perpignan, France, near the town swimming pool, a retired man was walking with his dogs when a luminous reddish sphere was seen to land about 30 meters from them and an individual in a diving suit walked around it. The dogs barked at the individual and he boarded the craft and it flew away without any noise. On this same day at 7:50 in the evening near the Nimes-Courbessac, France, airport, a yellow cigar-shaped object with brilliant "portholes," about 30 meters long, 6 meters in diameter, was seen on the ground. Figures with helmets covering their head could be seen inside the craft. A sort of haze was seen at both ends of the craft.

Also on October 15 in Saint-Pierre-Halte, near Calais, France, a baker saw a brilliant yellow craft which came down rapidly and landed on the railroad tracks. It was circular, about four meters in diameter and two meters in height. On that same afternoon in Po-di-Gnocca, Italy, farmers saw a disc-shaped machine which landed and then took off vertically. And on that night in Fouesnant,

186

France, a truck driver saw a disc-shaped craft fly very low towards the sea. A second disc followed shortly thereafter, going in the same direction. Both craft emitted a reddish glow.

On October 16 at nightfall, Dr. Henri Robert, who was driving through the village of Baillolet, France, saw four discs at about 300 meters altitude. They flew slowly one above the other, but all of a sudden one of them dropped to the ground with a dead-leaf motion about 100 meters ahead of the car. Then the witness felt an "electric shock" and the engine stalled and the headlights died. The car stopped as the disc touched the ground. Incapable of movement, Dr. Robert saw a short figure moving in the light of the object, then all went dark. Sometime afterward the car headlights came back on and Dr. Robert could see the craft taking off toward the north, along the road.

On October 17 at 2:30 in the afternoon in Cabasson, France, near Corbieres, a 65-year-old man was hunting with his dog near the junction of the Brillance Canal and the Durance river, when he suddenly found himself confronted with a grey-colored object, about four meters long and one meter high, plus it had a dome (and was a apparently a disc). The man saw two helmeted beings emerge from craft. The witness fled, but his dog ran towards the object but soon retreated and walked in an awkward way for some time, as if partially paralyzed. On the evening of the same day a man walking near Cape Massulo on the Italian island of Capri, is said to have observed a disc, about five meters in diameter, which landed on the property of writer Curzio Malaparte. The witness first thought it was a helicopter, but upon approaching the craft saw five short beings dressed in coveralls standing beside the craft. After about half an hour they entered the craft which made a soft whirring noise, rose lightly, and then flew away very fast.

On October 20 in the village of Jean-Mermoz, Algeria, a Mr. Gaston Blanquere was driving his car and saw a machine with a dome on top moving above the road. The dome gave off a yellow light while the underside emitted a beam of blue light. The light swept the countryside like a powerful searchlight.

On October 26 in Les Metaires, France, two farmers and their mother observed an orange craft 6 meters in diameter and 3 meters in height which flew over their tractor and the engine

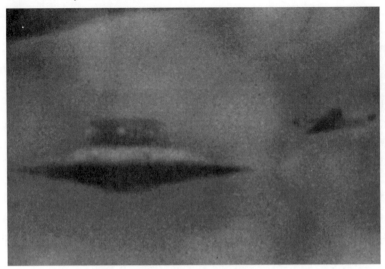

A Vril craft in flight with an Me-109 in the background.

died. Also on the evening of that day a 47-year-old farmer at La Madiere, France, was suddenly confronted with an individual of normal height wearing a sort of diving suit with a pale green light on either side of the helmet. This individual aimed a beam of two blue lights at the witness, who was thrown backwards. No craft was described.

On October 27 in Oye-Plage, France, a very bright cigar-shaped object was seen flying very low, following the turns of the road at 29 meters altitude. It was seen for 15 minutes then turned at right angles to the road and flew away.

On November 5 near La-Roche-en-Brenil, France, a craft (apparently a disc) which made a noise like a large transformer and gave off an orange light was seen in a pasture. Three men dressed in dark coveralls were standing near it. One was holding a sort of box "which emitted a beam of light three meters long." The other two were holding objects which looked like weapons. One of the witnesses fled, after feeling prickling on his face. Four photographs of the scene were allegedly taken by the third witness hidden in the bushes.

On November 7 in Monte Ortobene, near Nuoro on the island of Sardinia (Italy) a man fell from his motorcycle when he saw a disc-shaped machine land near the road. A taxi driver stopped and walked towards the object, which gave off a soft whirring sound,

188

and soon took off. Farmers on the other side of the mountain saw it fly away. It was given an approximate diameter of 15 meters. They said the disc was made of a silvery metal and had a dome with a porthole in it. Some elliptical ports were visible on the lower portion of the object which were covered with a grating similar to that of a radiator.

On November 8 in Monza, Italy, an amazing encounter occurred. Vallee says that a man saw a light in a stadium and soon a crowd of 150 people gathered, destroyed the barriers into the stadium, and rushed inside to have a closer look. They saw a flying disc set on three legs emitting a blinding white light. Figures dressed in light colors and wearing transparent helmets were standing close by. One of them had a dark face and sort of trunk or hose coming from his face. The three apparently human-size figures entered the craft and it flew away without any noise.

On November 10 near Porto Alegre, Brazil, an agricultural engineer and his family saw a disc from which two men, normal in height, with long hair and dressed in coveralls emerged. They came towards the car with their arms raised, but the frightened witnesses sped away.

On November 13 near Curitiba, Brazil, a lens-shaped object was seen on the railway tracks. Three small men wearing tight-fitting suits were looking at the tracks with a light. When witnesses approached the machine it took off very fast.

On November 22 in Santa Maria in the state of Rio Grande do Sul, Brazil, a radio operator at the air base nearby saw a huge dark object, about 30 meters in diameter, hovering at tree height. With four other persons, he saw it for several hours, sometimes softly glowing, sometimes coming down almost to the ground. However, it did not appear to land.

On December 9 a farmer in Linha da Vista, near Venancio Aires, Brazil, observed a stranger standing near a machine which was almost on the ground, shaped "like a tropical helmet," cream-colored and surrounded by haze, making a noise like a sewing-machine. Another individual was looking at the fence, while a third one was inside the craft with his head and arms visible. As the witness dropped his fork, one of the men picked it up and handed it back after examination. They went back inside the machine,

189

motioning the witness not to come close, and took off. They were of average height, had broad shoulders, long hair, very white skin and slanted eyes. They wore brown coveralls ending with shoes that had no heels.

On December 10 in Venezuela, a doctor from Caracas who was driving near Floresta stopped his car as two short men were seen running into the bushes beside the road. Soon thereafter a luminous disc rose from the side of the road with a sizzling sound and flew away.

Vallee ends his fascinating list of events on December 29, 1954, with an incident at 11 pm of a man going to Gardonne, France, who saw in the vicinity of Bru an oval, red object 50 meters away from him. When he approached it he was unable to move. When this paralysis ended he ran to the house where his brothers lived, 300 meters away, and came back with them. When they approached the object, apparently a flying saucer, it became white and then red and flew away to the east. It had been on the ground for 15 minutes at least.[33]

We must commend Jacques Valle for all of the work he has done over the years and his efforts to catalog and categorize the many unusual sightings he has accumulated over the years, only a few of which have been presented here.

But what are we to think of some of these sightings? It would seem that many of these are sightings of the small Vril craft which holds only two or three people.

But a larger saucer, such as the Haunebu is also indicated in many of these incidents which are occurring over a four-month period in 1954, mainly in France. Since Vallee is French it seems natural that he has carefully culled these many stories from French language newspapers.

Other stories are of the cigar-shaped Andromeda craft of which we can gather there were larger and smaller versions built. Supposedly the Andromeda craft held one of the larger Haunebu craft and four of the smaller Vril craft. It would seem that there were certain operations by the Black Sun in France, Italy and Algeria.

That some of the occupants were small in stature may have been due to the desire of the SS Black Sun to have the pilots of the small Vril craft be of short stature. But many of the occupants seem to be ordinary humans of normal height. It seems that wearing neoprene diving suits was popular during this time, or alternately, wearing coveralls. No insignia or numerals are seen on the craft.

One has to wonder if this amazing rash of sightings in France, particularly, had something to do with psychological warfare being run by the Black Sun to frighten and confuse the French public

Flying saucers (Vril craft?) in a circular formation over Czechoslavakia, circa 1955.

191

(and of other European countries as well)? Were the flying saucers with their powerful lights searching the dark roads of France at night meant to create confusion and panic in these early years after the war? This kind of UFO activity does not seem to be occurring in later decades with such frequency. One has to wonder, as well, whether these craft were on special missions, such as picking up certain individuals at carefully selected locations?

The incident at the stadium in Monza, Italy, is particularly interesting as it involves 150 witnesses. This appears to be an effort by the Black Sun and its SS pilots to get as much attention as possible by landing a brightly lit craft in an empty stadium at night and waiting for a crowd to gather. This was clearly not some sort of stealth operation but one designed to get as many witnesses as possible.

The UFO-Nauts

When looking at the old 1970s UFO books, one that stands out is *The UFO-Nauts* by Hans Holzer.[54] In this book Holzer examines some of the occupants of UFOs and gives us some curious information:

>...In July 1957, at 7:10 pm, an attorney and professor of Roman law at the Catholic faculty of law University of Santos, was sitting near the shore, when he observed what he described as a "luminous, hat-shaped craft" approach him from the sea and land on the water's edge near him. The craft opened and a metallic stairway came out, as well as a landing line with spheres attached to it. "Two tall men, over five feet ten inches in height, with long fair hair to their shoulders descended the stairway. Their complexions were fair, they had eyebrows, and their appearance was youthful and they had wise and understanding eyes. They wore greenish one-piece suits fitting closely at neck, wrists and ankles."
>
>The professor asked them in five different languages where they had come from, but they did not understand him. Instead, he received a telepathic invitation to come aboard and followed it. He noticed that the strangers were

able to jump up the stairway very lightly, while he had to to use both hands to ascend. The illuminated inside of the machine contained a circular seat on which he saw a crew of three or four people. They took him for a flight which by his estimation lasted about 30 or 40 minutes.

...In April 1957, a motorcyclist riding along a road near Cordoba, Argentina, saw a huge disc some 60 feet wide and fifteen feet thick, hovering above ground level ahead of him. In terror, he got off his motorcycle and hid in a ditch. When the disc came down to a height of about seven feet, a "sort of lift then descended from its base, coming down almost to the ground. In it was a man about five feet eight inches in height, who came over and gently coaxed the motorcyclist out of the ditch and then stroked his forehead to calm him. The stranger's garb was like a diver's suit, fitting the body closely, and seemingly of some sort of plastic."

...The Argentinian motorcyclist also was invited aboard the spacecraft that he entered via the lift shaft on which the astronaut had come down to him. He found himself inside the craft where there were five or six men dressed similarly to the first one, seated at instrument panels. He, too, noticed the extraordinary light which filled the cabin, and a series of large square portholes which he had been unable to see from outside.

Holzer then discusses the curious case of Reinhold Schmidt, who on November 5, 1957, while driving through a rural area near Kearney, Nebraska, saw a large, blimp-shaped object on the ground in a field. He claimed two men left the object and escorted him inside it. On board he witnessed a group of four men and two women, who appeared to be normal humans speaking a language he described as "High German." Schmidt was of German-American ancestry and spoke German, as did his parents. I detail Schmidt's unusual story in my book *Andromeda: The Secret Files*.

What Holzer finds particularly interesting is that on this same day a similar incident took place in Dante, Tennessee, a suburb of Knoxville, that involved a cylindrical craft, similar to the one seen by Schmidt. Says Holzer:

> On the same day the Schmidt incident took place in Nebraska, twelve-year-old Everett Clark of Dante, Tennessee saw a strange object in a field about one hundred yards from his home. Outside it were two men and two women, apparently normally dressed. One of the men tried to grab the boy's dog who growled and backed away. Then he tried to grab another dog that attempted to bite him, so he let it go. The strangers looked like German soldiers as Everett had seen them on television. When they got to the ship it looked as if they walked right through the side, as if the ship were made of glass. The object took off straight without sound. The boy described the strange craft as long and round, and of no particular color. There was no way the young Everett Clark could have heard of the Schmidt incident of the same day.

In these curious encounters we have normal looking humans, sometimes dressed in German uniforms, speaking German, and offering people tours and rides in their craft. In some of the stories the UFO-nauts do not speak at all, apparently choosing not to. It may be that some of these occupants may speak Croatian, rather then German, and Croatian is not a language that is spoken outside of Croatia or the Croatian communities in Argentina.

Also, the non-speaking occupant of the hat-like craft that apparently came out of the water onto a Brazilian beach may not necessarily have used telepathy to communicate with the Brazilian lawyer, but merely gestured slightly to the craft to invite him in. The diver's suit worn by the occupants of the craft in Argentina were probably neoprene suits similar to what surfers and divers wear today. I can't help thinking that these are all SS craft coming from the secret base in Tierra del Fuego and that the light inside and outside of the craft is essentially light from "Vril Power."

Holzer also tells us about a curious UFO encounter described by Mrs. Jennie Roestenberg, a housewife living in Ranton, near Shrewsbury, England:

On October 21, 1954, she and her two children "watched a dis-shaped object of aluminum color as it hovered over their house. Through two transparent panels she claimed she could see two men with white skin, long hair to their shoulders, and foreheads so high that all their features seemed to be in the lower half of their faces. They were wearing transparent helmets and tight blue clothing like ski suits."

...The description also jells with one given by a certain Jean Bertrand, who was driving on a road near Carcassonne, France, on October 9, 1954. Bertrand "saw on the road ahead of him a bright metallic sphere whose top half seemed to made of transparent plastic, for he could easily see two humanlike figures standing inside."

These small two-man craft would seem to be variants of the Vril saucers that we have the plans for, as we do for the Haunebu saucer and the Andromeda cigar-shaped craft. One wonders if the long hair is not a wig. The high foreheads could have been an illusion from the "transparent helmets."

What seems to be happening in these 1950s and 1960s UFO episodes is what a 1952 CIA memo described as "psychological warfare" and refers to a document that appears to be called 2AB. The memo is from Walter Bedell Smith, the director of the CIA. Walter Bedell Smith, whose nickname was "Beetle," was a Lieutenant General in the Army and a member of Dwight Eisenhower's Allied Supreme Command during WWII. He became the director of the CIA on October 7, 1950 when then-acting director Admiral Roscoe Hillenkoetter stepped down. Bedell Smith was the director of the CIA until February 9, 1953 when he was succeeded by Allen Dulles.

The 1952 memo, with the

Walter Bedell Smith.

195

CENTRAL INTELLIGENCE AGENCY
WASHINGTON 25, D. C.

19̂5̂

OFFICE OF THE DIRECTOR

MEMORANDUM TO: Director, Psychological Strategy Board

SUBJECT: Flying Saucers

1. I am today transmitting to the National Security
Council a proposal (TAB A) in which it is concluded that the
problems connected with unidentified flying objects appear to
have implications for psychological warfare as well as for
intelligence and operations.

2. The background for this view is presented in some
detail in TAB B.

3. I suggest that we discuss at an early board meeting
the possible offensive or defensive utilization of these
phenomena for psychological warfare purposes.

Walter B. Smith
Director

Enclosure

The 1952 CIA memo from Walter Bedell Smith on flying saucers.

subject: "Flying Saucers," says, "I am today transmitting to the
National Security Council a proposal (2AB A) in which it is
concluded that the problems connected with unidentified flying
objects appear to have implication for psychological warfare as
well as for intelligence and operations." It is signed Walter B.
Smith, Director.

So, who is conducting "psychological warfare" on the United
States with flying saucers? Is it extraterrestrials? Or is it some
earthly power such as the remnants of the SS now operating as
the Black Sun? Indeed, this seems to be the conclusion of the
CIA, as well as British Intelligence (MI-6): the flying saucers
and cylindrical craft were some sort of last battalion of Nazi-SS
craft that were terrorizing the residents of the United States, South
America, and Europe—as well as other areas of the world.

Where were these craft coming from? We don't know what
the CIA concluded but we may surmise that they thought that
they were coming from Antarctica and South America. Other craft

were apparently coming from the north, perhaps the secret bases in northern Norway and Greenland. There was a lot of UFO activity in Europe in the 1950s and 1960s and it would seem that there were certain places in Spain, France, Italy and Germany where flying saucers were landing frequently. Many of the SS survivors such as Otto Skorzeny had homes in Spain as well as Argentina.

While this "psychological warfare" was being conducted by flying saucers and such, a very real network called the Ratline was in operation. Otto Skorzeny was one of the heads of this shadowy organization that spanned many continents.

The Ratline and the ODESSA

The ODESSA, also known as the Ratline, was an organization that helped SS members escape from Europe after the declared end of the war. The term ODESSA is an American codename from the German: Organization der ehemaligen SS-Angehörigen (meaning: Organization of Former SS Members). The term was coined in 1946 to cover Nazi underground escape-plans by SS officers with the aim of facilitating secret escape routes, mainly to Argentina or other South American countries, plus aiding them at their destinations with employment of some sort.

According to Wikipedia the code word ODESSA appeared for the first time in a memo dated July 3, 1946, by the United States Army Counterintelligence Corps (CIC) whose principal role was to screen displaced persons for possible suspects. The CIC discovered that ODESSA was used at the KZ Bensheim-Auerbach internment camp for SS prisoners. Here they used this watchword in their secret attempts to gain special privileges from the International Red Cross.

So here we see that ODESSA was a real escape vehicle for the SS and other Nazis, but it seems that it was also an umbrella for a number of agencies, including the Vatican, that were providing new and other documentation for them. They were typically going to Argentina or the Middle East. A few were headed as far away as Indonesia. The Ratline became the network under the ODESSA umbrella.

The ratline was the final period of German immigration to Argentina and occurred between 1946 and 1950 when President

Juan Perón ordered the creation of a ratline for prominent Nazis, collaborators and other fascists from Europe. Perón supposedly issued 10,000 Argentine passports to the ODESSA during this period. Says Wikipedia:

> The ratlines were systems of escape routes for German Nazis and other fascists fleeing Europe from 1945 onwards in the aftermath of World War II. These escape routes mainly led toward havens in Latin America, particularly in Argentina, though also in Paraguay, Colombia, Brazil, Uruguay, Mexico, Chile, Peru, Guatemala, Ecuador, and Bolivia, as well as the United States, Spain, and Switzerland.
>
> There were two primary routes: the first went from Germany to Spain, then Argentina; the second from Germany to Rome, then Genoa, then South America. The two routes developed independently but eventually came together. The ratlines were supported by some controversial clergy of the Catholic Church. Starting in 1947, some U.S. Intelligence officers utilized existing ratlines to move certain Nazi strategists and scientists.

The Ratlines began in Finland in the fall of 1944. Finland had switched allegiances and was now a former Axis country sided with the Allies. Therefore, from 1944, there existed a network of extreme right-wing Finns and Nazis in Finland, founded by Sturmbannführer (Major) Alarich Bross. The original plan was for the network to engage in an armed struggle against the expected Soviet occupation. When that did not materialize, the most significant form of action the organization undertook was to smuggle out those who wanted to leave the country to Germany and Sweden for various reasons. A safe house network was built in Finland and the cover company "Great fishing cooperative" was established. Says Wikipedia:

> Hundreds of people were assisted in Sweden, including more than a hundred German prisoners of war who had fled the Finns. Transport to Germany took place after the

198

September 1944 break in German submarines, smuggling hundreds of people. At the same time Organization ODESSA brought refugees from Germany to the Finnish coast, sometimes in several submarines at the same time. They were transported along the safe house route to Sweden and further from there.

Wikipedia says that later, ODESSA developed in the prisoner of war camps and had the help of the Vatican. The origins of the first ratlines are connected to various developments in Vatican-Argentine relations before and during World War II. As early as 1942, Roman Cardinal Luigi Maglione contacted an ambassador of Argentina regarding that country's willingness to generously accept European Catholic immigrants in a timely manner, allowing them to live and work.

The "Roman ratline" was operated by a small but influential network of Croatian priests, members of the Franciscan order, led by Father Krunoslav Draganović, whose activities we have already discussed; organized a highly sophisticated chain with headquarters at the San Girolamo degli Illirici Seminary College in Rome, but with links from Austria to the port of Genoa where travellers would get a ship to Argentina. The ratline initially focused on aiding members of the Croatian Ustaše including its leader Ante Pavelić.

The operation of the Draganović ratline was an open secret among the intelligence and diplomatic communities in Rome. As early as August 1945, Allied commanders in Rome were asking questions about the use of San Girolamo as a "haven" for Ustaše.

A year later, a US State Department report of 12 July 1946 lists nine war criminals, including Albanians and Montenegrins as well as Croats, plus others "not actually sheltered in the Collegium Illiricum [i.e., San Girolamo degli Illirici] but who otherwise enjoy Church support and protection."

Draganovic's sponsorship of these Croat Ustashes definitely links him up with the plan of the Vatican to shield these ex- Ustaše nationalists until such time as they were able to procure for them the proper documents to enable them to go to South America.

In his 2002 book *The Real Odessa*,[55] Argentine researcher

Uki Goñi used new access to the country's archives to show that
Argentine diplomats and intelligence officers had, on Perón's
instructions, vigorously encouraged former SS officers and other
Nazis to make their home in Argentina.

According to Goñi, the Argentines not only collaborated
with Draganović's ratline, they set up further ratlines of their
own running through Scandinavia, Switzerland and Belgium.
According to Goñi, Argentina's first move into Nazi smuggling
was in January 1946, when Argentine bishop Antonio Caggiano,
leader of the Argentine chapter of Catholic Action, flew with
another bishop, Agustín Barrére, to Rome where Caggiano was
due to be anointed Cardinal. In Rome the Argentine bishops met
with French Cardinal Eugène Tisserant, where they passed on a
message that "the Government of the Argentine Republic was
willing to receive French persons, whose political attitude during
the recent war would expose them, should they return to France,
to harsh measures and private revenge."

During the spring of 1946, a number of French war criminals,
fascists and Vichy officials made it from Italy to Argentina. They
were issued passports by the Rome ICRC office; these were then
stamped with tourist visas for Argentina.

Shortly after this, Argentinian Nazi smuggling became
institutionalized, according to Goñi, when Perón's new government
of February 1946 appointed anthropologist Santiago Peralta as
Immigration Commissioner and former Ribbentrop agent Ludwig
Freude as intelligence chief. Goñi says that these two then set up a
"rescue team" of secret service agents and immigration "advisors,"
many of whom were themselves European war-criminals, with
Argentine citizenship and employment. This was the ratline.

In 2014, over 700 FBI documents were declassified (as part
of the Nazi War Crimes Disclosure Act), revealing that the US
government had undertaken an investigation in the late 1940s and
1950s into reports of the possible escape of Adolf Hitler from
Germany. Some leads purported that he had not committed suicide
in Berlin but had fled Germany in 1945, and eventually arrived in
Argentina via Spain.

Within the pages of these documents are statements, naming
people and places involved in Hitler's alleged journey to South

America, including mention of the ratlines. Additional CIA documents contain reported sightings and a photograph of a man alleged to be Hitler in 1954. The claim related to the photograph made by a self-proclaimed former German SS trooper named Phillip Citroen that Hitler was still alive, and that he "left Colombia for Argentina around January 1955." The CIA report states that neither the contact who reported his conversations with Citroen, nor the CIA station, was "in a position to give an intelligent evaluation of the information." The station chief's superiors told him that "enormous efforts could be expended on this matter with remote possibilities of establishing anything concrete," and the investigation was dropped.

ODESSA and the Gehlen Organization

The existence of Italian and Argentine ratlines has been only recently confirmed, mainly due to research in newly declassified archives. Until the work of Aarons and Loftus, and of Uki Goñi (2002), a common view was that ex-Nazis themselves, organized in secret networks, and ran the escape routes alone. The most famous such network is ODESSA founded in 1946 according to Simon Wiesenthal, which included SS-Obersturmbannführer Otto Skorzeny and Sturmbannführer Alfred Naujocks and, in Argentina, Rodolfo Freude. Alois Brunner, former commandant of Drancy internment camp near Paris, escaped to Rome, then Syria, by ODESSA.

Simon Wiesenthal, who advised Frederick Forsyth on the early 1970s novel/film script *The Odessa File* which brought the name to public attention, also names other Nazi escape organizations such as Spinne ("Spider") and Sechsgestirn ("Constellation of Six"). Wiesenthal describes these immediately after the war as Nazi cells based in areas of Austria where many Nazis had retreated and gone underground. Wiesenthal claimed that the ODESSA network shepherded escapees to the Catholic ratlines in Rome (although he mentions only Hudal, not Draganović), or to a second route through France and into Francoist Spain.

ODESSA was supported by the Gehlen Organization, which employed many former Nazi party members, and was headed by Reinhard Gehlen, a former German Army intelligence officer

201

employed postwar by the CIA. The Gehlen Organization became the nucleus of the BND German intelligence agency, directed by Reinhard Gehlen from its 1956 creation until 1968.

Frederick Forsyth's best-selling 1972 thriller *The Odessa File* brought the organization to popular attention. The novel was later turned into a film starring Jon Voight. In the novel, ODESSA smuggled war criminals to South America, but also attempted to protect those SS members who remained behind in Germany, and plotted to influence political decisions in West Germany.

In the 1976 thriller novel by Ira Levin, *The Boys from Brazil,* Dr. Josef Mengele, the concentration camp medical doctor who performed horrific experiments on camp victims during World War II, is involved in ODESSA. According to a young man and spy on his trail, Mengele is activating the Kameradenwerk for a strange assignment: he is sending out six Nazis (former SS officers) to kill 94 men, who share a few common traits. In *The Boys from Brazil,* the terms Kameradenwerk and ODESSA are used interchangeably.

The 2012 book *Ratline* by Peter Levenda[9] gives the history of the mechanisms by which thousands of Nazi war criminals fled to the remotest parts of the globe—including Adolf Hitler. The name of the infamous priest, Monsignor Draganovic, was discovered by Levenda in a diary found in Indonesia. Levenda then discusses a number of suspected ODESSA members living in Indonesia under assumed names.

Enter "The Spider"

An arm of the ODESSA was Die Spinne (German for "the spider") which was said to be the portion of the organization commanded by Otto Skorzeny, who had a home in Madrid, Spain. Die Spinne was led by Otto Skorzeny along with Reinhard Gehlen. Skorzeny, Gehlen and their network of collaborators gained significant influence in parts of Europe and Latin America. Skorzeny travelled between Francoist Spain and Peronist Argentina, where he acted as an adviser to President Perón and as a bodyguard of Eva Perón, while fostering an ambition for a "Fourth Reich" centered in Latin America. He was also a military advisor to the president of Paraguay.

Many historians claim that the idea for "The Spider" network began in 1944 when Gehlen, then working as a senior Wehrmacht intelligence officer as the head of Foreign Armies East, foresaw a possible defeat of Nazi Germany due to Axis military failures in the Soviet Union, particularly the failure to take the oil fields of Baku in Azerbaijan. Wikipedia says:

> T.H. Tetens, an expert on German geopolitics and a member of the US War Crimes Commission in 1946–47, referred to a group overlapping with Die Spinne as the Führungsring ("a kind of political Mafia, with headquarters in Madrid... serving various purposes.") The Madrid office built up what was referred to as a sort of Fascist international. The German leadership also included Dr. Hans Globke, who in 1936 had written an official commentary on the Nuremberg Laws of 1935. Globke held the important position of Director of the German Chancellery from 1953 to 1963, serving as adviser to Chancellor Konrad Adenauer.
>
> From 1945 to 1950, Die Spinne's leader Skorzeny facilitated the escape of Nazi war criminals from war-criminal prisons to Memmingen, Bavaria, through Austria and Switzerland into Italy. Certain US military authorities

In the 1930s and 40s The Spider was a pulp fiction crime fighter.

allegedly knew of the escape, but took no action. The Central European headquarters of Die Spinne as of 1948 was in Gmunden, Upper Austria.

A coordinating office for international Die Spinne operations was established in Madrid by Skorzeny under the control of Francisco Franco, whose victory in the Spanish Civil War had been aided by economic and military support from Hitler and Mussolini. When a Die Spinne Nazi delegation visited Madrid in 1959, Franco stated, "Please regard Spain as your second Fatherland." Skorzeny used Die Spinne's resources to allow notorious Nazi concentration camp doctor Joseph Mengele to escape to Argentina in 1949.

Skorzeny requested assistance from German industrialist tycoon Alfried Krupp, whose company had controlled 138 private concentration camps in Nazi Germany; the assistance was granted in 1951. Skorzeny became Krupp's representative in industrial business ventures in Argentina, a country which harbored a strong pro-Nazi political element throughout World War II and afterwards, regardless of a nominal declaration of loyalty to the Allies as World War II ended. With the help of Die Spinne leaders in Spain, by the early 1980s Die Spinne had become influential in Argentina, Chile and Paraguay, including ties involving Paraguayan dictator Alfredo Stroessner.

War Crimes investigator Simon Wiesenthal claimed Joseph Mengele had stayed at the notorious Colonia Dignidad Nazi colony in Chile in 1979, and ultimately found harbor in Paraguay until his death. As of the early 1980s, Die Spinne's Mengele was reported by Infield to have been advising Stroessner's ethnic German Paraguayan police on how to reduce native Paraguayan Indians in the Chaco Region to slave labor.

The Spider, SPECTRE and the Man From UNCLE

The Spider and the ODESSA has made its way into the popular mainstream consciousness as the organization featured in the

Ian Fleming, the creator of James Bond.

James Bond movies as SPECTRE, and the television series *The Man From U.N.C.L.E.* as THRUSH (the Terrestrial Hegemony for the Removal of Undesirables and the Subjugation of Humankind). THRUSH was opposed by the United Nations Counterintelligence League (UNCLE).

Ian Fleming, a former MI-6 agent in real life, had his fictional James Bond battle an SS-ODESSA network called SPECTRE (Special Executive for Counter-intelligence, Terrorism, Revenge and Extortion). This fictional organization featured in the James Bond novels and movies is led by criminal mastermind Ernst Stavro Blofeld. Blofield is essentially Bond's nemesis, and was the inspiration for the Dr. Evil character in the *Austin Powers* films.

This international organization of wealthy criminals and former Nazis first formally appeared in the 1961 novel *Thunderball* and in the 1962 film *Dr. No.* Like the SS and Black Sun operatives after the war, SPECTRE is not aligned with any nation or political ideology. The presence of former Gestapo members in the organization shows that Fleming knew about the ODESSA; he mentioned Nazi fugitives after the Second World War in his early novel *Moonraker* (1954).

Early Fleming novels used the term SMERSH instead of SPECTRE. SMERSH was a real spy organization created by the Soviets. Joseph Stalin coined the name "СМЕРШ" (SMERSH) as a combination of the Russian-language phrase Смерть шпионам (Smert' shpiónam, "Death to spies"). Originally focused on combatting German spies infiltrating the Soviet military, the

205

organization quickly expanded its mandate to finding and eliminating any subversive elements—hence Stalin's inclusive name for it. SMERSH was formed in late 1942 or even earlier, but officially announced only on April 14, 1943.

Fleming ultimately switched from using SMERSH as his organization of bad guys to SPECTRE. In the Bond films based on Fleming's works that featured SMERSH, the agency was either changed to SPECTRE or omitted altogether. However, SMERSH is mentioned in the film *From Russia with Love*.

In the James Bond novels, SPECTRE is an organized crime enterprise led by Blofeld. The top level of the organization is made up of twenty-one individuals, eighteen of whom handle day-to-day affairs. Members are drawn in groups of three from six of the world's most notorious organizations—the Nazi German Gestapo, the Soviet SMERSH, Yugoslav Marshal Tito's OZNA, the Italian Mafia, the French-Corsican Unione Corse, and KRYSTAL, a massive Turkish heroin-smuggling operation. The remaining three members are Blofeld himself and two scientific/technical experts who make their debut in the ninth Bond novel, *Thunderball*.

When Fleming was writing *Thunderball* in 1959, he believed that the Cold War might end during the two years it would take to produce the film, and came to the conclusion that the inclusion of a contemporary political villain would leave the film looking dated. Therefore, he thought it better to create a politically neutral enemy based on the Odessa, Ratline, and the Spider. In the film *You Only Live Twice* Blofeld asks for 100 million dollars "to be deposited to a bank in Buenos Aires."

The organization is mentioned in the tenth novel, *The Spy Who Loved Me* (1962), when Bond describes investigating their activities in Toronto before the story begins, though they play no part in the story itself. The organization's third appearance is in the eleventh novel, *On Her Majesty's Secret Service* (1963), where Blofeld is executing a plan to ruin British agriculture with biological warfare. Blofeld appears for the final time in the twelfth novel, *You Only Live Twice* (1964). By this point SPECTRE is focused on maintaining Blofeld's alias as Dr. Guntram von Shatterhand and his compound in Japan. Here we have a secret space base inside of a volcano.

The Third Power

In the films, SPECTRE often acts as a third party in the ongoing Cold War. They are the "third power" which is how the remnant SS-Black Sun operatives have been described by such authors as Joseph Farrell.[12] Their objectives ranged from supporting Dr. Julius No in sabotaging American rocket launches, holding the world to ransom, and demanding clemency from governments for their previous crimes. The goal of world domination is only ever stated in *You Only Live Twice* when SPECTRE was working on behalf of an unnamed Asian government, strongly implied to be Red China. Ian Fleming essentially introduced the term "ninja" to the English speaking world the 1964 book. Ian Fleming died of a heart attack in Canterbury, England that same year at the age of 56.

SPECTRE's long-term strategy is illustrated by the analogy of the three Siamese fighting fish Blofeld keeps in an aquarium aboard SPECTRE's yacht in the film version of *From Russia with Love*. Blofeld notes that one fish is refraining from fighting two others until their fight is concluded. Then, that cunning fish attacks the weakened victor and kills it easily. Thus SPECTRE's main strategy is to instigate conflict between two powerful enemies,

A poster for the 1965 film *Thunderball*.

James Bond plays baccarat with Largo who wears the SPECTRE ring.

namely the superpowers, hoping that they will exhaust themselves and be vulnerable when it seizes power.

In both the film and the novel *Thunderball*, the physical headquarters of SPECTRE are in Paris, operating behind a front organization that aids refugees named "Firco" (Fraternité Internationale de la Résistance Contre l'Oppression) in the novels and "International Brotherhood for the Assistance of Stateless Persons" in the films. Organizational discipline is notoriously draconian, with the penalty for disobedience or failure being death.

In both the film and the novel, Emilio Largo is the second in command. It is stated in the novel that if something were to happen to Blofeld, Largo would assume command. Largo appears in the 1961 novel *Thunderball*, the 1965 film version and its 1983 remake, *Never Say Never Again*.

In the film version of *Thunderball* Emilio Largo resides, among other places, on a yacht called the *Disco Volante* which translates to "flying saucer." Is this a nod to the Black Sun's possession of flying saucers? Largo early in his encounters with Bond is at a casino playing baccarat. During this scene we see that Largo is wearing a ring with the logo of SPECTRE: an octopus with a head that looks surprisingly like the head of a "grey alien."

At one point Largo kisses this ring and it can be clearly seen by the audience. This would appear to be an allegory for the Totenkopf (Death Head) rings that were worn and cherished by SS members. Himmler placed particular importance on the death's-head rings; they were never to be sold, and were to be returned to him upon the death of the owner.

The logo of SPECTRE.

As I said earlier, SPECTRE is the ODESSA which is the SS. Also, as noted, the SPECTRE cabinet in the Ian Fleming books had a total of twenty-one members. Blofeld was the chairman and leader because he founded the organization and Largo was elected by the cabinet to be second in command. A physicist named Kotze (who later defected) and an electronics expert named Maslov were also included in the group for their expertise on scientific and technical matters.

Members were typically referred to by number rather than by name. Members who failed missions were immediately executed, usually in gory and spectacular ways.

The film adaptation of *From Russia with Love* features the first on-screen appearance of Blofeld, although he is only identified by name in the closing credits of the film and his face is not seen at all. SPECTRE also serves as the primary antagonist of the film, orchestrating a plan to humiliate and kill James Bond as revenge for the death of Dr. No.

After being absent from the third film, *Goldfinger* (1964), SPECTRE returns in the fourth film, *Thunderball* (1965), which closely follows the events of the novel. During the events of the fifth film, *You Only Live Twice* (1967), they attempt to incite a war between the United States and Soviet Union. In film number six, On *Her Majesty's Secret Service* (1969), Blofeld develops a biological warfare program and plans to demand clemency and recognition of a claimed title of nobility.

SPECTRE's secret base inside a volcano on a Japanese island.

SPECTRE's final appearance is in the seventh film, *Diamonds are Forever* (1971), where the group attempts to forcibly disarm the Cold War powers. *Diamonds are Forever* is a particularly interesting Bond movie as it weaves into its plot the Gemstone File material of Aristotle Onassis being the head of the International Mafia, and the kidnapping of Howard Hughes by the American Mafia which held him captive in a Las Vegas penthouse. *Diamonds are Forever* also features a short segment where they are faking and filming the Apollo Moon missions.

Onassis was a Turkish-Greek who owned Monaco's Casino Royale in 1949 and made his money in smuggling Turkish heroin in Greek ships that were flagged out of Argentina. He then got into the oil tanker business, built a floating empire and owned his own island in northern Greece called Skorpios. *Skorpios* was the name of a later James Bond novel. Indeed, apparently Aristotle Onassis is the model for Ernst Stavros Blofeld.

Juan Perón and ODESSA

Uki Goñi's 2002 book *The Real Odessa. How Peron Brought the Nazi War Criminals to Argentina* (2002)[55] describes the role of Juan Perón in providing cover for Nazi war criminals with cooperation from the Vatican, the Argentinean government and the Swiss authorities through a secret office set up by Perón's agents in Bern, Switzerland. Heinrich Himmler's SS had prepared an escape-route through Madrid in 1944. In 1946, this operation moved to the Presidential palace in Buenos Aires. Goñi states that the operation stretched from Scandinavia to Italy, aiding war criminals and bringing in gold that the Croatian treasury had stolen.[55]

Goñi described how the Argentinian government dealt with war criminals who entered Argentina. However, during his research Goñi accidentally stumbled on British Foreign Office documents relating to the involvement of Vatican personnel in the smuggling of war criminals, the so-called post-war "ratlines." Goñi found out that the British Envoy D'Arcy Osborne had intervened with Pope Pius XII to put an end to these illegal activities. Furthermore, he discovered "that the Pope secretly pleaded with Washington and London on behalf of notorious criminals and Nazi collaborators."

> In Nuremberg at that time something was taking place that I personally considered a disgrace and an unfortunate lesson for the future of humanity. I became certain that the Argentine people also considered the Nuremberg process a disgrace, unworthy of the victors, who behaved as if they hadn't been victorious. Now we realize that they [the Allies] deserved to lose the war.
> —Argentine president Juan Perón on the Nuremberg Trials of Nazi war criminals

Goñi says that interest in a viable political alternative to Far Right Capitalism and Far Left Communism, the so-called Third Way, along with the inevitability of a Third World War, were all things in which the Argentine ruling elite and the Nazis believed. Argentina was also interested in a militarized Catholic state and saw Europe's loss as its gain.

His 'monolithic sense of military honor' offended by Nuremberg, Goñi says Perón became determined to rescue as many European Far Right fugitives as possible. And he would benefit from their military and technical expertise, as well as

211

whatever gold and cash they could manage to smuggle in.

Some of the Nazi war criminals who escaped using the ODESSA ratlines include:

Andrija Artuković, escaped to the United States; arrested in 1984 after decades of delay and extradited to SFR Yugoslavia in 1986, where he died in prison in 1988.

Klaus Barbie, fled to Bolivia in 1951 with help from the United States, as he had been an agent of the US Army Counterintelligence Corps since April 1947; captured in 1983; died in prison in France on September 23, 1991.

Otto Skorzeny, escaped an internment camp in 1948 and fled to Spain in 1950; in 1953 moved to Egypt and served as a military advisor to Gamal Abdel Nasser; travelled between Spain and Argentina serving as an advisor to Juan Perón; died in Spain in 1975.

Alois Brunner, fled to Syria in 1954; died around 2001.

Herberts Cukurs, fled to Brazil in 1945; assassinated by Mossad in Uruguay in 1965.

Léon Degrelle, fled to Spain in 1945; founded the neo-Nazi organization CEDADE in 1966 while under protection of the Franco regime; died in Spain in 1994.

Adolf Eichmann, fled to Argentina in 1950; captured 1960; executed in Israel on 1 June 1962.

Aribert Heim, disappeared in 1962; most likely died in Egypt in 1992 .

Aarne Kauhanen, fled to Venezuela in 1945; arrested 1947; died in mysterious circumstances in 1949.

Sándor Képíró, fled to Argentina; returned to Hungary in 1996. He stood trial for war crimes in Budapest in February 2011, before his death in September.

Josef Mengele, fled to Argentina in 1949, then to other countries; died in Brazil in 1979.

Ante Pavelić, escaped to Argentina in 1948; died in Spain, in December 1959, of wounds sustained two years earlier in an assassination attempt

Erich Priebke, fled to Argentina in 1949; arrested in 1994; died in 2013.

Walter Rauff, escaped to Chile; never captured; died in 1984.

Eduard Roschmann, escaped to Argentina in 1948; fled to Paraguay to avoid extradition and died there in 1977.

Hans-Ulrich Rudel, fled to Argentina in 1948; started the "Kameradenwerk," a relief organization for Nazi criminals that helped fugitives escape; died following a stroke in Rosenheim, Germany in 1982.

Dinko Šakić, fled to Argentina in 1947; arrested in 1998 and extradited to Croatia. He was tried and found guilty of war crimes and crimes against humanity, serving a 20-year sentence. He died in 2008.

Boris Smyslovsky, fled to Argentina in 1948 from Liechtenstein with the First Russian National Army. He returned to Liechtenstein in 1966, and died of natural causes in 1988.

Gustav Wagner, fled to Brazil in 1950; arrested in 1978; committed suicide in 1980.

Hans-Ulrich Rudel and the Argentine SS

Of particular interest in the list of ODESSA-Ratline escapees is Hans-Ulrich Rudel (July 2, 1916—December 18, 1982), a German ground-attack pilot during World War II. I discuss him at great length in my book *Haunebu: The Secret Files*, but some of the information bears repeating. Rudel was the most decorated German serviceman of World War II, being the sole recipient of the Knight's Cross with Golden Oak Leaves, Swords, and Diamonds in January of 1945. Rudel typically flew the Junkers Ju 87 "Stuka" dive bomber and his missions were exclusively on the Eastern Front. The Junkers Ju 87 "Stuka" was typically fitted with two anti-tank cannons beneath the cockpit of the fighter. Photos of armed Haunebu craft have these very same anti-tank cannons on them, mounted beneath the craft.

Rudel surrendered to US forces on May 8, 1945 and was released after a period of time. In 1948 he emigrated to Argentina and

Hans-Ulrich Rudel.

began to network with all of his former Nazi buddies. He was a committed and unrepentant National Socialist, and founded the "Kameradenwerk" (literally "comrades work" or "comrades act"), an organization that helped Nazi fugitives escape to Latin America and the Middle East, in other words, the ODESSA or the Ratline.

Together with another Nazi in South America, Willem Sassen, Rudel helped shelter Josef Mengele, the notorious former SS doctor who practiced at Auschwitz. Rudel worked as an arms dealer and a military advisor to the regimes of Juan Perón in Argentina, generals in Chile, and Alfredo Stroessner in Paraguay. These three nations in particular were suspected by US intelligence to be collaborating with the Nazis—before and after the war—and because of Rudel's activities, he was placed under observation by the newly formed Central Intelligence Agency. It is from this early period of the CIA following Rudel around South America that the curious CIA UFO files originate.[40]

In Argentina, Rudel lived in Villa Carlos Paz, roughly 36 kilometers (22 miles) from Cordoba City, where he rented a house and operated a brickworks. It is interesting that Rudel lived outside of Cordoba because this is a special area in Argentina. Cordoba is an industrial city in the north-central part of the country—and it is currently famous for UFO activity. Craft identical to the Haunebu have been seen in broad daylight, photographed and put on the local news.

This area is famous for a series of UFO disk sightings in the 1960s and early 1970s that occurred near the small city of Capilla del Monte, a short drive to the north of Cordoba. This small city is the center of Haunebu activity in northern Argentina and is well known for this. It is even a tourist destination because of the frequent sightings of flying saucers at the mountain on the edge of the city called Cerro Uritorco.

The CIA Releases a Photo of Hitler from 1954

In 2017 the CIA released a series of documents and a photo that might have been of Hitler taken in Colombia in 1954. A "fairly reliable" source contacted the agency's base in Venezuela in 1955, according to a CIA memo, and shared a photograph of two men taken in Colombia the previous year.

The clean-shaven man on the left was a former German SS

trooper named Phillip Citroen, according to the source. And the man on the right was supposed to be Hitler. He had apparently changed his name to "Adolf Schüttelmayor" but was not so worried about discovery that he felt it necessary to shave his mustache.

Hitler's alleged presence in Colombia was an open secret in some circles, a subsequent CIA investigation found. In a city "overly populated with former German Nazis," the former SS officer told an agency source, Schüttelmayor was idolized by those who knew his real identity. They called him "Der Führer" and honored him with the old Nazi salutes.

The CIA station chief continued to pursue the case but, as we have noted, was eventually told by his superiors that "enormous efforts could be expended on this matter with remote possibilities of establishing anything concrete." So Schüttelmayor, whoever he was, was thereafter left alone.

The photo was received by the CIA and classified on October 3, 1955 and microfilmed on July 26, 1963. The document, classified as "Secret" also said that Hitler left Colombia for Argentina around January 1955. Phillip Citroen also said that "inasmuch as ten years have passed since the end of World War II, the Allies could no longer prosecute Hitler as a criminal of war."

This fits in with the story of Hitler's survival as portrayed in the 2011 book *Grey Wolf: The Escape of Adolf Hitler*.[4] In this book, which we discussed in detail in another chapter, the authors maintain that Hitler, whose code name was Grey Wolf, escaped out of Berlin with Eva Braun and his daughter.

It was said that Hitler and Braun, with their daughter, lived on an island in a lake near Bariloche, Argentina for some years. Supposedly Braun left Hitler in 1950 to live with her daughter in another city to the north called Neuquén. Hitler continued to live on the island in the lake and reportedly died in 1960. Therefore, he could be the man in the 1954 photograph taken in Colombia. It would seem normal that Hitler might make the occasional trip from his secret island home. The fascinating question is how did Hitler get from Bariloche, Argentina to Colombia? Did he go by private plane? Was he possibly taken there, and back, via a Haunebu or Vril craft? Indeed, seemingly laughable phrase "Hitler drives a flying saucer" may have some truth in it after all.

The 1954 photograph of "Hitler" in Colombia from newly released CIA documents.

Chapter 6

The Marconi Connection

I have not worked 30 years to become the assassin of mankind.
—Guglielmo Marconi

The height of cleverness is to be able to conceal it.
—Francois de La Rochefoucauld (1613 - 1680)

While Nikola Tesla has become an important figure with a new generation of techies with the special mystique of his work on death rays, free energy, anti-gravity airships and such, so has Guglielmo Marconi become a similar figure for a small group of UFO enthusiasts in Latin America, Italy and Germany. Marconi and his followers are thought to have created a secret city in South America from which flying saucers were said to come and go. His is a strange story not well known to English readers.

Guglielmo Marconi was born into the Italian nobility in Bologna on April 25, 1874, the second son of Giuseppe Marconi (an Italian aristocratic landowner) and his Irish wife Annie Jameson. Annie Jameson was the daughter of the wealthy Andrew Jameson of Daphne Castle in County Wexford, Ireland, and granddaughter of John Jameson, founder of the Jameson & Sons whiskey company, still a famous brand today. Marconi spoke Italian and English fluently and between the ages of two and six Marconi and his elder brother Alfonso lived with their mother in the English town of Bedford, a pleasant spot north of London.

Marconi was homeschooled by private tutors who were hired by his parents. Marconi said he had an important mentor who was professor Vincenzo Rosa, a high school physics teacher in Livorno.

Rosa taught the 17-year-old Marconi the basics of physics and chemistry as well as new theories on electricity.

Guglielmo Marconi.

At the age of 18 Marconi moved back in his home town, Bologna, and became acquainted with University of Bologna physicist Augusto Righi, who had done research on the work of Heinrich Hertz. Righi permitted Marconi to attend lectures at the university and to use the University's laboratory and library for his researches.

Interested in science and electricity since his early youth, in the early 1890s Marconi began working on the idea of "wireless telegraphy"—the transmission of telegraph messages without connecting wires as required by the electric telegraph then in use.

A relatively new development in the field of wireless telegraphy came from Heinrich Hertz, who, in 1888, demonstrated that one could produce and detect electromagnetic radiation, based on the work of James Clerk Maxwell. At the time, this electromagnetic radiation was called "Hertzian" waves, and is now generally referred to as radio waves.

With Hertz's death in 1894 there were published reviews of his earlier discoveries including a demonstration on the transmission and detection of radio waves by the British physicist Oliver Lodge. There was also an article about Hertz's work by Marconi's mentor Augusto Righi. Professor Righi's article renewed Marconi's interest in developing a wireless telegraphy system based on radio waves. Marconi noted other inventors did not seem to be pursuing this line of inquiry.

Supported by his father, Marconi, now 20 years old, began building his own equipment in the attic of his home at the Villa Griffone in Pontecchio, Italy, with the help of his butler, Mignani. Marconi began to conduct experiments in radio waves and built on Hertz's original experiments. At the suggestion of Righi, he began using a coherer, an early detector used in Lodge's experiments. The coherer changed resistance when exposed to radio waves.

In the summer of 1894, Marconi built a storm alarm made up of a battery, a coherer, and an electric bell, which went off when it picked up the radio waves generated by lightning. Then one night, in December 1894, Marconi demonstrated a radio transmitter and receiver to his mother, a set-up that made a bell ring on the other side of the room by pushing a telegraphic button on a bench. Marconi continued to study scientific literature and picked up on the ideas of physicists who were experimenting with radio waves. He developed devices, such as portable transmitters and receiver systems, that could work over increasingly longer distances.

In the summer of 1895, Marconi moved his experiments outdoors on his father's estate in Bologna. A breakthrough came in the summer of 1895, when Marconi found that much greater range could be achieved after he raised the height of his antenna and, borrowing from a technique used in wired telegraphy, grounded his transmitter and receiver. With these improvements, the system was capable of transmitting signals up to two miles (3.2 km) over hills through the country.

Marconi concluded that a device could become capable of spanning even greater distances. He needed additional funding and research. Marconi travelled to London in early 1896 at the age of 21, accompanied by his mother, to seek support for his work. Marconi arrived at Dover, and the customs officer opened his case to find various apparatus. The customs officer immediately

Guglielmo Marconi with his wireless signal in 1901.

219

contacted the Admiralty in London. While there, Marconi gained the interest and support of William Preece, the Chief Electrical Engineer of the General Post Office (the GPO).

During this time Marconi decided he should patent his system, and filed an application on June 2, 1896 titled "Improvements in Transmitting Electrical Impulses and Signals, and in Apparatus Therefor," which would become the first patent for a radio wave based communication system.

Marconi made the first demonstration of his system for the British government in July 1896. A further series of demonstrations for the British followed, and, on May 13, 1897, Marconi sent the first ever wireless communication over open sea—a message was transmitted over the Bristol Channel from Flat Holm Island to Lavernock Point near Cardiff, a distance of six kilometers (3.7 miles). The message read, "Are you ready." Another demonstration at Brean Down Fort on the Somerset coast stretched the range to 16 kilometers (9.9 miles).

Impressed by the many demonstrations that could facilitate communications between ships at sea and the shore, Preece and the GPO introduced Marconi's ongoing work to the general public at two important London lectures: "Telegraphy without Wires," at the Toynbee Hall on December 11, 1896; and "Signaling through Space without Wires," given to the Royal Institution on June 4, 1897.

Numerous additional demonstrations followed, and Marconi began to receive international attention. In July 1897, he carried out a series of tests at La Spezia, Italy, for the Italian government. On July 6, 1898 Marconi conducted a test for Lloyd's between The Marine Hotel in Ballycastle and Rathlin Island in County Antrim, Ireland.

Marconi set up an experimental base at the Haven Hotel at Poole Harbour in Dorset, England, where he erected a 100-foot-high mast. On March 17, 1899, the East Goodwin lightship sent the first wireless distress signal on behalf of the merchant vessel *Elbe* which had run aground at the Goodwin Sands near the lighthouse. The message was received by a radio operator at the South Foreland lighthouse who summoned the aid of lifeboats. Later on March 27, 1899, Marconi sent a transmission across the English Channel from Wimereux, France to the South Foreland

Lighthouse, England.

In the autumn of 1899, his first demonstration in the United States took place. Marconi had sailed to the US at the invitation of *The New York Herald* newspaper to cover the America's Cup international yacht races off Sandy Hook, New Jersey. The transmission was done aboard the SS *Ponce*, a passenger ship of the Porto Rico Line. Marconi left for England on November 8, 1899 on the American Line's SS *Saint Paul*, and he and his assistants installed wireless equipment aboard during the voyage. On November 15, the SS *Saint Paul* became the first ocean liner to report her arrival to Great Britain by the newly installed wireless aboard, which contacted Marconi's Royal Needles Hotel radio station 66 nautical miles off the English coast.

Marconi continued investigating a means to signal across the Atlantic to compete with the transatlantic telegraph cables. Marconi established a wireless transmitting station in Ireland at Marconi House, Rosslare Strand, County Wexford, in 1901 to act as a link between the new high-power station at Poldhu in Cornwall, England, and Clifden in Connemara, County Galway, Ireland. He soon made the announcement that the message was received at Signal Hill in St. John's, Newfoundland on December 12, 1902, using a 500-foot (150 m) kite-supported antenna for reception—signals transmitted by the station at Poldhu.

On December 17, 1902, a transmission from the Marconi station in Glace Bay, Nova Scotia, Canada, became the world's

Marconi setting up his station in Newfoundland, Canada in 1902.

221

British postal engineers set up a Marconi receiving station in 1897.

first radio message to cross the Atlantic from North America. The first from the United States was from a station near South Wellfleet, Massachusetts that Marconi had built in 1901; it sent a message of greetings on January 18, 1903 from President Theodore Roosevelt to King Edward VII in the United Kingdom.

Marconi began to build high-powered stations on both sides of the Atlantic to communicate with ships at sea, in competition with other inventors. In 1904, he established a commercial service to transmit nightly news summaries to subscribing ships, who would use these news stories for their on-board newspapers that were typically issued daily on cruise ships of the time. A regular transatlantic radio-telegraph service began on October 17, 1907 between Marconi's Clifden station in Ireland and the Glace Bay station in Nova Scotia.

The Titanic and Marconi's Super Yacht

Marconi's efforts continued in the years to come and the role played by Marconi Co. wireless in maritime rescues raised public awareness of the value of radio and brought fame to Marconi, particularly the sinking of RMS *Titanic* on April 15, 1912.

The *Titanic* radio operators, Jack Phillips and Harold Bride, were not employed by the Marconi International Marine Communication Company. After the sinking of the *Titanic*, survivors were rescued by the RMS *Carpathia. Carpathia* took a total of only 17 minutes to both receive and decode the SOS signal sent by Titanic. There was a distance of 58 miles between the two ships and the quick communication between the vessels aided in the rescue effort. When the *Carpathia* docked in New York, Marconi went aboard with a reporter from *The New York Times* to talk to Bride, the surviving operator. After this incident, Marconi was again in the news and gained popularity, becoming more recognized for his contributions to the field of radio and wireless technology.

As World War I came about Marconi was made a Senator in Italy and appointed Honorary Knight Grand Cross of the Royal Victorian Order in the UK in 1914. Italy was on the British-French side during WWI and fought against the Germans and Austrians. During this war against Germany Marconi was placed in charge of the Italian military's radio service as a lieutenant in the Italian Royal Army.

Marconi's superyacht the *Elettra* circa 1928.

223

After the war Marconi bought a naval patrol boat for £21,000 in 1919 that he would use as his floating laboratory. The vessel was built in the shipyards near Edinburgh, and was launched on behalf of Archduke Charles Stephen of Austria under the name of *Rovenska* in 1904. The vessel sailed under the flag of the Austro-Hungarian Empire until 1909 but was then sold to Sir Max Waechter for £26,000, at which point she sailed under the British flag while still retaining her original name.

At the outbreak of WWI, the vessel was requisitioned by the British government and converted into an escort ship for the Royal Navy as part of the Channel Fleet, plying between England and the French ports of Brest and Saint Malo. At the end of the war, the vessel was decommissioned and auctioned at Southampton, England, where it came into the hands of Guglielmo Marconi.

Marconi named the yacht *Elettra* (not *Electra*) and it became his floating laboratory superyacht for his experiments. From this seaborne laboratory he conducted his many experiments with wireless telegraphy, wireless telephony and other communication and direction-finding techniques during the interwar period. These experiments also included so-called "deathrays."

Marconi's original intention was to rename his yacht *Scintilla* ("Spark") but it was felt this would prove too difficult to pronounce in English. The yacht was accordingly renamed *Elettra* and was entered into the Italian Registry of Shipping 1921.

Shortly after it was purchased by Marconi, the vessel sailed from London in July 1919. Off the coast of Portugal, Marconi startled the operators at a coast station with transmissions of music from his gramophone records. The yacht arrived at Naples in mid-August, and then was transferred to the massive port of La Spezia in northwestern Italy, where the vessel was converted for service as a laboratory.

Modifications at the La Spezia shipyards included increasing the height of the masts in order to rig the various wireless aerials that would be required. It was also arranged that Marconi's private cabin would lead directly onto the laboratory. On deck and aft of the laboratory was a large dining room with space at table for 12 to 14 diners. Further aft was a large and well-appointed saloon complete with a piano and billiards table.

224

In April 1920 the luxurious yacht was sailing across the Bay of Biscay north to England; an interesting "first" was established when guests danced in the yacht's saloon to a broadcast of music coming from the ballroom of the Savoy Hotel in London. Later that year on June 15, the voice of a famous soprano of the time, Nellie Melba, was heard at a distance of 2000 miles during a broadcast from the Marconi transmitting station at Chelmsford in England to the yacht.

The yacht was outfitted with luxurious accommodation that was deemed necessary to impress distinguished guests that would later include King Victor Emmanuel III of Italy and King George V of the United Kingdom. In September 1920 another guest on board was Marconi's friend, the Italian poet and nationalist Gabriele D'Annunzio.

The vessel soon became famous and known in Italian as *il nave dei miracoli* ("the ship of miracles"). On March 31, 1930 Benito Mussolini visited the yacht when she was lying off Fiumicino. This was followed with another visit in June 1930 when she was off Ostia. Mussolini, who was greatly interested in long distance wireless telegraphy and telephony, expressed a wish to be put through to London and communication was made via the Marconi wireless station, with its receivers at Bridgeport and transmitters and beam aerials at Dorchester in Dorset. This formed part of the Imperial Wireless Chain that linked London with the British Empire.

The *Elettra* had a crew of 30 and was able to sail long distances without needing to refuel. In 1922 she first crossed the Atlantic to New York, surviving the effects of a severe storm. An important crewmember was the radio officer, Adelmo Landini, who was known as the "marconista," the Italian term equivalent to "sparks" in English. Landini, who sailed with Marconi from 1927 to 1931, had been a wireless operator decorated for gallantry in the army during the Great War. He was the yacht's radio officer and also assisted Marconi with his experiments. Landini became an experimenter and inventor in his own right, registering seven patents for his inventions. In 1938/39, he registered a patent concerning the bouncing of radio waves off the surface of the moon—a phenomenon that he had first become aware of while serving on *Elettra*.

Marconi continued to experiment from his superyacht, concentrating his efforts on the short wave spectrum. In April 1923, he sailed from Falmouth to the Cape Verde Islands and monitored signals from the station at Poldhu in England.

In 1924 thanks to an improved aerial at Poldhu, two-way communication from the yacht was established from the Mediterranean and the Atlantic on a wavelength of 32 meters. The same experiment also proved successful when *Elettra* was in port

A radio dance with headphones on Marconi's yacht in 1922.

at Beirut that same year.

At this time a successful contact was made from the yacht while in the Mediterranean to Sydney, Australia enabling Marconi to speak to the managing director of the Amalgamated Wireless Company. This was an astonishing feat! These experiments using beamed transmissions convinced the British government of the viability of shortwave (as opposed to the current use of longwave) and resulted in a contract with Marconi's company for a communications network, the aforementioned Imperial Wireless Chain, linking the many stations in the British Empire with London. A two-way communications link was officially inaugurated between Britain and Canada in 1926.

Marconi did many marvelous experiments while aboard the *Elettra* and had this to say on the advantages of a seaborne laboratory:

> Without *Elettra* it would have been impossible to carry out my experiments in the Mediterranean and in the Atlantic; I would not have been able to continue and develop my research into short wave transmissions. With my seaborne laboratory—unique in the world—I have been able to realize my dreams. For example, how to beam (direct) a radio signal and to use radio for navigational purposes. This yacht has not only made me independent, but also freed me from distractions and the curiosity of others. I have been able to work at any time of the night and day and move around in a way that would have been quite impossible on dry land.

In 1929 the wireless equipment aboard *Elettra* was replaced by technicians from Marconi's company with updated equipment. Early in 1930 wireless telephony contact was made with Amalgamated Wireless in Sydney and on March 26 of that year, Marconi achieved publicity worldwide when, by pressing a Morse key on his yacht in Genoa harbor, he remotely switched on the lights in Sydney for the opening of the World Exhibition.

In 1931 *Elettra* completed a round-the-world voyage. On July 30, 1934, with a 60 cm transmitting beacon on shore and a receiver in the chartroom, the windows of which had been covered, Marconi successfully navigated the yacht between two buoys off Santa Margherita Ligure, near Genoa, Italy.

A four-way contact was established in November 1936 when the *Elettra* (at Santa Margherita Ligure) made contact with New York and two aircraft flying over that city. *Elettra* sailed the seas of the world until Marconi died on July 27, 1937, of a heart attack. Marconi was working on microwave technology the last years of his life and he suffered nine heart attacks in his last three years. He was 63 years old when he died and Italy held a state funeral for him.

After Marconi's death the *Elettra* was acquired by the Italian Ministry of Communications for the sum of 820,000 lire. In 1943, the *Elettra* was commandeered and refitted as a warship by the German Navy. During the autumn of 1943 Professor Mario Picotti obtained permission from the Germans to dismantle and remove all of Marconi's wireless equipment. This was carried away in 19 large packing cases and deposited safely in the vaults of the Castello di San Giusto in Trieste. The equipment remained there until the end of 1947 before coming into the hands of the Milan Museum of Science and Technology

The vessel, now designated NA-6, sailed from Trieste on December 28, 1943 for a patrol along the Dalmatian coast. On January 21, 1944 she arrived off Diklo, near Zadar on the Croatian coast. The following morning she was spotted and attacked by RAF fighter-bombers. The ship was badly damaged and the captain decided to run her aground before she sank. After the war the wreckage was removed to Italy and was cut into pieces which were distributed amongst Italian museums

One might think that Marconi's death would put an end to the Marconi saga, but apparently the story is only beginning.

Marconi's Death Ray

In the 1977 book *The Mysteries of the Andes,*[24] the French author Robert Charroux says that Marconi demonstrated a death ray device to Mussolini. Says Charroux:

In 1937 the great Italian scientist's death from a heart

228

attack seemed mysterious to many of his compatriots.

Marconi was certainly one of the greatest geniuses of his time, since, with the aid of Hertz's spark arrester, Popov's antenna and Branly's coherer, he made the first radio transmission in 1895. What is less well known about his work is his discovery of what would now be called a death ray, as reported by Rachele Mussolini, widow of the Italian dictator Benito Mussolini.

One afternoon in June 1936 she was traveling by car to Ostia, where she had a small estate. That morning her husband, who knew about her trip, had told her to be on the road from Rome to Ostia between three o'clock and three-thirty. "You'll see something that will surprise you," he had said with a mysterious expression.

Intrigued, she did as he said, and at exactly three o'clock her car stopped for no apparent reason. At first she thought it was an ordinary mechanical breakdown, especially since her chauffeur lifted the hood of the car and began tinkering with the engine. But then she saw that all the other cars on the road had also stopped. Dozens of drivers were calling out to each other, unscrewing parts of their cars, blowing into tubes, activating fuel pumps. As far as the eye could see, not a single car was moving. It was bewildering and a little frightening.

"I don't understand what's happened," said Rachele's chauffeur. "It's as if someone cast a spell on this road!"

After what her husband had told her, she felt confident. She shrugged her shoulders and said that if the car did not start within half an hour they would have a wrecker come and tow it away. Around her, drivers were swearing and looking puzzled.

At three-thirty-five she told her chauffeur to try the engine again. To his amazement it started and ran perfectly. The other cars also began moving. After half an hour of suspense, everything resumed as if nothing had happened.

That evening Mussolini gave his wife the key to the mystery by telling her that an ultrasecret experiment had been performed with an invention by Marconi, who had devised a system of rays that could disrupt the electrical circuits of engines. Mussolini believed that this would give Italy decisive superiority in case of war. He even believed that, with further research, Marconi's invention could be made effective against living beings and would then become a death ray.

Charroux goes on to say that Marconi attempted to send and receive messages from Mars and that the pope was not very keen on this death ray stuff:

In March 1936, assisted by the physicist Landini, Marconi performed experiments aboard his yacht *Electra*, [sic] which had been made into a floating laboratory. He is said to have succeeded in sending wave trains from Genoa to Australia, where electric lights went on for no discernible reason.

It is said that Pope Pius XI learned about the invention of paralyzing rays in 1936 and that, regarding it as satanic, he took steps to have Mussolini order Marconi to stop such research and destroy all records of it. A year later Marconi died in a way that many of those who knew him considered unclear, but it may be assumed that his close collaborators knew about his work and had a copy of his records. It can probably be stated that Marconi was keenly interested in the question of extraterrestrial civilizations and had received signals, if not messages, from space people.

Charroux then says that a group of Marconi's followers created a "secret city" in South America called the Ciudad Subterranea de los Andes (CSA). Charroux then gives us the story of the Kingdom of Two Craters that seems to come from newspaper accounts from the 1960s and 70s. Says Charroux referring to the legendary underground city in Mongolia or Tibet called Agartha and the possibility that there is such an underground city in South America:

The Agartha, that mysterious underground kingdom

230

that, according to the writer Ossendowski, lies under the Himalayas, is now in South America if we are to believe certain traditions. It was perhaps this South American Agartha that Harry Gibson, a Venezuelan pilot, saw during a routine flight in 1964, at the bottom of two craters in the jungle somewhere between the Sierra Maigualida and the Orinoco River.

It is a strange story, and one would be tempted to place it in the same category as reports of imaginary kingdoms— El Dorado, Paititi, Moricz's tunnel—if it had not been taken very seriously by two respected archeologists, David Nott of Liverpool and Charles Brewer Carias of Caracas, assisted by the Venezuelan Air Force and ten scientists from different nations.

The craters are near the sources of the rivers Caura and Ventuari, and two mountains known as Pava and Masiati, at the edge of the Sierra Pacaraima. The volcanoes have been extinct for thousands or perhaps millions of years, so scientists hope to find plant and animal life in them that has long since disappeared from the rest of the world.

In January 1974 a first three-member team went down into one of the craters, about a thousand feet deep and twelve hundred feet wide. They brought back living plants and animals of species that were either unknown or had been thought extinct sine the Mesozoic.

The two craters are connected by an underground passage nearly a mile long. According to unverified rumors, it is still in use, because traces of recent activity were found in it.

So much for the openly announced part of the discovery. The most important results are being kept secret by the Venezuelan scientific authorities for mysterious reasons. This secrecy has given rise to private inquiries among the people living in the surrounding mountains, whose local names are Jaua-Jidi and Sari Inama-Jidi. Fantastic legends concerning the mystery of the two craters have been gathered.[24]

231

Charroux says that these craters were apparently occupied by people with powerful lights and flying saucer craft that were brilliantly lit by a mysterious power source:

> The region of Jaua-Jidi is a dense, very sparsely inhabited forest. It has been difficult for Venezuelan investigators to make contact with the primitive people who live there. They shun outsiders, speak an unknown language and do not understand Spanish. Half-breeds from the town of Esmeralda, on the Orinoco, have been able to approach them, however.
>
> "Strange people wearing strange clothes have been seen several times in the forest of Jaua-Jidi," one of them reported. "They seem unwilling to approach the Indians and they venture only a short distance away from the craters. Their skin is the color of yellowed ivory; they have big eyes, like a jaguar's, and long hair of different colors.

A map showing the major rivers flowing into the Amazon.

They seem fearful and run away whenever they hear an unusual sound. They are thought to live at the bottoms of the craters and in vast underground rooms, with secret entrances in the forest."

Other reports would seem to indicate that the people of the "Kingdom of Two Craters" are in almost constant contact with space beings, but it should be pointed out that sightings of flying saucers are more common in Central and South America than anywhere else in the world.

The Indians of the forest say that at night the trees on the rim of each volcano are illuminated by a soft green light that apparently comes from the bottom. Occasionally something that looks like a "little round airplane" comes out of the darkness, enters the green halo and disappears into the volcano.

Two or three nights before David Nott, Brewer Carias, G. Dunsterville and their companions came to the site, intense activity by the flying "things" was observed. They were as numerous as a swarm of bees but, perhaps because of their distance from the observers, they flew without making any discernible sound.

The Indians felt that the strange people were receiving heavy reinforcements, or else that they were moving out before the archeologist came. In any case they left little trace of their presence in the underground passages, but enough to give convincing evidence that their existence is not a myth. The Indians believe that the "Kingdom of Two Craters" extends under the mountains and that, for the time being, its entrances are tightly closed.

In Lima Zizi Ghenea told me that a little forest of trees extinct everywhere else grew inside the caves and the craters, and that in it lived animals from the Tertiary.

What is strange about this whole affair, in which legend is mingled with fact, is the Venezuelan government's inexplicable silence and the secrecy in which the expedition's report has been kept.[24]

Charroux is essentially saying that the Kingdom of Two

Craters was in a mountainous area of southern Venezuela near the borders of Brazil and possibly of Guyana. He mentions the Sierra Pacaraima, which is a mountain range that is part of the Guyana Highlands in southeastern Venezuela bordering Guyana and Brazil. The highest mountain in this range is the tabletop peak Mount Roraima which is 9,220 feet high.

But he also mentions the town of Esmeralda. The town of La Esmeralda is a jungle-river town that is in southern Venezuela but is farther to the west in the Sierra Parima, which is an outlying range of the Guyana Highlands. The peaks in the Sierra Parima are largely unexplored; the tallest is Cerro Marahuaca at 5,000 feet (1,500 meters). The range connects with the Pacaraima Mountains in the northeast.

In the area is the famous Casiquiare River. The Casiquiare River is a distributary of the upper Orinoco flowing southward into the Rio Negro. As such, it forms a unique natural canal between

A map of Venezuela showing the major towns.

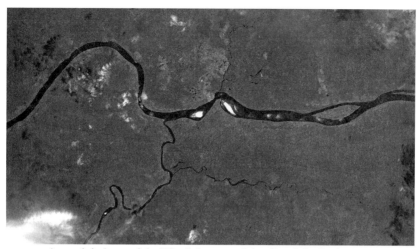

An aerial photo of the Rio Orinoco and the Canal do Casiquiare.

the Orinoco and Amazon River systems. It is the world's largest river of the kind that links two major river systems, a so-called bifurcation. The area forms a water divide, more dramatically at regional flood stage. It is assumed that this river is not a manmade canal and is a natural connection between two major river systems.

Curiously, this Casiquiare River "canal" was investigated in the 1920s by an American explorer named Alexander Hamilton Rice Jr. from Massachusetts. Rice was born in 1875 to a wealthy and influential family and went to Harvard where he became a medical doctor and where he ultimately became a professor.

In 1914–15 he volunteered for the Paris surgical staff of the Ambulance Américain, a group of American civilian doctors serving in Europe prior to the United States' entry into World War I. From 1915 to 1917 he directed the Hôpital 72, Société de Secours aux Blessés Militaires, a French charity hospital also in Paris.

He is best known for his expeditions into the Amazon where he explored remote areas of northern Brazil and southern Venuzuela. As a geographer and explorer Rice specialized in rivers. On seven expeditions, beginning in 1907, he explored 500,000 square miles (1,300,000 km2) of the Amazon Basin, mapping a number of previously unmapped rivers in the northwestern area of the Amazon Basin reaching into Colombia and Venezuela.

Like Marconi, Rice had a specially modified yacht (named

235

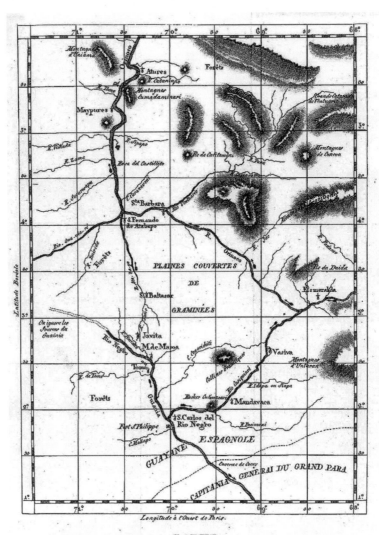

CARTE

De l'Interieur de la Guayane Espagnole dressée sur les lieux
d'après des observations astronomiques
par A. de Humboldt.

A map of the Rio Orinoco and the Canal do Casiquiare.

Alberta) for the Amazon explorations. It left from New York then made the journey to the Amazon. He used this special yacht on all of his Amazon expeditions.

Alexander H. Rice in 1920.

After his 1915 marriage, his socialite wife accompanied him on several expeditions to South America that were chronicled by the popular press. During a 1920 trip, it was reported that "the party warded off an attack by savages and killed two cannibals" "scantily clad ... very ferocious and of large stature." A subsequent headline read: "Explorer Rice Denies That He Was Eaten By Cannibals."

In 1913, the Harvard College Class of 1898 Quindecennial Report had noted: "An interesting feature of [Rice's] work in South America is frequent reports to the effect that he has been eaten by cannibals or has been a victim of the snakes which are said to be laying in wait for him all the time."

On an expedition in 1919 he ascended the Orinoco to its upper reaches in Venezuela, but had a disastrous battle with a group of Yanomami. That expedition continued, in 1920, to traverse the Casiquiare canal, and descend the Rio Negro to the Amazon at Manaus.

His most important exploration in 1924-25 was the first to use aerial photography (from a Curtis Sea-Gull biplane with floats) and shortwave radio for mapping. This four-month expedition ascended the Rio Branco and its Uraricoera headwater (past Maraca Island and the mighty Purumame waterfall) and then, leaving their boats, the explorers cut trails into the Parima hills. The team had a peaceful encounter with another group of Yanomami whom Dr. Rice found poor and repellent but was impressed by their magnificent conical yano hut.

Rice also established hospitals for Indians in Brazil, researched tropical diseases, and conducted expeditions in Alaska and Hudson Bay. His explorations of the Amazon and Orinoco Rivers won him honors which included: the 1914 Gold Medal of the Royal

Alexander H. Rice's specially built yacht the *Alberta*.

Geographical Society, London; Gold Medalist, Geographical Society of Philadelphia; Gold Medalist, Société Royale de Géographie d'Anvers; and gold medalist, Harvard Travelers Club. He led his last expedition in 1924–1925. He died in 1956 after teaching at Harvard from 1929 to 1952.

What is interesting is that Rice had many similarities to Marconi and similar interests. Is it possible that Rice did some explorations that helped the Marconi group mentioned by Charroux find a suitable place for their "secret city" (CSA)? Was information from Rice used by the Marconi group to locate and construct their secret city? Did Marconi's group come to these remote mountain ranges in flying saucers? All of this area, including Sierra Parima and Sierra Pacaraima, is remote and only reachable by the air or by boat. There are no roads.

What Charroux seems to believe is that this Marconi group had come to these remote areas and set up "cities" or laboratories or camps. This explains the activity of all the lights in the crater that Charroux mentions—it was the Marconi group packing up their stuff and moving to another location.

Indeed, it would seem that there is more than one of these secret jungle locations and there can be literally dozens of mountaintop camps or bases for such craft. Even today the mountainous jungle areas of Venezuela, Colombia Ecuador, Peru, Bolivia and Brazil are largely unexplored. Such a secret Marconi city could be in Guyana

238

as well. This might partly explain the intense UFO activity seen in South America since WWII. It may be partly a combination of the secret Marconi craft and the SS craft brought from Antarctica and secret bases in Argentina.

I Have Been to Mars

Robert Charroux discusses this secret city in his book *The Mysteries of the Andes*[24] and says:

> Is there a correlation between the Kingdom of Two Craters and the Underground City of the Andes, or, as it is called in Spanish, the Ciudad Subterranea de los Andes (CSA), which is discussed in private from Caracas to Santiago?

Charroux then discusses a curious book published in Mexico in 1958 that was titled in Spanish "*Yo He Estado en Marte*" which translates to "I have been to Mars" in English. This book claimed that a group of followers of Marconi—all scientists and inventors— went to Venezuela and built a secret laboratory inside an extinct volcano in the remote mountain jungles of that country. This is most likely the mountain ranges in the very south of the country.

Yo He Estado en Marte is said to have been written by an Italian Marconi scientist named Narciso Genovese.[25] The 168-page book was first published in Mexico (and apparently Italy) by a publisher called Editorial Posada in 1958. According to my 1987 edition of the book, it was reprinted three times: in 1966, 1977, and 1987. This is approximately every ten years, but the book is barely known in the English world. Curiously, an edition of this book appeared in German in 1964, published by

The book *I Have Been to Mars*.

Ventla-Verlag.

Charroux tells us that the real author of the book is a Mexican journalist named Mario Rojas Avendaro, who investigated the story of the CSA, interviewed Narciso Genovese, and wrote his book while adding his own embellishments and inventions.

Says Charroux:

[Mario Rojas Avendaro] wrote his story on the basis of statements supposedly made to him by a former disciple of Guglielmo Marconi: Narcisso Genovese, a physicist, philologist and teacher at a high school in Baja California, Mexico.

According to Genovese, when Marconi died in 1937 his students decided to continue his work on the utilization of solar or cosmic energy, taking all possible precautions to make sure it would not be used for war or criminal purposes. Ninety-eight scientists and technicians from various countries formed an organization ...and withdrew to a deserted region of the Andes (or of the forest), where they lived isolated and unknown.

Their work consists in taming the electrical forces of space in the service of a peaceful, universal goal. The community is governed by three basic principles:

•One religion on Earth: that of the true God, or Universal Intelligence.

•One nation: the planet Earth.

•One policy: worldwide peace and an alliance with the peoples of space.

Possessing large financial resources (taken, it is said, from the war treasuries of Benito Mussolini and Adolf Hitler), the association has built an underground city with better research facilities than any other installation in the world.

...In 1946 the center was already using a powerful collector of cosmic energy, the essential component of all matter, in Marconi's theories.

Genovese states that at the first stage of research, the physicists of the CSA counted on the antagonism between matter and antimatter. They now draw energy directly from the sun.

"In 1952," he says, "we traveled above all the seas and continents in a craft whose energy supply was continuous and practically inexhaustible. It reached a speed of half a million miles an hour and withstood enormous pressures, near the limit of resistance of the alloys that composed it. The problem was to slow it down at just the right time.

"We had our first contact with extraterrestrials from Mars on December 16, 1955, at five o'clock in the afternoon. We had already sent radio and light signals. We were surprised to see a formation of five craft flying over our camp."

(The CSA is sometimes a secret city and sometimes a "camp." The whole story is extremely dubious. The technical and scientific details are vague and would seem to indicate that the CSA is behind European and American technology, rather than ahead of it. I am publishing the story without attaching any value to it, other than as a messianic and premonitory phenomenon and as an expression of desire-images.)

"When we sent radio signals to them, one of the craft prepared to land while the others hovered above us, keeping watch and ready to serve as a cover if necessary. The craft we contacted was a flying saucer. It radiated phosphorescent light that disappeared when its propulsion system was turned off. On the ground it took on a fantastic, opaque, light brown color."

Genovese continues his account by describing the saucer. It had a diameter of about twenty-five feet and was surrounded by a smooth rim that rotated when the craft was in motion.

As in many stories of this kind, the extraterrestrial visitors were tall, pale and blue-eyed and wore tight one-piece costumes made of an unknown material. And, of course, they had higher, broader and more rounded foreheads than earthlings.

Conversation took place by means of a computer that

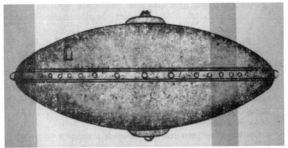

A drawing of one of the Martian craft.

"reflected the electric waves of the earthlings' brains, thus transmitting their thoughts, which were naturally decoded by the better-organized brains of the extraterrestrials."

A celestial map and globe were used to show the location of the planet from which the visitors had come: Mars, known as Loga in their language.

This part of the story clearly shows that it was fabricated: Mars is said to have a larger population than Earth, one that is technologically far superior to us. But after the photographs sent back by Mariner 9, we can consider it certain that Mars is uninhabited, at least on its surface, since its sandy soil, swept by horrendous winds, does not lend itself to any kind of construction.

The pseudo-Genovese nevertheless assures us that Martians and earthlings now exchange scientific information and visits in flying saucers propelled by solar energy. On Mars there is only one nation, one social class and one universe-god, whose name is Sundi.

All this would be wonderfully encouraging if Genovese, a "learned physicist, philologist and humanist," did not show himself to be an inept geographer by adding: "A month later the Center for Space Studies, located in the tropical forest of the Andes at an altitude of thirteen thousand feet, was visited a second time."

I have traveled in the Andes from the Chilean border to the region of San Agustin and from Bogota in Colombia, and I have flown over their entire length many times. I can state from personal observation that there are no tropical forests at an altitude of thirteen thousand feet, but only

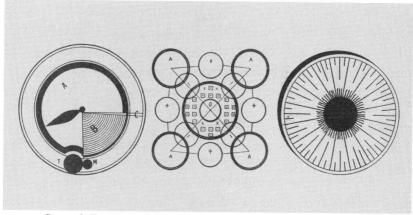

Several diagrams of the propulsion system of the Martian craft.

bare rocks and stunted vegetation.

My conclusion is that the stories of Genovese and Mario Rojas are false, *even if they are not totally groundless.*[24]

Indeed, this book, "I Have Been to Mars" is a curious book and one that is clearly fabricated in certain parts. But is some of it true? Charroux clearly thinks that Mario Rojas has fabricated part of the book, and calls him the pseudo-Genovese in the sense that the second portion of the book—the meeting with the Martians—is clearly fabricated.

The full text of this book in Spanish can be found online and I have also an English summary of the book. What seems to be clear when reading the text is that there are two different books here. Book One is the story of Marconi's secret city somewhere in South America. Book Two is apparently Mario Rojas' fabricated story of a Martian civilization and their perfect system of government. Indeed, much of the second half of the book is a detailed look at the social structure and politics of the Martians who have a superior civilization to us.

There are a few drawings in the book. One is of a craft that looks like a flying saucer, and

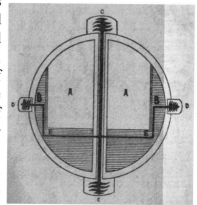

A diagram of the propulsion system.

other illustrations are of spherical Martian craft. There is a drawing of Tage, who is the chief Martian that visits the Marconi city and he looks like any normal human. Tage is married and has a daughter named Dile. The youngest of the Marconi group, a Frenchman named Lavoisier, "fell in love with her, and Tage gave him hope that on the next voyage the two could marry."[25]

The Martian named Tage.

At the very end of the book the author (Genovese with Mario Rojas) discusses the Martian alphabet and finally says that Tage gave the director of the Marconi group, a man named Martinelli, 25 sheets of pure gold. He promised Martinelli that the Martians would continue to give the group whatever they needed to continue their work at the secret city.

Finally, in the last four pages of the book the author turns back to Marconi's work and legacy:

> The applications of solar energy are astonishing. Marconi had done many experiments with surprising results. What intrigued him most was the ease of concentration of electricity in clods which discharged it as rays without any mechanical device.
>
> It was rumored that there was a death ray that would affect human organs. But the majority of of his studies would remain tightly sealed secrets inside a reduced circle of close collaborators, among whom was the eminent

Inside the Martian craft.

Jesuit priest Gianfreschi, of the Academy of Science of the Vatican.

Given the circumstances of the moment—WWII— the findings were considered too dangerous to be in the hands of certain governments, so Pope Pius XI, who was an admirer and protector of Marconi, held the information in reserve. The violent pressures of Mussolini caused the catastrophe in the life of Marconi, who died on July 20, 1937.

His last words, thrown into the face of Il Duce were, "I have not worked 30 years to become the assassin of mankind."

Since 1936 Marconi had sent out powerful electric waves to attract the attention of hypothetical inhabitants of Mars and Venus.

After his death a few of his disciples decided to initiate a scientific college, and to take his studies out of reach of hunters of inventions for warlike aims. One of the results of that is this. Other things will be made public at the appropriate time.[25]

So here we have the Vatican's involvement with Marconi and the secret city. As Charroux reported earlier in this chapter Marconi had demonstrated a death ray to Mussolini and the pope had been alarmed. The quote from Marconi that he had not worked for 30 years to be the assassin of mankind seems to refer to the death rays that Mussolini was so interested in and would use to further his expansionist wars in Africa and the Balkans.

The book ends with a plea for peace and oneness for the planet:

In all of history we find authentic geniuses: Archimedes, Solon, Aristotle, Cesar, Augustus, Homer, Cicero, Dante, Leonardo, Michelangelo, and Marconi.

We also find monsters: Heliogabalos, Attila, and Stalin; there are also hybrid geniuses: Alexander, Napoleon, and Hitler.

How can we estrange ourselves to the progress made by Martians?

If we sacrifice the spirit to the material? If we dispose of scientific sensibility? If we coordinate our investigations? If we cancel all global dividing lines that separate us physically and morally? The Earth has only one frontier, its circumference; it has only one limit, marked by the Sun.

Inhabitants of the Earth, throw your weapons of destruction in the face of the tyrants. Lets make hate into a pyre over the ashes of which we will raise an altar of granite columns of union and incense the spirit to recognition of Supreme God, maker of all things.

…The Martians visit our planet, and the object of this publication is to invite all the inhabitants of Earth to look for their alliance. Amend the erroneous concepts of certain movies, newspapers and magazines. Display desires of alliance, peace, and friendship.

In the serene night we elevate our gate to the firmament where millions of stars sing marvelous hymns of harmony and peace. Join with them in the universal chorus and we will see how great God is and how beautiful his work. The End.

The book ends with the last page giving an important note: "Studious persons interested in obtaining more data can direct their inquiries to the author. Address below."

Guissepe Gianfraneschi at his office in the Vatican.

Guissepe Gianfraneschi and Marconi in Rome, 1934.

This address was that of Mario Rojas Avendaro in Baja, Mexico.

The Heliogabalos (also known as Elagabalus) referenced is a disgraced Roman Emperor of 204-222 AD who was assassinated for his sexual excess and lack of interest in actually governing the Roman Empire as he was supposed to do. The author calls Hitler a hybrid genius—whatever that is—and does not mention Mussolini at all in this section.

The reference to Jesuit priest Gianfreschi, of the Academy of Science of the Vatican, is curious. This may be the Jesuit priest Guissepe Gianfraneschi, an Italian physicist and priest (1875-1934). He was the first director of Vatican Radio and knew Marconi well. He apparently died a few years before Marconi, but did he fake his death? It has been suggested that Marconi faked his death as well and they both joined the group in South America.

But anyway, the last half of the book consists of political and social science fiction about the peace and prosperity achieved on Mars by the very human Martians. It is clearly made up by the Mexican journalist and schoolteacher. Much like the Peruvian book *I Visited Ganymede*, it is a political treatise on a perfect Socialist system in the guise of a UFO book. Charroux clearly sees this and rejects the rather silly Martian aspect to this curious 1958 book. But he suspects that the secret city created by Marconi's followers is true. He says that the city "…is discussed in private from Caracas to Santiago."

247

Secret Cities of the Vril

So, we now have a group of Marconi followers who have moved their camp and experiments to a secret city in southern Venezuela (or elsewhere) and we have the SS moving into Argentina from Antarctica and directly from Europe via Spain (or submarine).

The Marconi group went to South America before the war and the Germans had already established their base in Antarctica. With their extraterritorial activities in the Arctic, the Canary Islands, Antarctica, and South America, the Germans had laid the foundation for a postwar Reich that would include submarines, flying saucers and other craft. Did they ever meet up with the Marconi group?

It would seem that Rojas is giving us a chronicle of a group of Marconi followers with their anti-gravity technology in the mode of Nikola Tesla. What is real in this story?

We have them going to South America and building a city in a crater. They are flying their craft around the world: "In 1952," he says, "we traveled above all the seas and continents in a craft whose energy supply was continuous and practically inexhaustible."

Here we have Charroux's Ciudad Subterranea de los Andes as a place where secret technology was being developed and this technology involved energy, electric power, and aerospace technology (flying saucers). The Martian stuff should be ignored but the secret city of Marconi adepts is possibly real. It would seem to be so.

South America is a hotbed of UFO activity. I have mentioned this in other books and for those who have not been to South America I can tell you that UFO reports are very common in all of the countries there including on the mainstream news in the capital cities. UFOs are a common topic and accepted as a real phenomenon.

Mussolini Had a Crashed UFO in 1933

An Italian researcher claims to have proof that backs up recent allegations that a crashed UFO was recovered in Italy in 1933. It adds to a growing interest in Unidentified Anomalous Phenomena (UAPs) that now includes elected officials and a NASA panel—even in the face of broad scientific skepticism.

248

In an interview published by the *Daily Mail* (July 3, 2023), Italian ufologist Roberto Pinotti says that fascist dictator Benito Mussolini got his hands on a flying saucer after it crashed on June 13, 1933. But the alien craft, Pinotti said, was captured by American forces at the end of World War II and sent to the United States.

Roberto Pinotti.

Pinotti showed documents to the newspaper that he claims are evidence of both the crash and a secret department set up by Mussolini to study the alleged saucer.

"I and my colleague Alfredo Lissoni began investigating the story of the 1933 UFO crash in Lombardy in 1996 when we received some original secret documents about the case," Pinotti told the newspaper.

Pinotti's claims appear to dovetail with the spectacular accusations of former U.S. intelligence officer David Grusch, who recently claimed that the Italian flying saucer was the first such object recovered by the United States. The ex-National Reconnaissance Office staffer also said that he has evidence of a secret U.S. program that has obtained multiple "non-human" flying saucers. Says the *Daily Mail* article:

"I thought it was totally nuts, and I thought at first I was being deceived, it was a ruse," Grusch said. "People started to confide in me. Approach me. I have plenty of senior, former, intelligence officers that came to me, many of which I knew almost my whole career, that

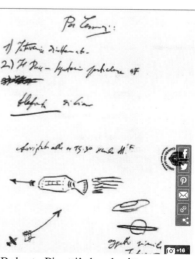

Roberto Pinotti's handwritten memo.

249

David Grusch testifying before Congress.

confided in me that they were part of a program."

The House Oversight Committee is planning a hearing to discuss Grusch's allegations. Florida senator Marco Rubio has said that other intelligence community members besides Grusch have come forward with "firsthand" accounts of UFO hardware.

The renewed UAP interest doesn't stop at the alleged Italian flying saucer. An independent NASA panel has been studying the mysterious phenomena, and said in May that a lack of high-quality data and a lingering stigma are hampering research. And a Pentagon report found images containing objects that could not be identified, but did not conclude that the images had anything to do with aliens.

Pinotti was also sent handwritten memos on paper with a government agency letterhead dated August 22, 1936 which include a sketch and description of a cylindrical aircraft with portholes on the sides and white and red lights spotted flying over Northern Italy.

The documents include two June 1933 telegrams in Italian demanding "absolute silence" over an 'alleged landing on national soil of unknown aircraft'

Another, dated June 13, 1933, threatens the "immediate arrest" and "maximum penalties" for any journalists reporting news of an "aircraft of unknown nature and origin."

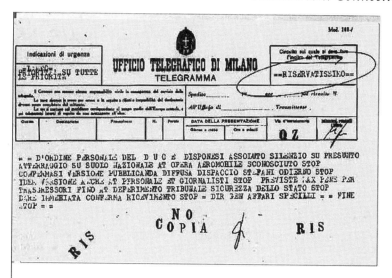

BY PERSONAL ORDER OF THE D U C E ABSOLUTE SILENCE IS ORDERED
ON PRESUMED LANDING ON NATIONAL SOIL OF UNKNOWN AIRCRAFT
STOP
VERSION TO PUBLISH DIFFUSED WITH TODAY'S DISPATCH BY STEFANI IS
CONFIRMED. SAME VERSION ALSO FOR STAFF AND JOURNALISTS STOP
MAXIMUM PENALTIES FORESEEN FOR TRANSGRESSORS UP TO
DEFERMENT TO STATE SECURITY SUPREME COURT STOP
IMMEDIATE CONFIRMATION OF RECEIPT REQUESTED STOP
- DIRECTOR SPECIAL AFFAIRS - ENDS
STOP.

An order from Mussolini about media silence on the landing of a craft.

Other documents sent to Pinotti refer to a mysterious government department called "Gabinetto RS/33," or the RS (Special Research) 33 Cabinet, supposedly set up by the Italian dictator.

So here we have a report of a cylindrical craft with portholes that apparently crashed in 1933. We also have an Italian department called "Gabinetto RS/33." This is apparently the Italian version of MJ-12 or some super-secret military panel to look into UFOs and such. It is known that Mussolini was interested in Marconi's death rays.

Also, we have a report dated June 13, threatens the "immediate arrest" and "maximum penalties" for any journalists reporting news of an "aircraft of unknown nature and origin."

However, the documents sited do not talk about any occupants of the craft. It seems to be presumed that any craft that is a UFO, or UAP as they like to call them these days, must be extraterrestrial. As we have seen in this book, that is not necessarily the case. Flying saucers and cigar-shaped airships may be one thing, but who is piloting this craft may be ordinary humans with an extraordinary technology—a technology that they are using to shape the cultural consciousness of the world with.

Chapter 7

Yellow Submarine: Argentina and British Intelligence

I saw a film today, oh boy
The English Army had just won the war
...I'd love to turn you on.
—The Beatles, *A Day in the Life*

There's a party at the end of world
Flying machines, yellow submarines
French girls in cowboy decor, d'accord
— Jimmy Buffet, *Party at the End of the World*

Starting in the early 1930s Germany began an extended quest for extra-territorial land and military bases. Some of these extra-territorial military bases were submarine bases, some were air bases, and others were a combination of both. These bases existed in areas of the world that the Germans did not directly control, and ranged from friendly countries that were officially neutral in the war to remote territories in the Arctic and Antarctic such as the German Colony of New Schwabenland and the secret bases in Tierra del Fuego and Greenland.

It is well known that Japanese submarines were meeting with German submarines in the Atlantic Ocean during the war. German submarines were also carrying cargos to Indonesia that were apparently of the liquid metal Mercury. So we know that there was a connection between Japan and Germany throughout the war, mainly via submarine. The Germans had many hundreds of them, far more than any other country.

However, these German and Japanese submarines never made the trip all the way to Japan or Germany, it seems. They would meet somewhere in the Atlantic, Indian or Pacific Ocean and exchange cargo. Often it was bars of gold and secret plans for the latest German weapons. Germany had always excelled in making destructive weapons of the worst kind. The famous Krupp Arms group are proof of that.

One can only surmise what British Intelligence thought of the missing U-boats, the secret base in Antarctica or the flying saucers

One of four photos of a Vril craft over New Jersey, 1952.

suddenly appearing in Argentina and all over the world in the late 1940s.

The British and Americans had won the war at great cost and the British economy was in difficult straits. The war had officially ended but there were plenty of problems out on the international stage, including the independence and partition of India and Pakistan, Korea, Vietnam, and other colonies. On top of this was the SS remnant of the Third Reich that controlled various military assets including submarines, secret bases, and UFO-type aircraft.

The British had their hands full and Argentina, as well as Antarctica, were virtually impenetrable locations for them. They still controlled the Falkland Islands, but Argentina never recognized this. Aside from building many of the railroads in South America, Britain has always had difficult relations with the continent's powers. They have their own colony at Guyana which is largely kept isolated from other South American countries.

Yet, the British were keenly interested in the escaped Nazis and such groups as the ODESSA. Prince Philip of the British royal family was a well-known UFO enthusiast who bought numerous UFO books and subscribed to virtually all the UFO newsletters that were available. He amassed a considerable library of UFO material and bequeathed this library to Prince William.

One might assume that Prince Philip's interest in UFOs might have to do with his knowledge of the remains of the Third Reich with their submarines, advanced flying craft and secret bases. Prince Philip was essentially the head of British Intelligence during his lifetime. He is a very interesting person indeed, and perhaps one of the most knowledgeable persons on UFOs in the world at the time of his death.

He Blew His Mind Out in a Car

In December of 1966 there was a terrible crash involving a British sports car in South Kensington, London. Killed in that crash was Tara Browne, a wealthy socialite, swinger, and rumored MI-6 agent.

While Tara is often a girl's name, Tara Browne was a male. He was born on March 4, 1945 and was an heir to the Guinness fortune, being the son Oonagh Guinness who was an heiress to the

255

family enterprise. His father was Dominick Browne, 4th Baron Oranmore and Browne. His father was an Anglo-Irish peer and member of the House of Lords who served in that house for 72 years, longer than any other peer up to that time.

Tara was to inherit one million British pounds on his 25th birthday. He only lived to be 21 years old.

Browne was a member of Swinging London's counterculture of the 1960s and in August 1963, at age 18, he married Noreen "Nicky" MacSherry. The couple had two sons, Dorian and Julian. For his 21st birthday in March 1966, he threw a lavish party at Luggala, the Gothic Browne family seat in the Wicklow Mountains, where two private jets flew the 200 or so guests from London to Ireland. These guests included John Paul Getty, Mick Jagger, Brian Jones and Jones' then-girlfriend Anita Pallenberg, who was said to be the muse of the Rolling Stones. The Beatles did not attend.

Browne had a home in the Belgravia section of London and this abode was the place of many "swing parties," with LSD as depicted in such movies as the 1967 *Bedazzled* with Peter Cook and Raquel Welch. Browne is believed to have been working for MI5 or MI6 when he held these parties and essentially gave away free LSD to all his friends. He famously introduced his friend Paul McCartney to LSD in 1966 at his house in Belgravia.

So we see that Browne was the life of the party and was a fun, intelligent guy who had a lot of money. He was also part of British

Tara Browne with his wife Nicki shortly after their marriage.

Intelligence and was helping to turn everyone on to LSD.

His life was captured in Paul Howard's biography *I Read the News Today, Oh Boy*, published in 2016.[41] Howard says that few people rode the popular wave of the sixties quite like Tara Browne. One of Swinging London's most popular faces, he lived fast, died young and was immortalized for ever in the opening lines of "A Day in the Life," a song that many critics regard as The Beatles' finest. But who was John Lennon's lucky man who made the grade and then blew his mind out in a car?

Howard gives us the story of a young Irishman who epitomized the spirit of the times: racing car driver, Vogue model, friend of The Rolling Stones, style icon, son of a peer, heir to a fortune and the man who turned Paul McCartney on to LSD. Browne was a child born into Ireland's dwindling aristocracy, who spent his early years in an ancient castle in County Mayo, and who arrived in London just as it was becoming the most exciting city on the planet.

The Beatles and the Stones were about to conquer America, Carnaby Street was setting the style template for the world, and rich and poor were rubbing shoulders in the West End in a new spirit of classlessness. Among young people, there was a growing sense that they could change the world. And no one embodied the ephemeral promise of London's sixties better than Tara Browne.

Browne tragically died on December 17, 1966, while he was driving with his girlfriend, model Suki Potier, in his Lotus Elan sports car through South Kensington, London, late at night and at high speed. He was under the influence of alcohol and other drugs at the time. Browne failed to see a traffic light and proceeded through the junction of Redcliffe Square and Redcliffe Gardens and collided with a parked truck. Badly injured, Browne died of his injuries the following day. Suki Potier claimed that Browne was a hero and swerved the car to absorb the impact of the crash in order to save her life.[41]

Tara Browne's body was brought back to Ireland and buried on the Guinness family's Luggala Estate. His grave is one of three situated on the shore of Lough Tay, next to an ornamental building known as the Temple. He was sadly missed by the swinging London scene, which nevertheless continued on without him.

257

A *Daily Mirror* story on the death of Tara Browne with a photo of the car.

While he had been a major distributor of LSD to the swinging London scene, others would take up his role.

That British Intelligence was tied into The Beatles and that LSD was their big promotion is shown by the famous 1967 Beatles album *Sgt. Pepper's Lonely Hearts Club Band*, an album that exposed a very important British Intelligence agent named John Arthur Reid Pepper.

Will the Real Sgt. Pepper Please Stand Up

No photographs are known to exist of John Arthur Reid Pepper, but it is known that he headed the British Security Coordination

(BSC) after World War II. The BSC was a covert organization set up in New York City by the British Secret Intelligence Service (MI6) in May 1940 upon the authorization of the Prime Minister, Winston Churchill.

MI6, properly known as the Secret Intelligence Service (SIS), is the UK's external intelligence agency, and is responsible for protecting and promoting British interests and security overseas. One of the methods by which it does this is espionage. Although the "MI" in MI6's informal title stands for "Military Intelligence," the SIS is a Crown Service that is formally responsible to the Foreign and Commonwealth Office.

MI5 and MI6 are both intelligence agencies of the UK government, but there is a crucial difference. MI5 is responsible for protecting UK citizens and interests at home, notably against threats to national security.

MI6 (SIS) is based in an iconic building on the Thames at Vauxhall and is answerable to the foreign secretary. MI5 is based separately in another building (Thames House) and answerable to the Home Secretary. In some ways they are similar to the FBI and CIA; one is concerned with events inside the United States and the other focuses on foreign events and actors. The Germans similarly had two intelligence services, the SS and the Abwehr.

MI6 has its origins in the Secret Service Bureau, founded in 1909 to control the UK's intelligence activities. Originally split into naval and army sections, these branches rapidly came to focus on overseas and domestic security respectively. This division was formalized with the separation of the Secret Intelligence Service in 1911. The "MI" designations were introduced in 1916, with the organizations' transfer to the Directorate of Military Intelligence.

After the Russian Revolution, the threat posed by communism became a central focus for MI6—leading it on occasion into sensitive political areas. In the 1930s, MI6's attention switched to Nazi Germany. It has been alleged that a number of foreign intelligence figures at this time were sympathetic to Hitler, in their opposition to the USSR. MI6 also spied on the US and Latin America through a front organization set up in New York City called the British Security Coordination.

Says Wikipedia about the British Security Coordination (BSC):

Its purpose was to investigate enemy activities, prevent sabotage against British interests in the Americas, and mobilize pro-British opinion in the Americas. As a "huge secret agency of nationwide news manipulation and black propaganda," the BSC influenced news coverage in the *Herald Tribune,* the *New York Post, The Baltimore Sun,* and Radio New York Worldwide. The stories disseminated from the organization's offices at Rockefeller Center would then be legitimately picked up by other radio stations and newspapers, before being relayed to the American public. Through this, anti-German stories were placed in major American media outlets to help turn public opinion.

Its cover was the British Passport Control Office. BSC benefitted from support given by the chief of the US Office of Strategic Services, William J. Donovan (whose organization was modeled on British activities), and US President Franklin D. Roosevelt who was staunchly anti-Nazi.

The declaration of war upon Germany by the British in September 1939 forced a break in liaison between SIS (MI-6) and the FBI because of the Neutrality Acts of the 1930s. William Stephenson was sent to the US by the head of SIS to see if it could be rekindled to an extent that SIS could operate effectively in the US. While J. Edgar Hoover was sympathetic, he could not go against the State Department without the President's authorization; he also believed that if it was authorized, it should be a personal liaison between Stephenson and himself without other departments being informed. However, Roosevelt endorsed co-operation.

Stephenson's deputy at BSC was Australian-born British intelligence officer Dick Ellis. The pair had been introduced by Sir Ralph Glyn.

Ellis said Stephenson "had been providing a great deal of information on German rearmament to Churchill at that time he was not in office [prior to May 1940] but was playing quite an important role in providing background information to members of [the] House of Commons who were much more concerned with what was happening than the administration [of Prime Minister Neville Chamberlain] seemed to be at the time... I introduced him to my own channels, to heads of intelligence. And that led to his being asked if he was going to America... if he would do what he could to reestablish a link between security authorities here and the FBI."

The liaison was necessary because Britain's enemies were already present in the US and could expect sympathy and support from German and

William Stephenson in 1942.

Italian immigrants, but the authorities there had no remit or interest in activities that were not directly against US security.

Stephenson's report on the American situation advocated a secret organization acting beyond purely SIS activities and covering all covert operations that could be done to ensure aid to Britain and an eventual entry of the US into the war. Stephenson was given this remit and the traditional cover of appointment as a "Passport Control Officer" which he took up in June 1940. Although the existing setup in New York was lacking, Stephenson could call upon his personal liaison with Hoover, the support of Canada, the British ambassador, and his acquaintances with US interventionists.

The office, which was established for intelligence and propaganda services, was headed by Icelandic-Canadian industrialist William Stephenson. Its first tasks were to promote British interests in the United States, counter Nazi propaganda, and protect the Atlantic convoys from enemy sabotage.

The Rockefeller Center in New York held the BSC.

The BSC was registered by the State Department as a foreign entity. It operated out of Room 3603 at Rockefeller Center and was officially known as the British Passport Control Office from which it had expanded. BSC acted as administrative headquarters more than operational one for SIS and the Special Operations Executive (SOE) and was a channel for communications and liaison between US and British security and intelligence organizations.

In a rare article on the BSC in *The Guardian* on August 19, 2006, British novelist William Boyd wrote that it was 1940 and the Nazis were in the ascendant, the Blitz at its deadliest, and Britain's last hope was to bring a reluctant United States into the war. So it happened that the largest covert operation in UK history was launched. Boyd said:

BSC was set up by a Canadian entrepreneur called William Stephenson, working on behalf of the British Secret Intelligence Services (SIS). An office was opened

262

in the Rockefeller Centre in Manhattan with the discreet compliance of Roosevelt and J Edgar Hoover of the FBI. But nobody on the American side of the fence knew what BSC's full agenda was nor, indeed, what would be the massive scale of its operations. What eventually occurred as 1940 became 1941 was that BSC became a huge secret agency of nationwide news manipulation and black propaganda. Pro-British and anti-German stories were planted in American newspapers and broadcast on American radio stations, and simultaneously a campaign of harassment and denigration was set in motion against those organizations perceived to be pro-Nazi or virulently isolationist (such as the notoriously anti-British America First Committee—it had more than a million paid-up members).

Stephenson called his methods "political warfare," but the remarkable fact about BSC was that no one had ever tried to achieve such a level of "spin", as we would call it today, on such a vast and pervasive scale in another country. The aim was to change the minds of an entire population: to make the people of America think that joining the war in Europe was a "good thing" and thereby free Roosevelt to act without fear of censure from Congress or at the polls in an election.

BSC's media reach was extensive: it included such eminent American columnists as Walter Winchell and Drew Pearson, and influenced coverage in newspapers such as the *Herald Tribune, The New York Post* and *The Baltimore Sun*. BSC effectively ran its own radio station, WRUL, and a press agency, the Overseas News Agency (ONA), feeding stories to the media as they required from foreign datelines to disguise their provenance. WRUL would broadcast a story from ONA and it thus became a US "source" suitable for further dissemination, even though it had arrived there via BSC agents. It would then be legitimately picked up by other radio stations and newspapers, and relayed to listeners and readers as fact. The story would spread exponentially and nobody

263

suspected this was all emanating from three floors of the Rockefeller Centre. BSC took enormous pains to ensure its propaganda was circulated and consumed as bona fide news reporting. To this degree its operations were 100% successful: they were never rumbled.

Nobody really knows how many people ended up working for BSC—as agents or sub-agents or sub-sub-agents—although I have seen the figure mentioned of up to 3,000. Certainly at the height of its operations in late 1941 there were many hundreds of agents and many hundreds of fellow travellers (enough finally to stir the suspicions of Hoover, for one). Three thousand British agents spreading propaganda and mayhem in a staunchly anti-war America. It almost defies belief. Try to imagine a CIA office in Oxford Street with 3,000 US operatives working in a similar way. The idea would be incredible—but it was happening in America in 1940 and 1941, and the organization grew and grew.

In the summer of 1941, the BSC sent a bogus Hungarian astrologer called Louis de Wohl to the US. At a press conference in New York de Wohl said he had been studying Hitler's astrological chart and could see nothing but disaster ahead for the German dictator. De Wohl became a minor celebrity and went on tour through the US, issuing similar dire prognostications about Hitler and his allies. De Wohl's wholly bogus predictions were widely published.

The False Map of South America

Much of the BSC's activities were focused on South America. Latin America was an important neutral source of trade for the Axis forces and many Latin American countries were pro-Germany and the Axis. The Italian airline LATI operated a transatlantic service—between Rome and Rio de Janeiro—which was a conduit for high-value goods (platinum, gems, etc.), plus Axis agents and diplomatic bags. London instructed the BSC to do something about the airline.

The airline had connections with the Brazilian government

through the president's son-in-law. Accordingly, the BSC constructed a forged letter of such accuracy that its authenticity could not be questioned even under forensic examination. The letter purported to come from LATI's head office to an executive of the company stationed in Brazil. The contents included disparaging references to the Brazilian president and to the US, and implied connections with a fascist opposition party in Brazil.

Following a "burglary" of the executive's house, a photostat of the letter was placed with an American Associated Press reporter, who immediately took it to the American Embassy, which then showed the letter to the President of Brazil, Getúlio Vargas. LATI's operations in Brazil were confiscated and its personnel interned— the airline ceased transatlantic flights in December 1941. Brazil broke off relations with the Axis and joined the Allies in 1942. They were the only South American country to declare war on Germany and the Axis. Portugal and Spain were officially neutral during the war but Spain was known as a safe haven for Nazis and SS officers.

Says Boyd in his *The Guardian* article:

> One of BSC's most successful operations originated in South America and illustrates the clandestine ability it had to influence even the most powerful. The aim was to suggest that Hitler's ambitions extended across the Atlantic. In October 1941, a map was stolen from a German courier's bag in Buenos Aires. The map purported to show a South America divided into five new states—Gaus, each with their own Gauleiter—one of which, Neuspanien, included Panama and "America's lifeline" the Panama Canal. In addition, the map detailed Lufthansa routes from Europe to and across South America, extending into Panama and Mexico. The inference was obvious: watch out, America, Hitler will be at your southern border soon. The map was taken as entirely credible and Roosevelt even cited it in a powerful pro-war, anti-Nazi speech on October 27 1941: "This map makes clear the Nazi design," Roosevelt declaimed, "not only against South America but against the United States as well."

The news of the map caused a tremendous stir: as a piece of anti-Nazi propaganda it could not be bettered. But was the South America map genuine? My own hunch is that it was a British forgery (BSC had a superb document forging facility across the border in Canada).

The story of its provenance is just too pat to be wholly believable. Allegedly, only two of these maps were made; one was in Hitler's keeping, the other with the German ambassador in Buenos Aires. So how come a German courier, who was involved in a car crash in Buenos Aires, happened to have a copy on him? Conveniently, this courier was being followed by a British agent who in the confusion of the incident somehow managed to snaffle the map from his bag and it duly made its way to Washington.

The story of the South America map and the other BSC schemes was written up (in an extensive document of some hundreds of pages) after the war for private circulation by three former members of BSC (one of them Roald Dahl, interestingly enough). This secret history was a form of present for William Stephenson and a selected few others; it was available only in typescript and only 10 typescripts ever existed. Churchill had one, Stephenson had one and others were given to a few high officials in the SIS but they were regarded as top secret.

This secret document of all of the BSC's schemes is fascinating indeed. Roald Dahl went on to be a famous writer whose works include *Charlie and the Chocolate Factory*. Like his friend Ian Fleming, Roald Dahl was British Intelligence with a great deal of knowledge of the inner workings of this operation. Yet, he chose to become a writer and publish material that had to conform to British Intelligence's strict censorship.

Roald Dahl clearly had his own copy of this manuscript, privately circulated (by him), and may have in his later years photocopied it and given it to friends. It would seem that Ian Fleming must have had a copy. That John Lennon was given a copy of the "book" is quite likely. At any rate the book and its contents were widely known to those who were part of the circle.

266

This circle included The Beatles.

The Case of the Missing Sgt. Pepper
   Wikipedia has a list of notable BSC employees. This fascinating list includes a number of media personalities but also people you probably would never have heard of, including Sir John Pepper. This notable BSC employees list is (with my notes):

Cedric Belfrage—British film critic, writer, cofounder of *National Guardian*
Roald Dahl—after he was transferred to Washington, DC as Assistant Air Attaché.
Dick Ellis—deputy-head; post-war accused of being spy for the Germans and the Soviets
Ian Fleming—author and Intelligence corps officer
Alexander Halpern—Russian Menshevik and ex-Freemason
Gilbert Highet—historian, professor of Greek and Latin at Columbia University
H. Montgomery Hyde—counter-espionage Intelligence Corps officer
Dorothy Maclean—Canadian spiritual writer and cofounder of Findhorn
Eric Maschwitz—screenwriter (Dr. Who), broadcaster, and Intelligence Corps officer
David Ogilvy—creator of modern advertising
John Arthur Reid Pepper—Director BSC 1947 to ?
Ivan T. Sanderson—author, zoologist, and Intelligence Corps officer
Herbert Sichel—South African statistician who made great advances in applied statistics
Betty Thorpe—spy, codenamed "Cynthia" in plot to seduce Vichy French officials in Washington DC
Harold Phillips—officer in the Coldstream Guards who protect the monarchy

   Every single person on this list has their own Wikipedia entry and link except for John Arthur Reid Pepper. There is no link to a biography of him. There is no photo of him to be found. He is a profoundly missing player in the BSC scheme and he is nowhere to be found on the Internet. He is a ghost person who was known to exist but virtually nothing is known about him. He must be dead by now, but we do not know when he was born or when he died. We know nothing of his activities except that The Beatles immortalized him with their 1967 album. In this album we are told that Sgt. Pepper taught the band to play, and that was 20 years before today. This date would be 1947, the year that John Pepper became the director of the BSC, apparently.

In 2004 a new head of MI6 was appointed whose name was Sir John Scarlett. It was noted that he was a recognized public figure with plenty of photos, but his predecessor, Sir Richard Dearlove, was a mystery and no public photo can be found of him since his graduation from university many decades before.

Why is there no information on Sir John Pepper? Is it because he was exposed by The Beatles with their sonic masterpiece album? British Intelligence was to suppress all information about Pepper as part of their pattern of keeping secret things secret.

Other people on this list are various Anglo-American operatives and media stars. Of special interest is Dick Ellis, an early James Bond character.

Colonel Charles Howard "Dick" Ellis was an Australian-born British intelligence officer credited with drawing the blueprint for the United States' wartime intelligence agencies—Coordinator of Information and Office of Strategic Services (OSS), which would become the CIA. For his contribution to the United States in World War II, he received the Legion of Merit from President Harry S. Truman. Colonel David K. E. Bruce said that "without [Ellis's] assistance... American intelligence could not have gotten off the ground in World War II."

Dick Ellis in 1919.

Ellis was born in Sydney, Australia in 1895. Following the outbreak of the WWI (1914–18), Ellis enlisted as a private in the 100th Provisional Battalion, later known as the 29th (City of London) Battalion. Ellis entered the "theatre of war" in October 1916 in France, where he fought in the First Battle of the Somme and was wounded on several occasions

After convalescing in a British hospital and further training in Troon, Scotland, Ellis joined the 4th Battalion Middlesex Regiment, was commissioned as a junior officer in September 1917, and later promoted to captain. In 1918, Ellis left Europe for Egypt and India, via Italy. While stationed with the South Lancashire Regiment 1st Battalion in Quetta (now Pakistan), he volunteered for the Intelligence Corps in Persia and Transcaspia. Ellis was later sent to Georgia and Armenia as part of a mission against the Bolsheviks in what is now Turkmenistan. Here he saw the oilfields of Baku that the Nazis attempted to seize during WWII. I describe this in my book *Haunebu: The Secret Files*.

In June 1940 Ellis was appointed deputy head to William Stephenson at British Security Co-ordination in New York, after the two men were introduced in 1938 in London by Sir Ralph Glyn. Ellis was officially appointed His Britannic Majesty's Consul in New York. He arrived in the United States in July 1940.

Ellis continued working closely with Donovan and the OSS during 1942 and was involved in the setting up of OSS training centers and the infamous Camp X in Whitby, Ontario, to be discussed shortly. In 1943 Ellis briefly went to Cairo, Egypt, where he served under Richard Casey but travelled frequently to the United States and Canada. In September 1944 he returned home to England but visited Washington, DC in 1946 for talks with General John Magruder of Strategic Services Unit, the successor to OSS. It soon disbanded and the CIA was formed in 1947.

At MI6, Ellis was promoted to Chief Controller Pacific (Far East and the Americas), making him, in the words of one biographer, "effectively one of the most powerful intelligence agents in the world, with responsibility for North and South America and those regional hotbeds of communism, East Asia and South-East Asia." Ellis became No. 3 in the entire secret service hierarchy, controlling its activities in about half the world.

Ellis also headed MI6's Combined Intelligence Far East, based in Singapore and Hong Kong. What did Ellis know about Argentina and South America? His agents must have been very active but we know very little of their activities.

In the late 1940s Ellis went to Australia on behalf of MI6 and helped found the Australian Secret Intelligence Service. Ellis retired from MI6 in 1953 and accepted a two-year contract with the Australian Security Intelligence Organization to act as a liaison between the Australian intelligence services and MI6. Ellis returned to England on February 11, 1954. He died in 1975 in England at the age of 80.

Following the defection of MI6 agent Kim Philby to the Soviet Union in 1963, Ellis was the subject of an internal MI5-MI6 investigation, during which he allegedly made a confession that he had supplied information to the Nazis prior to World War II. He denied anything to do with the Soviet Union.

Some of the intelligence that may have originated with Ellis, who knew that Admiral Wilhelm Canaris, chief of the Abwehr (military intelligence, different from the SS), had secret plans to use the White Russians in operations in Ukraine and southern Russia. Canaris was cooperating with many of the same organizations as those sponsored by the British, and there is evidence that on occasion they worked in concert, abetted by Ellis. The Abwehr had apparently collaborated with the British in central Europe and the Balkans, including Georgia, in counterintelligence operations against "communist agents" who had begun to flood into Western Europe to provoke revolutions in support of the Kremlin.

Dick Ellis was something

Dick Ellis during WWII.

of a James Bond and notably was in charge of British Intelligence operations in North and South America. Working with him at this time was the mysterious John Pepper of Beatles fame.

Also a candidate for James Bond was William Stephenson, who as we have seen, was a Canadian soldier, fighter pilot, businessman and spymaster who served as the senior representative of the British Security Coordination (BSC) for the western allies during World War II. He is best known by his wartime intelligence code name, Intrepid. Many people consider him to be one of the real-life inspirations for James Bond. Ian Fleming himself once wrote, "James Bond is a highly romanticized version of a true spy. The real thing is… William Stephenson."

As head of the BSC, Stephenson handed British scientific secrets over to Franklin D. Roosevelt and relayed American secrets back to Winston Churchill. In addition, Stephenson has been credited with changing American public opinion from an isolationist stance to a supportive tendency regarding the United States' entry into World War II.

After World War I, Stephenson returned to Manitoba and with a friend started a hardware business inspired largely by a can opener that Stephenson had taken from his POW camp. The business was unsuccessful, and he left Canada for England. In England, Stephenson soon became wealthy, with business contacts in many countries. In 1924, he married American tobacco heiress Mary French Simmons, of Springfield, Tennessee. That same year, Stephenson and George W. Walton patented a system for transmitting photographic images via wireless that produced £100,000 a year in royalties for the 18-year run of the patent (about $12 million per annum adjusted for inflation in 2010).

In addition to his patent royalties, Stephenson swiftly diversified into several lucrative industries: radio manufacturing; aircraft manufacturing; Pressed Steel Company that manufactured car bodies for the British motor industry; construction and cement; as well as Shepperton Studios and Earls Court studio. Here we see how Stephenson was involved in the entertainment industry.

Stephenson had a broad base of industrial contacts in Europe, Britain and North America, as well as a large group of contacts in the international film industry. Shepperton Studios were the

271

largest film studios in the world outside of Hollywood.

As early as April 1936, Stephenson was voluntarily providing confidential information to British MP Winston Churchill about how Adolf Hitler's Nazi government was building up its armed forces and hiding military expenditures of £800,000,000. This was a clear violation of the terms of the Treaty of Versailles and showed the growing Nazi threat to European and international security. Churchill used Stephenson's information in Parliament to warn against the appeasement policies of the government of Neville Chamberlain.

After World War II began, now-Prime Minister Winston Churchill sent Stephenson to the United States in June 1940 to covertly establish and run BSC in New York City, over a year before the US entry into the war.

Stephenson's initial directives for BSC were to:

•investigate enemy activities;
•institute security measures against sabotage to British property; and
•organize American public opinion in favor of aid to Britain.

Later this was expanded to include "the assurance of American participation in secret activities throughout the world in the closest possible collaboration with the British." Stephenson's official title was British Passport Control Officer. His unofficial mission was to create a secret British intelligence network throughout the western hemisphere, and to operate covertly and broadly on behalf of the British government and the Allies in aid of winning the war. South America was under his control for MI6 (SIS).

Stephenson was soon a close adviser to Roosevelt, and suggested that he put Stephenson's good friend William J. "Wild Bill" Donovan in charge of all US intelligence services. Donovan founded the US Office of Strategic Services (OSS), which in 1947 would become the Central Intelligence Agency (CIA). As senior representative of British intelligence in the western hemisphere, Stephenson was one of the few persons in the hemisphere who were authorized to view raw Ultra transcripts of German Enigma ciphers that had been decrypted at Britain's Bletchley Park facility. He was trusted by Churchill to decide what Ultra information to pass along to various branches of the US and Canadian governments.

While the US was still neutral, agreement was made for all transatlantic mail from the US to be routed through the British colony of Bermuda, 640 miles off the North Carolina coast. Airmail carried by both British and American aircraft landed at RAF Darrell's Island and was delivered to censors working in the Princess Hotel.

All mail, radio and telegraphic traffic bound for Europe, the US and the Far East were intercepted and analyzed by 1,200 censors, of British Imperial Censorship, part of British Security Coordination (BSC), before being routed to their destination with no indication that they had been read. With BSC working closely with the FBI, the censors were responsible for the discovery and arrest of a number of Axis spies operating in the US. After the war, Stephenson lived at the Princess Hotel for a time before buying his own home in Bermuda.

Once the US had entered the war in December 1941, BSC went on to train US propagandists from the United States Office of War Information in Canada at Camp X. BSC covert intelligence and propaganda efforts directly affected wartime developments in Brazil, Argentina, Colombia, Chile, Venezuela, Peru, Bolivia, Paraguay, Mexico, the Central American countries, Bermuda, Cuba and Puerto Rico. Stephenson worked without salary.

As we have noted, Stephenson employed Amy Elizabeth Thorpe, codenamed Cynthia, to seduce Vichy French officials into giving up Enigma ciphers and secrets from their Washington embassy. As part of Canada's contribution to the war effort, at the height of the war Pat Bayly, a University of Toronto professor from Moose Jaw, created the Rockex, the fast secure communications system that would eventually be relied on by all the Allies.

Camp X

One of Stephenson's contributions to the war effort was the setting up by BSC of Camp X, the unofficial name of the secret Special Training School No. 103, a paramilitary installation for training covert agents in the methods required for success in clandestine operations. Located in Whitby, Ontario, this was

An aerial photo of Camp X in Ontario during WWII.

the first such espionage training school in North America. It is estimated that up to 2,000 British, Canadian and American covert operators were trained there from 1941 to 1945.

Established December 6, 1941, the training facility closed before the end of 1944; the buildings were removed in 1969 and a monument was erected at the site.

Wikipedia says that historian Bruce Forsyth summarized the purpose of the facility thusly: "Trainees at the camp learned sabotage techniques, subversion, intelligence gathering, lock picking, explosives training, radio communications, encode/ decode, recruiting techniques for partisans, the art of silent killing and unarmed combat." Communication training, including Morse code, was also provided. The existence of the camp was kept such a secret that even Canadian Prime Minister William Lyon Mackenzie King was unaware of its full purpose.

Reports indicate that Camp X graduates worked as "secret agents, security personnel, intelligence officers, or psychological warfare experts, serving in clandestine operations. Many were captured, tortured, and executed; survivors received no individual recognition for their efforts." Camp X graduates operated in Europe (Spain, Portugal, Italy and the Balkans) as well as in Africa, Australia, India and the Pacific.

Graduates of Camp X may have included Ian Fleming, future author of the James Bond books. While in Toronto, Fleming stayed at a hotel near St. James-Bond United Church, and it is thought that this is where he got the name for his fictional 007 character. He was visiting Camp X at the time.

It has been said that the fictional Goldfinger's raid on Fort Knox was inspired by a Stephenson plan to steal $2,883,000,000 in Vichy French gold reserves from the French Caribbean colony of Martinique. The plan was never carried out.

Later, until the buildings were destroyed in 1969, Camp X became the Oshawa Wireless Station under operation by the Royal Canadian Corps of Signals as a secret listening location. Records that had not been previously destroyed were stored in Ottawa under the Official Secrets Act.

Stephenson worked as the director of the BSC until 1947. At this time the directorship was taken over by Sir John Pepper. It is not known how long the BSC continued to operate or how long John Pepper was the director. Information on the later activities after the war are very sketchy, if not totally unknown. However, it seems that it lasted until the mid-1960s and that The Beatles were introduced to John Pepper at some point.

Perhaps at this meeting it was explained to The Beatles that British Intelligence was actively promoting LSD as a way for college students and young adults to forget about politics and nationalism and think about other things. The British were keen on focusing on two areas: the nationalism in Ireland and parts of the UK and the growing Nazi threat in Argentina and other South American countries.

John Pepper, as a high-ranking MI6 officer, would probably have been briefed on the missing subs and the suspicious activities in Antarctica and Argentina. He might have known about the supposed battle near Iceland between the British Fleet and the black submarines that refused to surrender. Haunebu craft from the German Peary Land base in the very north of Greenland were also said to have been present at this sea battle.

It is possible that there was a battle between UK submarines and black U-boats in Tierra del Fuego shortly after the war but this seems unlikely. These secret bases in the Chilean fjords have probably remained undiscovered and may still be operated by SS Black Sun officers. One also wonders if the song *Yellow Submarine* was somehow a nod to the notion that U-boats were still out there as mystery subs.

Yes, British Intelligence, with the help of John Pepper and the BSC, would flood Argentina, Chile, and Uruguay with rock and roll and LSD. This would create a new atmosphere of peace and brotherly love where young people gathered for concerts instead of political rallies of the left or the right. As Keith Richards famously said, "Rock concerts are the one big venue where everyone comes together for the same purpose—to have fun."

The first thing that John Pepper and the BSC needed to do was get The Beatles to Argentina. They did this by sending a fake band to Buenos Aires in 1964.

The Beatles and British Intelligence in Argentina

I have said before that UFO activity in Argentina and other South American countries was very heavy in the 1950s and 60s. The SS had created a new Reich in Argentina and British Intelligence was aware of that. American Intelligence and other NATO states were aware of this as well. They have kept this a secret but intelligence documents tell a different story.

While American intelligence has been compelled to release some of their files, the British have not been compelled to do so. We do know that Prince Phillip, when he was alive, was an avid UFO enthusiast. Some of the books and reports he read would have been about UFO activity in Argentina and elsewhere on the South American continent. He must have been aware of some of the reports that the SS was operating flying saucers and secret submarine craft after the war—and that it was coming from Argentina, a de facto Nazi state.

The British needed to penetrate the SS-created Nazi-Neo-State that was postwar Argentina with rock and roll and drugs. And that penetration was ultimately to made by The Beatles, but the Fab Four didn't show up. So, apparently MI6 cooked up their own plan: a fake Beatles invasion. We can only suppose that John Pepper cooked up the plan to send a fake Beatles band to Argentina, but this was the sort of operation that the BSC was known for.

In the spring of 1964 as Beatlemania was making its way around the world, a newspaper in Buenos Aires announced that The Beatles would be travelling to South America. Millions awaited their arrival with bated breath—and in July, when four young moptops arrived in Buenos Aires Airport, it seemed that the teenage dreams of young Argentinians were about to come true. The Beatles however were thousands of miles away in London.

The youth of Argentina and nearby countries were thrilled that the Fab Four were coming to South America for a series of concerts. Unfortunately for the concertgoers in Argentina the group that showed up was not the real Beatles. It was a group called "The American Beetles."

Originally a doo-wop harmony band from Florida called The Ardells, "The American Beetles" consisted of Bill Ande (guitar), Tom Condra (guitar), Vic Gray (bass) and Dave Hieronymus (drums). They began their career at a nightclub in Miami under the guidance of manager Bob Yorey.

Bob was quick to capitalize on the success of The Beatles,

A promotional photo for The American Beetles.

277

Vril: Secrets of the Black Sun

claiming; "They're the English Beatles. I'm going to make up a group called The American Beetles." So, Bob managed to recruit the four musicians, asked them to grow their hair, dress the same as the Fab Four wearing similar suits. This was the same look given to The Beatles by British intelligence.

The American Beetles on stage.

Both a joke and a timely cash-grab, the group's rebrand had won them big crowds and fresh attention from promoters in the US.

An Argentinian named Rudy Duclós saw the band perform in Bob Yorey's Miami club and told Yorey he wanted to book them on a tour of South America. However when pitching the group to venues and promoters, Rudy forgot to mention the "American Beetles" part. He pitched them as the real Beatles. The agreement was done, press were alerted and Beatlemania was turned up a notch. The Fab Four were coming to Argentina! It didn't matter to British intelligence that the real Beatles weren't going to Argentina. What mattered was that Beatlemania would be cultured in South America.

Their arrival in Buenos Aires was met with commotion—a number of TV channels were vying for them to perform on their shows so getting the band and their instruments from the plane into a car and onto a hotel proved chaotic.

They were the main act booked for a concert called *The Laughter Festival* on July 8, 1964. The band waited behind the stage, hidden from view by a curtain with their guitars and drumsticks at the ready as the host delivered his opening dialogue. As soon as he introduced "Los American Beetles" the band arrived on stage and began to play *Twist and Shout*.

It didn't take long till viewers at home realized they had been deceived by the televised concert. However, at the concert it was the same screaming and yelling in mirth at the mop tops on stage. Beatlemania had come to Buenos Aires.

The South American press felt like they had been treated as

278

a laughing stock with headlines like, "They sing bad but they act worse!" and "The Beetles showed that all the talent they have is in their hair."

However, the band continued to tour—with shows in Lima, Sao Paolo and Rio de Janeiro where they played to packed crowds of excited Beatles fans, happy to see the next best thing. It had been a success and rock and roll was the winner. Nazi music and German-themed parties were no longer in vogue and it was the swinging London scene with The Beatles, Rolling Stones, Jimi Hendrix and the like painting a psychedelic picture of love, peace, and happiness.

After their tour of South America the band returned to Miami and changed their name to Razor's Edge. Interestingly, the group had a chance meeting with The Beatles at Bob Yorey's Miami club later that year. John, Paul, George and Ringo had landed in Florida and made the short journey to see their doppelgänger's perform. It is said that George and Paul even got up to dance.

Turn Me On Dead Man

Meanwhile, back in London the *Sgt. Pepper's Lonely Hearts Club Band* album was changing the music industry and "Lucy in the Sky with Diamonds" was the thing. And then, suddenly, Paul was dead. He was the one who "blew his mind out in a car," not the MI6 agent Tara Browne. British intelligence did not want anyone to know who "Sgt. Pepper" was or who Tara Browne was. Apparently they cooked up the fake conspiracy, with the help of John Lennon, that Paul was dead.

Suddenly, the amazing cover of the Sgt. Pepper's album, which included a number of British intelligence agents, including Alastair Crowley, and was essentially an exposé of British intelligence and the drug scene, was really a cryptic hint at the answer to the puzzle of "Paul is dead."

According to the rumor, McCartney died in a car crash and to spare the public from grief, the surviving Beatles, aided by Britain's MI6, replaced him with a McCartney look-alike, subsequently communicating this secret through subtle details of their albums.

It all began in early 1967, a rumor circulated in London that Paul McCartney had been killed in a traffic accident while driving along the M1 motorway on January 7 of that year. McCartney then alluded to the rumor during a press conference held around the release of *Sgt. Pepper's Lonely Hearts Club Band* in May. By 1967, the Beatles were known for sometimes including backmasking in their music. Analyzing their lyrics for hidden meaning had also become a popular trend in the US. In November 1968, their self-titled double LP (also known as *"The White Album"*) was released containing the track "Glass Onion." John Lennon wrote the song in response to "gobbledygook" said about Sgt. Pepper. In a later interview, he said that he was purposely confusing listeners with lines such as "the Walrus was Paul"—a reference to his song "I Am the Walrus" from the 1967 album *Magical Mystery Tour*.

In September 1969, Tim Harper, an editor of the *Drake Times-Delphic*, the student newspaper of Drake University in Des Moines, Iowa, published an article titled "Is Beatle Paul McCartney Dead?" The article addressed a rumor being circulated on campus that cited clues from recent Beatles albums, including a message interpreted as "Turn me on, dead man," heard when the *White Album* track "Revolution 9" is played backwards. Also referenced was the back cover of *Sgt. Pepper*, where every Beatle except McCartney is photographed facing the viewer, and the front cover of *Magical Mystery Tour*, which depicts one unidentified band member in a differently colored suit from the other three. This character looks like a walrus. Rumor had it that Paul had been replace by a look-alike named Billy Shears.

In late September 1969, the Beatles released the album *Abbey Road* as they were in the process of disbanding. The cover of the album added fuel to the fire, in that Paul is pictured crossing road barefoot while the others are shod. The Beatles' press officer, Derek Taylor, commented on the rumor stating: "Recently we've been getting a flood of inquiries asking about reports that Paul is dead. We've been getting questions like that for years, of course, but in the past few weeks we've been getting them at the office and home night and day. I'm even getting telephone calls from disc jockeys and others in the United States."

Throughout this period, McCartney felt isolated from his bandmates in his opposition to their choice of business manager, Allen Klein, and distraught at Lennon's private announcement

280

that he was leaving the group. With the birth of his daughter Mary in late August, McCartney had withdrawn to focus on his family life. On October 22, 1969, the day that the "Paul is dead" rumor became an international news story, McCartney, his wife Linda and their two daughters travelled to Scotland to spend time at his farm near Campbeltown.

McCartney returned to London in December 1969 and, bolstered by Linda's support, he began recording his debut solo album at his home in St John's Wood. Titled *McCartney*, and recorded without his bandmates' knowledge, it was "one of the best-kept secrets in rock history" until shortly before its release in April 1970. This led to the announcement of the Beatles' break-up. In his 1971 song "How Do You Sleep" Lennon attacked McCartney's character, and described the theorists as "freaks" who were "right when they said you was dead."

The Beatles were partly responsible for the phenomenon due to their incorporation of random lyrics and effects. *The White Album* track "Glass Onion" has Lennon inviting clue-hunting by including references to other Beatles songs.

A 2010 mockumentary, *Paul McCartney Really is Dead: The Last Testament of George Harrison*, purports to tell the story of George Harrison, believing himself to be on his deathbed after being stabbed on December 30, 1999, revealing that Paul had died in a car crash with a girl named Rita and that British intelligence agencies had orchestrated a cover-up through which Paul was replaced by a look-alike. The film is narrated by a voice actor purporting to be George Harrison (but is obviously not), describing over archival footage the clues left behind in songs and album art that Paul was dead. This cover-up was because British intelligence had decided that too many young women would commit suicide if Paul was dead. This ridiculous premise is promoted during the entire 90-minute film with a menacing MI5 character known as "Maxwell" constantly fighting with The Beatles over their "leaking" clues of Paul's death to their millions of listeners. Maxwell was the handler for the group, threatening them with retaliation and even death if they exposed the fact that Paul was dead and that MI5 is part of the cover-up. John Lennon was ultimately killed for this reason says the film.

281

Yet, while this documentary is satire, it does create a sense that some of it is true, particularly that British Intelligence was involved with The Beatles. No, Paul is not the person who didn't notice that the light had changed. Billy Shears is Ringo, not Paul, as each of The Beatles took on a new persona for the *Sgt. Pepper's* album. "Lucy in the Sky with Diamonds" was about LSD and The Beatles and their friends got their hits in the thousands from various MI5 or MI6 friends. Various celebrities such as Cary Grant, Timothy Leary, Jimi Hendrix and John Lennon were known for taking LSD on a daily basis. It has been said that every CIA agent of this time period was required to take LSD. The CIA did many famous experiments with LSD including bombs that would release LSD or some other psychoactive agent and even infecting an entire village in France.

One has to wonder whether British Intelligence was also required to take LSD during this period of the 60s and 70s? It would seem that this would be the case. LSD is something of a truth serum and mind control drug. The CIA wanted its operatives to be aware of the LSD experience—a state of heightened awareness and cosmic awareness where the core ego is not important—and know when something like it was being used against them.

Its Only Rock and Roll But I Like It

So where does the search for Sgt. Pepper lead us? It leads through WWII, to Camp X, the BSC, covert operations in South America (and Antarctica), to manipulating the American public through advertising and propaganda, to the secret war with the dark subs and the SS that went on until 1947 or so.

After this, things calmed down for a few years and then suddenly, around 1950 flying saucers started buzzing farmers and city folk alike in a new universe of psyops. The Buck Rogers and Flash Gordon era of the 1930s was back, this time with flying saucers! The extraterrestrials may have suddenly shown up as well, but at least some of these flying saucer and cylindrical craft sightings and interactions are with German-designed craft that are basically electric in nature.

The clear daylight photos of the Vril craft, as published in this book, are proof that one of the most common flying saucers is the small Vril, made for one or two people. The many sightings of these craft in the 1950s created a hysteria that was only calmed by official Air Force investigations and Hollywood movies bringing it to us as science fiction, making it more normal to see flying saucers. "Well, I've seen flying saucers in the movies."

Flying saucers were still popular as the 60s came on and with the assassination of John F. Kennedy, the time was ripe to "turn on" and give peace a chance. Enter Sir John Pepper and the Beatles. And, this was a plot that was wildly successful.

> I was drowned, I was washed up and left for dead
> I fell down to my feet and I saw they bled
> I frowned at the crumbs of a crust of bread
> I was crowned with a spike right through my head
> —The Rolling Stones, *Jumping Jack Flash* (1968)

The British, aware of the Nazi survival in South America and the SS psyops of "flying saucers on the attack," were busy doing some psyops of their own. They created a movement of rock and roll and LSD, taking the 1960s by storm and reversing a terrible trend of wars and assassinations around the world, including the assassination of President Kennedy. They turned the flying saucer invasion into Lucy in the Sky with Diamonds and the dark U-boats became Yellow Submarines.

Rock and roll was banned in the Soviet Union during the 1960s and 1970s, but it was popular all over the world including in Germany, Argentina and all over Latin America where many Beatles and Jimi Hendrix-themed bars, cafes and music shops abide. Bob Marley arrived in the 1970s and an entire new culture of reggae and rock and roll took over countries in Africa, Asia and Latin America. Rock and roll is still banned in a number of countries including North Korea, Iran, and other Middle East countries. It is feared that this culture out of hip London would corrupt their youth. They are right.

Paul McCartney played a concert in Buenos Aires on December 12, 1993, and played other concerts in Argentina in 2010, 2016 and 2019. The Rolling Stones finally came to Argentina in 1995 to play sell-out concerts on their Voodoo Lounge Tour. The song

"Jumping Jack Flash" is something that the former U-boat crews could identify with as they had all been drowned and left for dead. As I said earlier, Keith Richards says that rock concerts are where everybody gets together to root for the same thing and a splendid time is guaranteed for all.

By the 1970s, Nazi and fascist ideals were defeated, as was the fear of an alien invasion. Submarines were now yellow and a lot of fun.

One of the reasons that British intelligence and the CIA have promoted the use of LSD and other psychedelics is to get people who are indoctrinated in various forms of "thought control" to envision something else from what they have been taught. This "thought control" can be from the Catholic Church or other religions, or from political sources such as communist or fascist indoctrination. We are all victims of thought control, as long as we interact with society at large.

This thought control extends as well into scientific realms and this includes the subject of UFOs and secret technology. Overt efforts sought to erase the name and inventions of Nikola Tesla for decades, but now his work is recognized and celebrated and the Tesla car corporation is one of the most successful and well known companies in the world today. But after losing the giant oil war of WWII, with the failure of Germany to take Moscow and the oilfields at Baku, where would these defeated SS fanatics go with their Haunebu and Vril craft—the dark side of the Moon? It would seem that they would have to come in out of the cold.

As we live a life of ease
Every one of us has all we need
Sky of blue and sea of green
In our yellow submarine
—The Beatles, *Yellow Submarine*

The Cash-Landrum Case
On the evening of December 29, 1980, Betty Cash (aged 51), Vickie Landrum (57), and Vickie's grandson Colby Landrum were driving home to Dayton, Texas, a small rural town to the northeast of Houston. They were in Cash's Oldsmobile Cutlass after dining out.

284

They have said that at about 9 pm, while driving on an isolated two-lane road in dense woods, they saw a light above some trees. They at first thought it was an airplane approaching Houston Intercontinental Airport (about 35 miles away) and gave it little notice.

A few minutes later on the winding roads, they saw what they believed to be the same light as before, but it was now much closer and brighter. They said that the light came from a huge diamond-shaped object, which hovered at about treetop level. The craft's base was expelling some sort of electric flame and emitting significant heat that they could sense inside their car.

Cash to stopped the car, fearing they would be burned if they got closer to the flaming object. An evangelical Christian, Landrum interpreted the object as a sign of the Second Coming of Jesus Christ, and told young Colby, "That's Jesus. He will not hurt us."

Cash said she was anxious, and considered turning the car around, but abandoned this idea, because the road was too narrow and she presumed the car would get stuck on the dirt shoulders, which were soft as it had rained earlier in the evening. Cash and Landrum said that they got out of the car to examine the object, but that Colby was terrified inside the car, and so Landrum said she quickly returned to the car to comfort him.

Cash remained outside, mesmerized by the bizarre sight. The object, intensely bright and a dull metallic silver, was shaped like a huge upright diamond, about the size of the Dayton water tower, with its top and bottom cut off so that they were flat rather than pointed. The center of the craft was ringed by small blue lights, and periodically over the next few minutes flames shot out of the bottom, flaring outward to create the effect of a large cone. Every time the fire dissipated, the craft floated a few feet downward toward the road. But when the flames blasted out again, the craft rose about the same distance.

Cash and Landrum said that the craft then ascended over the treetops, and rose higher in the sky. Suddenly a group of helicopters approached the craft, surrounding it in tight formation. Cash and Landrum counted 23 helicopters, and later identified some of them as tandem-rotor Boeing CH-47 Chinooks used by American military forces worldwide.

With the road now open, Cash says she drove on, and saw

glimpses of the object and the helicopters receding into the distance. From first sighting the object to its departure, they said the encounter lasted about 20 minutes.

We do not know where these helicopters would have come from as there are no known military bases in the area. The closest one would be Joint Forces Reserve Center at the Ellington Airport in Houston. This is a small facility and it is doubtful that 23 helicopters would have come from this base in metro Houston.

Another possibility is Fort Johnson, formerly Fort Polk, in west central Louisiana. Fort Johnson is a very large military base that is some 100,000 acres (160 square miles) and is adjacent to 98,125 acres (153 square miles) of the Kisatchie National Forest. According to Wikipedia, in 2013 there were 10,877 troops stationed at Fort Johnson.

After the UFO and helicopters left, Cash took the Landrums back to their home, then retired for the evening. That night, they reportedly all experienced nausea, vomiting, diarrhea, generalized weakness, a burning sensation in their eyes, and felt as though they were suffering from sunburn.

Over the next few days, Cash said her symptoms worsened, with many large, painful blisters forming on her skin. When taken to a hospital emergency room on January 3, 1981, Cash could not walk, and had lost large patches of skin and clumps of hair. She was released after 12 days, though her condition was not much better, and she later returned to the hospital for another 15 days. The doctors switched from treating her for burns to treating her for radiation sickness. Later, she was treated for cancer.

Eventually, Cash and Landrum contacted their US Senators, Lloyd Bentsen and John Tower, who suggested that the witnesses file a complaint with the Judge Advocate Claims office at Bergstrom Air Force Base. Bergstrom Air Force Base is a large Air Force base near Austin, Texas, quite a bit south of where the incident occurred. In August 1981, personnel at Bergstrom Air Force Base interviewed Cash, Landrum, and young Colby at length and they were told that they should hire a lawyer, and seek financial compensation for their injuries.

They hired an attorney named Peter Gersten who took on the case pro bono. The case wound its way through the US courts for several years. Cash and Landrum sued the federal government for $20 million. Testimony from officials at NASA, the Air Force, the Army and the Navy was given. Each maintained that no agency of the US government possessed any such UFO, and that no military personnel had operated any of the reported helicopters. None could explain the incident in any way. Where the 23 helicopters had come from they had no idea but were certain that they were not piloted by military personnel. But who was piloting these craft, if they were not military personnel?

In the end a US District Court judge dismissed the Cash/ Landrum case on August 21, 1986 and the three "victims" plus their lawyer received no compensation for this bizarre incident which caused serious health problems to all three. The case remains one of the great unsolved UFO cases of the 70s and 80s.

What concerns us here is that despite what the military has to say (who cares what NASA has to say?) this would appear to have been some experimental craft that was electric and gave off strong radiation. This shows that, probably beginning in the 1950s, the US military has been secretly developing what we call "flying saucer" or "UFO" technology—that is technology that has anti-gravity or gravity control technology that allows to a craft to move quickly and hover in place.

The Cash-Landrum case happened in 1980, and may represent 30 years of experiments and special projects of the US military. How much of this technology came from the German flying discs and cylindrical craft? Was there to be some cooperation between the Black Sun forces and the US government?

The Final Integration of the Black Sun
The Black Sun with its secret SS labs and secret cities in South America managed to last for decades as a Third Power that controlled whole countries in South America at various times. We can easily put Argentina, Chile and Paraguay into this category, and other countries such as Uruguay, Brazil, Colombia, Bolivia and Peru were heavily influenced by this Third Power that apparently used secret saucer bases in remote mountainous and jungle areas.

Henry Stevens[46] says that the Third Power ultimately came to a truce and made an agreement of sorts with the United States military

287

during the second term of President Ronald Reagan. Stevens says that about the same time as his famous "Mr. Gorbachev, tear down this wall" speech on June 12, 1987, Reagan made a side trip to an obscure town in far western Germany named Bitburg.

At a ceremony at a cemetery Reagan placed flowers at the graves of German soldiers who had died there defending their country from the invading Western Allies near the end of the war. At the small cemetery in Bitburg are buried a large number of Waffen SS (the military branch of the SS organization) soldiers buried. These SS officers had fought against the British and Americans at the end of war.

Why would President Ronald Reagan do this? Stevens suggests that this was a formal integration of the former Waffen SS and its many tentacles into the US military's secret space program. President Reagan also ordered that all Pershing missiles based in Germany be removed. Reagan had a very pro-German foreign policy while at the same time offering overtures to the Russians, who also wanted the Pershing missiles removed from Germany.

The United States was at this time given some special technology by the Third Power, Stevens claims, including maser and laser technologies that the United States didn't have. They also gave the Americans klystron technology that can be used to produce positrons for space travel. We might think that some of the space technologies were developed at the secret SS labs in the Arctic, Antarctica and South America.

This klystron technology may be what creates the bright "vril" lighting around the various craft. Says Stevens about klystron anti-gravity technology in which beams of positrons are projected above or below a discoid or cylindrical craft:

> Then let us suppose a flying craft powered by positrons generated via klystron technology. How would this look? Well, how about mounting the klystron-positron projectors as swivel heads, mounted on the wing tips of a flying triangle? At the point where the three beams converge, that is the point into which the flying triangle moves, pushed and pulled by this super Biefield-Brown Effect. At low power, for instance, with the three beams converging over

the center of the craft's gravity, it would just hang there, motionless. With variations in power and focus, any type of three-dimensional movement is possible.

If this were the technology the Reagan Administration had received, it would account, temporally, for the appearance of flying triangles in Belgium only a couple years after "payment" had taken place. Likewise, beyond Belgium this new shape seemed to be the predominant UFO shape from that time to the present.[46]

This was also a time period when the last officers of the Third Reich, including Operation Paperclip Nazis like Wernher von Braun, were dying of old age. Says Henry Stevens:

> And this time-line ties into what was happening internally within the Third Power itself. The Third Power remained intact until sometime around the 1990's, in the technological sense. Wilhelm Landig had kept in contact with expatriate Reich insiders who informed him of the situation. The reader will remember the "Ruestungsesoteriker," the armament esoterics, the ultimate geeks who kept the . postwar Nazi high technology, including the field propulsion flying discs in good operation. They worked out of these secret bases and through a network supplying parts and know-how toward the perpetuation of these technological wonders which resided in huge underground caverns connected to the outside world by tunnel-entrances. Well, it seems even they had limits. All machines eventually wear out.[46]

Stevens then tells us that the German SS officer and novelist Wilhelm Landig commented on the postwar situation through an informant, Heiner Gehring, who managed a peek into Landig's private files:

> Actually, after the war, there were efforts made to build a military-technical power outside of Germany. The Base 211 in Neuschwabenland, which really was established,

was certainly given up after some time. Besides the immunity situation it may have also been the dropping of the atom bomb of the USA during the Geophysical Year 1954 as a reason for the handing over of the base. Garrison and materiel of the Base 211 were sent to South America. Likewise, more German U-boat bases were available [such as the ones in Tierra del Fuego].

German flying discs, so the Landig particulars let it be known, are still warehoused in South America but perhaps may not be flight worthy any more. Their propulsion was unconventional. The development of the "Haunebus" through the "Vril" Society did, in collaboration with the SS, actually take place. Certainly some of those topics that are found in the video-films in circulation are partially completely humbug. False are the reports concerning moon and Mars flights of German flying discs, the equipment was not developed for such effort. In the USA and USSR, attempts after the Second World War were made to replicate flying discs. This replica has, on propulsion, failed, which cannot be reconstructed.[46]

So Landig admits that the Antarctic base was probably abandoned after it was "nuked" in 1954. However, it would seem that other bases in Antarctica, south as in the Palmer Archipelago and the South Shetland Islands, continued to operate well into the 1960s.

Landig mentions that the craft are warehoused in South America, probably at the Tierra del Fuego bases, and may be unusable. This does not seem to be the case, as South America continues to be a hotbed of UFO stories and sightings and it would seem that craft of different sorts, even newer models, are still being flown in South America as well as Antarctica.

Landig is probably incorrect when he says that Americans were unable to reconstruct the field effect propulsion that propelled the Haunebu and other craft. It seems likely that the Americans, who had allegedly teleported a battleship in the Philadelphia Experiment, moved forward with their own secret anti-gravity projects immediately after the war. It is interesting to note as well

290

that Landig dismisses any flights to the Moon or Mars during the war or afterward, stating that the craft are for terrestrial flights.

Says Stevens on the aging of the generals of the Black Sun Third Power:

> Dr. Hans Kammler was said to have died in 1972 according to Hans Rittermann. Otto Skorzeny died in 1975. Reinhard Gehlen died in 1979. Afterward, certainly, a younger generation of Nazis took over management of the Third Power. By the early-mid 1980's the Cold War was moving into its fourth decade with no end in sight or in contemplation in the minds of anyone on planet earth. Even the younger men running the Third Power must have been thinking about their own retirement as they were doubtless already in their 60s. It is no wonder they were more willing to divulge their secrets at this time. They were not sought criminals or marked men in any sort of way. They were free to fly first-class on commercial jets, they had no need of flying discs at this point.
>
> The point is this postwar Nazi subculture existed in parallel alongside of both the Eastern and Western blocs of the Cold War, interacting and influencing both of them in ways which we are now only beginning to understand. Just as Farraday and Tesla postulated a self-inducting homopolar generator, these Nazis self-inducted the Cold War to a greater or lesser extent. And in some ways, especially in terms of technology, this postwar Nazi subculture was the focus of the conflict. And yet on the other hand, in terms of their middle position regarding communications, they were the glue which kept the Cold War from overheating. Was the Third Power a balance-point, a fulcrum? Maybe this is overstating things but in the more narrow scope, especially in Europe and with high technology, it must have been important.
>
> The Third Power was as much a child of the Cold War as were the Eastern and Western blocs and when one power got off this teeter-totter, shifting the world order, the existence of the Third Power as an active world-player

became redundant. Now, twenty years later, their flying saucers rest in cold mountain storage, their U-boats rust in still-secret places, and their microfilm slowly deteriorates in hidden caches.

Today the Third Power is not trying to take over the world or even become a Fourth Reich. The Third Power was a concept for its members, and lives within friendly government officials and organizations of several countries as well as corporations and financial entities that owed a measure of their success to this Third Power. It also lives in the organizations who owe their roots or at least a greater part of their nourishment to Nazi ideas. This includes the Vril Society and the Karoteckia both of which, I am told by reliable sources, still exist. It also lives in the technology of those times, some of which must still be secret.[46]

And what now for the former power of the Black Sun? Are the bases in Antarctica just empty bunkers waiting for intrepid explorers to find their dark caverns and light them up one more time? Were they destroyed by the Americans? Other secret bases in Antarctica and Tierra del Fuego seem to be untouched.

One wants to think that the Black Sun and its Thule and Vril Society beliefs have tempered over the decades and they are not the cruel racist fascists that made WWII such a hideous war. The Japanese were equally cruel in the Pacific theater. Gehlen was part of the plots to assassinate Hitler, but he managed to escape Hitler's wrath when the plots failed. This helped him gain favor with the Americans when he surrendered to them at the end of the war.

Gehlen spent most of his time in West Germany and rarely left the country. Indeed, his main focus during WWII was Eastern Europe and Russia. It would seem that he continued to focus on this area after the war. With the dissolution of the Soviet Union in 1989 Gehlen had finally achieved his goal, even though he was dead.

What would happen as far as the Black Sun was concerned in Eastern Europe with the fall of the Soviet Union? Could the Black Sun have a resurgence?

Chapter 8

Ukraine and the
Battalion of the Black Sun

Yea, they're all bold as love,
Just ask the Axis,
He knows everything.
— *Bold As Love*, Jimi Hendrix

Sometimes the best map will not find you
You can't see what's around the bend
Sometimes the road leads through dark places
Sometimes the darkness is your friend
—*Pacing the Cage*, Jimmy Buffet (written by Bruce Cockburn)

The theme of this book, and my last three books, is about the survival of the SS and the awesome facilities and vehicles that they obtained. It has been proven that the SS continued to operate in Argentina, Chile, Paraguay and other Latin American countries.

But what has been overlooked over the past 50 years is the SS activities in Austria, Eastern Europe, the Ukraine and Russia. Indeed, the SS operated freely in Finland and the Ukraine during the war. Many Ukrainian SS officers immigrated to the Chicago area after the war, facilitated by the OSS and later the CIA. Openly neo-SS groups operate in the Ukraine today, and apparently in Russia as well, as we shall see.

But first, let us look at some curious UFO incidents that occurred near Russia or happened to Soviet pilots. In the *Fortean Times* compilation book *UFOs: 1947-1987: The 40-Year Search for an Explanation*,[6] there is a chapter entitled "UFOs in the Soviet Union" by the Spanish researcher Enrique Vicente. In this chapter are a number of curious UFO encounters that may have something to do with SS activities, including the following:

In 1956, while the famous pilot, Commanding Officer of the polar routes, Valentin Akkusatov, was exploring a strategical region near Greenland, a huge inverted saucer-shaped object flew parallel to them for an hour, avoiding all attempts to evade or approach it. Later a second, similar object joined the first; finally both vanished at unbelievable speed.

In spring 1959 panic was provoked when "saucers" visited the Sverdlovsk rocket base over a 24-hour period. They were detected by radar, and at times could be seen hovering stationary over the launch platforms.

In August 1961 a pilot flying over Kiev was accosted by a UFO which seemed to be playing games with him, flying round his plane in ever closer spirals, then moving away. The pilot followed the object, which seemed to stop, but as he came near it rapidly moved off. After some 12 minutes of aerial antics it disappeared at a speed of 10,000 km/h.

In 1962 Italian journalist Alberto Fenoglio relayed the story of a Russian female parachutist who jumped at an altitude of 9000 m near Santov—and vanished for two days. When she reappeared, she reported having been kidnapped by a flying saucer in the course of her descent. She had been very well treated by its three occupants, who showed her our planet from a great height, and entrusted her with a case containing a message for the authorities, which she handed to the police on her return.

On 26 July 1965 astronomers Robert and Esmeralda Vitolniek and Yan Meideris, at the Ogre Observatory in Latvia, saw a star-like triangular object. Through the telescope they could see a combination of three smaller green balls which spun round a central sphere some 100 meters in diameter, then went away; they estimated the objects could have been at an altitude of 100km.

During 1966 an intense wave was registered in the USSR, Poland, Czechoslovakia, as well as in other parts of the world. In April, Air Force Major Baidukov obtained visual and radar sighting over the Odessa region of a UFO that descended from an altitude of 50 to 18 km; this was confirmed by ground radar. On 17 June B.G. Krylov and a team of geophysicists at Blista (northern Caucasus) saw a small reddish disc which descended from 48 to 17 km in 45 minutes. In October V.I. Duginov, director of the Hydromagnetic School at Kherson, with 45 other witnesses, observed a saucer-shaped object with an apparent diameter three times that of the sun.

During 1967 *Soviet Weekly* reported some 200 UFO sightings in southern Russia. On 18 August astronomer Anatoli Sazanov, and 11 colleagues of the astrophysical station near Kislovodsk in the Caucasus, watched the movements of a yellowish crescent-shaped, asymmetrical object at least 150 meters long, moving at 18,000 km/h; it emitted a puff of what looked like steam, and was accompanied by a luminous point. Similar phenomena were seen by some of his colleagues, and other inhabitants of the area, on 18 July, 4 September and 18 October; the sighting were confirmed by the staff of Kazan Observatory.[6]

Later in the chapter Vicente has a brief subchapter entitled "UFOs over Strategic Installations… or a Military Intelligence Game?":

Devious official policy could account for several otherwise inexplicable incidents, such as the 1978 publication of an article by the young astrophysicist Juri Poslepov, in which he states that on 7 June 1976, just before the launch at Plesetsk of a Kosmos communications satellite, technicians photographed a chain of luminous cylinders flying over the launch platform. They remained there for 20 minutes, but fighters sent to intercept them could do nothing because their controls were mysteriously de-activated as also were the ground radar installations which had previously been able to detect and follow the UFOs.

295

Repeated reports came from Plesetsk of strange green or red balls which were unharmed by shots from jet fighters. Poslepov adds that in November 1977, just before the launch of a satellite containing orbital bombs at Turyatam, several egg-shaped luminous balls danced over the launch area for more than a quarter of an hour, finally coming and leaving. During this time, electrical equipment failed to function and three jet fighters were unable to take off. The records and photograph were being kept secret in order not to frighten the population.[6]

These remarkable UFO incidents seem to fit neatly into the SS survival hypothesis, with a UFO encounter over Greenland where a secret SS laboratory was said to be. The story of the female Russian skydiver is a curious one, and it would seem that in many of the stories the UFOs—both saucers and cylindrical craft—wanted to be seen by the observers. The green fireballs are a common occurrence and I write about them in my book *Andromeda: The Secret Files.*[36]

Much of this activity seems to be some sort of psychological warfare—basically screwing with the minds of the local military with their aerial acrobatics. This was happening around the world—in Europe, Australia, North America, South America, and in the Soviet Union.

A Massive USO Rises Next to Oil Rig in 1997

We also have to mention the ability of these craft to go into the water, as they are submarines as well as airships. The book *UFO Odyssey*[11] chronicles a number of interesting incidents of apparent SS craft emerging from the water and got this story from the "UFO Updates" column of Toronto researcher Ben Field on January 14, 1998:

In December 1997, a massive craft was seen emerging from the sea next to an oil platform in the Gulf of Mexico. According to engineer Jeremy Packer, the sighting was witnessed by 250 oilrig workers.

At about 7:58 am, Packer said that everyone got frightened when they heard a rumbling noise that they

296

knew couldn't be the engines that ran the platform bore. Looking toward the west, they sighted 25 to 35 helicopters on maneuvers. This was not unusual, Packer said, except that the rig commander said that he had not received the usual alert regarding Coast Guard operation in the area.

Then, according to Packer, they all saw something that totally changed their lives. All of the helicopters stopped in midair and a huge metal cigar-shaped object about the size of the oil platform surfaced beneath them. The massive craft, about as long as two football fields, soared straight out of the water and into the air, where it hovered above the helicopters for about two minutes.

Packer described the object as concave on its underside with four large domes on its bottom. The topside of the cigar-shaped craft was encircled by beautiful lights of every imaginable color.

And then, as if someone had turned off a light switch, the giant craft disappeared. One second everyone was studying the object through binoculars or telescopes; then, in the literal blink of an eye, it was gone.

As an interesting side-note, Packer said that the crew noticed that their watches were 30 minutes later than the actual time when they got back to the mainland.[11]

This amazing story has to have us wondering who was on this gigantic cigar-shaped craft? Was it an SS crew demonstrating one of the craft to the American military at a given time and place? Was it actually an American military craft that they were witnessing? Was this massive craft being piloted by extraterrestrials?

That the craft apparently went into hyperspace and caused a temporal anomaly on the crew of the oil rig suggests possible alien technology, although the US Navy allegedly teleported a battleship out of Philadelphia harbor in 1943. Was this craft perhaps a collusion between the US military and the SS scientists who continued to improve the Andromeda craft? We will probably never know.

These huge cigar-shaped craft, often glowing with "vril" energy, have been seen in Eastern Europe and Russia and the Black Sun, or sonnenrad, symbol is a popular one in Ukraine and other

Eastern European countries.

The Black Sun Symbol and the Ukrainian Military

It seems that the Ukraine, plus other regions of the former Soviet Union, have seen an uptick in anti-Russian SS activity. Not only has there been UFO activity in Ukraine but there has been a rise in groups who openly use the Sonnenrad and other SS symbols such as the Wolfsangel.

The Sonnenrad or "Black Sun," is composed of 12 repeated runes—letters from ancient Germanic languages—arranged in a wheel. Each rune represents a sound, like in the Latin alphabet, but they also have a meaning when they stand alone. The symbol originated with Himmler and the SS and is used by a number of SS-affiliated groups (and non-SS-affiliated groups). It was apparently first seen at the Wewelsburg castle as the previously described floor mosaic.

According to the German-language author Wilhelm Landig, the Sonnenrad replaced the swastika on the Haunebu and Vril saucers being assembled at the secret bases in Greenland and the Canadian Arctic. He wrote the Thule trilogy *Götzen gegen Thule* (1971), *Wolfszeit um Thule* (1980) and *Rebellen für Thule—Das Erbe von Atlantis* (1991). His books, beginning in 1971, inspired the idea of the continuance of the Black Sun, a substitute swastika and a mythical source of energy. This energy is called vril.

The name "Black Sun" came into wider use after the publication of a 1991 occult thriller novel, *Die Schwarze Sonne von Tashi Lhunpo* (The Black Sun of Tashi Lhunpo), by the pseudonymous author Russell McCloud. The book links the Wewelsburg mosaic with the neo-Nazi concept of the "Black Sun" as an occult form of energy.

Along with other symbols from the Nazi era such as the Wolfsangel, the Sig Armanen rune, and the Totenkopf, the Black Sun is employed by some neo-Nazi adherents of Satanism. Scholar Chris Mathews writes:

The Black Sun motif is even less

The Black Sun Sonnenrad.

ambiguous. Though based on medieval German symbols, the Wewelsburg mosaic is a unique design commissioned specifically for Himmler, and its primary contemporary association is Nazi occultism, for which Nazi Satanic groups and esoteric neo-Nazis adopt it.

The Ukrainian Azov Regiment, founded in 2014, used the Black Sun symbol as part of its logo. Political scientist Ivan Gomza wrote in *Krytyka* that the illiberal connotations of the symbol in that logo are lost on most people in Ukraine, and the logo rather has an association with "a successful fighting unit that protects Ukraine." WotanJugend, a neo-Nazi group based in Kyiv and connected to the broader Azov political movement, has also used the Black Sun symbol to promote its group.

During the 2022 Russian invasion of Ukraine, NATO tweeted a photo of a female Ukrainian soldier for International Women's Day. The soldier wore a symbol on her uniform that "appears to be the black sun symbol." After receiving complaints from social media users, NATO removed the tweet and stated, "The post was removed when we realized it contained a symbol that we could not verify as official."

A number of far-right groups and individuals have utilized the symbol in their propaganda, including the Christchurch mosque shooter Brenton Tarrant and the Australian neo-Nazi group Antipodean Resistance, and the symbol was displayed by members of several extremist groups involved in the August 2017 Unite the Right rally in Charlottesville, Virginia.

In May 2022, a mass shooting in Buffalo, New York occurred. The shooter, a white supremacist, wore the Black Sun symbol on his body armor and placed it on the front of his digital manifesto. Pro-Kremlin *Telegram* channels and influencers subsequently spread misinformation linking the shooter with the Ukrainian Azov Regiment and the Ukrainian nation more broadly. However, the shooter makes no reference to the Azov Regiment in his manifesto, and Ukraine receives only a single mention in a section plagiarized from an earlier mass shooter's manifesto that predates the Russian invasion of Ukraine.

Meanwhile, back in Argentina, on September 1, 2022, a man

with a Black Sun tattoo on his elbow named Fernando André Sabag Montiel attempted to assassinate Argentinian vice president Cristina Fernández de Kirchner. He attempted to shoot her as she got into her car outside of her home in Buenos Aires among a large crowd. For reasons unknown the pistol failed and did not fire. Montiel was arrested on the spot. Kirchner escaped unharmed.

In a lengthy article titled "Kyiv Walks Fine Line as Fighters Embrace Use of Nazi Symbols" journalist Thomas Gibbons-Neff writes in *The New York Times* (June 6, 2023):

> Since Russia began its invasion of Ukraine last year, the Ukrainian government and NATO allies have posted, then quietly deleted, three seemingly innocuous photographs from their social media feeds: a soldier standing in a group, another resting in a trench and an emergency worker posing in front of a truck.
>
> In each photograph, Ukrainians in uniform wore patches featuring symbols that were made notorious by Nazi Germany and have since become part of the iconography of far-right hate groups.
>
> The photographs, and their deletions, highlight the Ukrainian military's complicated relationship with Nazi imagery, a relationship forged under both Soviet and German occupation during World War II.
>
> That relationship has become especially delicate because President Vladimir V. Putin of Russia has falsely declared Ukraine to be a Nazi state, a claim he has used to justify his illegal invasion.
>
> Ukraine has worked through legislation and military restructuring to contain a fringe far-right movement whose members proudly wear symbols steeped in Nazi history and espouse views hostile to leftists, LGBTQ movements and ethnic minorities. But some members of these groups have been fighting Russia since the Kremlin illegally annexed part of the Crimea region of Ukraine in 2014 and are now part of the broader military structure. Some are regarded as national heroes, even as the far-right remains marginalized politically.

300

The iconography of these groups, including a skull-and-crossbones patch worn by concentration camp guards and a symbol known as the Black Sun now appears with some regularity on the uniforms of soldiers fighting on the font line, including soldiers who say the imagery symbolizes Ukrainian sovereignty and pride, not Nazism.

In the short term, that threatens to reinforce Mr. Putin's propaganda and give fuel to his false claims that Ukraine must be "de-Nazified"—a position that ignores the fact that Ukraine's president, Voldymyr Zelensky, is Jewish. More broadly, Ukraine's ambivalence about these symbols, and sometimes even its acceptance of them, risks giving new, mainstream life to icons that the West has spent more than a half-century trying to eliminate.

...In April, Ukraine's Defense Ministry posted a photograph on its Twitter account of a soldier wearing a patch featuring a skull and crossbones known as the Totenkopf, or Death's Head. The specific symbol in the picture was made notorious by a Nazi unit that committed war crimes and guarded concentration camps during World War II.

The patch in the photograph sets the Totenkopf atop a Ukrainian flag with a small no. 6 below. That patch is the official merchandise of "Death in June," a British neo-folk band that the Southern Poverty Law Center has said produces "hate speech" that "exploits themes and images of fascism and Nazism."

The Anti-Defamation League considers the Totenkopf "a common hate symbol." But Jae Hyman, a spokesman for the group, said it was impossible to "make an inference about the wearer or the Ukrainian Army" based on the patch.

"The image, while offensive, is that of a musical band," Mr. Hyman said.

The band now uses the photograph posted by the Ukrainian military to market the Totenkopf patch.

The New York Times asked the Ukrainian Defense Ministry on April 27 about the tweet. Several hours later, the post was deleted. "After studying this case, we came to the conclusion that this logo can be interpreted ambiguously," the ministry said in a statement.

The soldier in the photograph was part of a volunteer unit called the Da Vinci Wolves, which started as part of the paramilitary wing of Ukrainian's Right Sector, a coalition of right-wing organizations and political parties that militarized after Russia's illegal annexation of Crimea.

At least five other photographs on the Wolves' Instagram and Facebook pages feature their soldiers wearing Nazi-style patches, including the Totenkopf.

NATO militaries, an alliance that Ukraine hopes to join, do not tolerate such patches. When such symbols have appeared, groups like the Anti-Defamation League have spoken out, and military leaders have reacted swiftly.

Last month, Ukrainian's state emergency services agency posted on Instagram a photograph of an emergency worker wearing a Black Sun symbol, also known as a Sonnenrad, that appeared in the castle of Heinrich Himmler, the Nazi general and SS director. The Black Sun is popular among neo-Nazis and white supremacists.

In March 2022, NATO's Twitter account posted a

Soldiers from the Azov Battalion in front of a building with a swastika and the red-and-black UPA flag at the battalion's base in Urzuf, Mariupol Raion, July 2014.

photograph of a Ukrainian soldier wearing a similar patch. Both photographs were quickly removed.

In November, during a meeting with *Times* reporters near the front line, a Ukrainian press officer wore a Totenkopf variation made by a company called R3ICH (pronounced "Reich"). He said he did not believe the patch was affiliated with the Nazis. A second press officer present said other journalists had asked soldiers to remove the patch before taking photographs.

Ihor Kozlovskyi, a Ukrainian historian and religious scholar, said that the symbols had meaning that were unique to Ukraine and shold be interpreted by how Ukrainians viewed them, not by how they had been used elsewhere.

"The symbol can live in any community or any history independently of how it is used in other parts of Earth," Mr. Kozlovskyi said.

Russian soldiers in Ukraine have also been wearing Nazi-style patches, underscoring how complicated interpreting these symbols can be in a region steeped in Soviet and German history.

The Soviet Union signed a nonaggression pact with Germany in 1939, so it was caught by surprise two years later when the Nazis invaded Ukraine, which was then part of the Soviet Union. Ukraine had wilted under a Soviet government that engineered a famine that killed millions. Many Ukrainians initially viewed the Nazis as liberators.

Factions from the Organization of Ukrainian Nationalists and its insurgent army fought alongside the Nazis in what they viewed as a struggle for Ukrainian sovereignty Members of those groups also took part in atrocities against Jewish and Polish civilians. Later in the war, though, some of the groups fought against the Nazis.

Some Ukrainians joined Nazi military units like the Waffen-SS Galizien. The emblem of the group, which was led by German officers, was a sky-blue patch showing a lion and three crowns. The unit took part in a massacre of hundreds of Polish civilians in 1944. In December, after a years-long legal battle, Ukraine's highest court ruled that a government-funded research institute could continue to list the unit's insignia as excluded from the Nazi symbols banned under a 2015 law.

Today, as a new generation fights against Russian occupation, many Ukrainians see the war as a continuation of the struggle for independence during and immediately after World War II. Symbols like the flag associated with the Ukrainian Insurgent Army and the Galizien patch have become emblems of anti-Russian resistance and national pride.

That makes it difficult to easily separate, on the basis of icons alone, the Ukrainians enraged by the Russian invasion from those who support the country's far-right groups.

The Azov regiment was celebrated after holding out during the siege of the southern city of Mariupol last year. After the commander of the Da Vinci Wolves was killed in March, he received a hero's funeral, which Mr. Zelensky attended.

"I think some of these far-right units mix a fair bit of their own mythmaking into the public discourse on them," said Mr. Colbourne, the researcher. "But I think the least that can and should be done everywhere, not just Ukraine, is not allowing the far right's symbols, rhetoric and ideas to seep into public discourse."

This last sentence is interesting as it implies that we should not allow symbols such as the Black Sun into public discourse. Why is that? The authors of this article seem to be completely unaware of the flying saucer component to the Black Sun mythos. But the Ukrainian people are not unaware of this—they know because of the many books published on the subject in

The former emblem of the Azov Battalion.

Poland, Czech, Finland, Estonia, and Russia, that the Third Reich was building flying saucers. Books in these countries that discuss UFO Nazi technology have been very popular. Models of the Haunebu have been made by Revell, a German model

Zelensky guard spotted with Totenkopf.

company. These models were banned in Germany but not in other countries. This author bought one through Amazon and it came from a warehouse in Turkey.

CNN showed a segment in early 2023 of a wounded Ukrainian soldier in a hospital recovering from wounds he had suffered from the front lines. He wearing a t-shirt that had the plans for two flying saucers on it: the Vril craft and the Haunebu craft, one on top of the other. These were the famous plans of the Haunebu and the Vril released in 1989. CNN did not comment on the t-shirt, but this was obviously a commercially printed shirt that was sold to the people of Ukraine. Yes, they know about the Black Sun flying saucers.

Even more bizarre is the fate of the Russian mercenaries Yevgeny Prigozhin and Dmitry Utkin.

The SS and Mercenaries in the Ukraine

Yevgeny Prigozhin and Dmitry Utkin were Russian mercenaries who formed what is known as the Wagner Group. They died with

A surrendered Azov Battalion at Mariupol, formerly part of Ukraine.

eight other people when their airplane exploded and crashed in Russia on August 23, 2023.

According to Russia's emergency ministry, the airplane was en route from Moscow to Saint Petersburg when it crashed, killing all 10 people on board. Russian state-owned media agency TASS reported that Prigozhin had been on the passenger list of the flight. The passengers' deaths were officially confirmed by the Investigative Committee of Russia on August 27, following genetic analysis of the remains recovered from the wreckage.

A Wagner-associated Telegram channel claimed the jet was shot down by Russian air defenses over Tver Oblast. However, this assertion was contested due to the lack of visible missile trails in the released footage of the crash, which was filmed by numerous people. Western intelligence agencies surmised that an explosion on board likely brought down the aircraft in Russia.

On December 22, 2023, *The Wall Street Journal* cited sources within the Western and Russian intelligence agencies as saying that the Wagner Group plane crash was orchestrated by Putin's right-hand man Nikolai Patrushev. The newspaper alleged that Patrushev presented to Putin a plan to assassinate Prigozhin in early August 2023, which led to intelligence officials inserting a bomb under the wing of Prigozhin's plane during pre-departure safety checks.

As the head of the Wagner Group, Prigozhin was a former criminal, caterer, Russian mercenary leader and oligarch. He led the Wagner Group private military company and was a close confidant of Russian president Vladimir Putin until launching a rebellion in June 2023. Prigozhin was sometimes referred to as "Putin's chef" because he owned restaurants and catering businesses that provided services to the Kremlin. Once a convict in the Soviet Union, Prigozhin controlled a network of influential companies whose operations, according to a 2020 investigation, were "tightly integrated with Russia's Defense Ministry and its intelligence arm, the GRU."

In 2014, Prigozhin reportedly co-founded the Wagner Group with Dmitry

Yevgeny Prigozhin.

Utkin to support pro-Russian paramilitaries in Ukraine. Funded by the Russian state, it played a significant role in Russia's invasion of Crimea and supported Russian interests in Syria and in Africa. In February 2023, Prigozhin confirmed that he was the founder and long-time manager of the Internet Research Agency, a Russian company running online propaganda and disinformation campaigns.

Prigozhin rose to international prominence during the 2022 Russian invasion of Ukraine. During the initial stages, the Russian Ground Forces suffered significant casualties. As a result, authorities actively sought to enlist mercenaries for the invasion, which led to heightened influence and power for Prigozhin and the Wagner Group. Prigozhin was allocated substantial resources, including helicopters and airplanes. Starting in the summer of 2022, he gained the authority to recruit inmates from Russian prisons into the Wagner Group in exchange for their freedom. Western intelligence estimated that the number of Wagner mercenaries increased from "several thousand" fighters around 2018 to approximately 50,000 fighters by December 2022. The majority were criminal convicts recruited from prisons.

On June 23, 2023, Prigozhin claimed in a video that the government's justifications for invading Ukraine were based on falsehoods, and that the invasion was designed to further the interests of the Ministry of Defense and Russian oligarchs. He accused the Ministry of Defense of attempting to deceive the public and President Vladimir Putin by portraying Ukraine as an aggressive and hostile adversary which, in collaboration with NATO, was plotting an attack on Russian interests. Prigozhin had basically turned on the Russian military and accused them of creating this war under false pretenses.

Specifically, he denied that any Ukrainian escalation took

A Russian Special Ops suit.

place prior to February 24, 2022, which was one of the central points of Russian justification for the war. Prigozhin alleged that General Shoigu and the "oligarchic clan" had personal motives for initiating the war. Furthermore, he asserted that the Russian military command intentionally concealed the true number of soldiers killed in Ukraine, with casualties reaching up to 1,000 on many days.

The next morning, early on June 24, 2023, Wagner forces crossed into Russia's Rostov Oblast from Luhansk, encountering no apparent opposition. In response, criminal charges were filed against Prigozhin by the Federal Security Service (FSB) for inciting an armed rebellion. The Wagner Group proceeded to capture the Russian city of Rostov-on-Don, and began an advance on the Russian capital at Moscow. During the fighting the Wagner Group shot down an Ilyushin Il-22M airborne command post plane plus several military helicopters.

With the seizure of Rostov-on-Don, Russian President Vladimir Putin addressed the nation, denouncing Wagner's actions as "treason" and vowing to take "harsh steps" to suppress the rebellion. He stated the situation threatened the existence of Russia itself. Furthermore, Putin made an appeal to the Wagner forces who "by deceit or threats" had been "dragged" into participating in the rebellion.

Prigozhin apparently made efforts to establish contact with the

Prigozhin's Embraer Legacy 600 aircraft.

presidential administration in Moscow on the afternoon of June 24, 2023, including reaching out to Putin himself, who refused to speak with him. Negotiations were reportedly conducted by top generals and the Russian ambassador to Belarus. Belarusian president Alexander Lukashenko reportedly spoke with Prigozhin upon Putin's request, acting as a mediator to broker a settlement.

Charges were dropped and Wagner ceased its march on Moscow. As part of the agreement, Prigozhin moved to Belarus and Wagner troops were slated to return to Ukraine, but those plans were cancelled because of Wagner's refusal to sign contracts with the military giving them authority over the Wagner Group.

Prigozhin and Utkin were then presumed to be living in Belarus. The BBC said they tracked Prigozhin's private jet flying from Belarus to Russia in late June, 2023. The jet made several flights between St. Petersburg and Moscow, but whether Prigozhin was on board was unknown. On July 6, Lukashenko stated: "As for Prigozhin, he's in St Petersburg. He is not on the territory of Belarus."

On July 28, 2023, a confirmed sighting of an Embraer Legacy 600 in the aftermath of the failed mutiny emerged, showing Prigozhin meeting with Freddy Mapouka, a presidential advisor in the Central African Republic, and the head of the Cameroonian pro-Russian media outlet *Afrique Média*, at the Trezzini Palace hotel in St. Petersburg during the 2023 Russia–Africa Summit. Prigozhin told *Afrique Média* that the Wagner Group was ready to increase its presence in Africa.

Then on August 23 Prigozhin's Embraer Legacy 600 aircraft (made in Brazil) was en route from Moscow to Saint Petersburg. A bomb on board the plane caused it to lose a wing and it crashed straight into the ground, killing all 10 people on board.

Aboard this plane with Prigozhin on this doomed flight was Dmitry Utkin, a Russian mercenary with SS tattoos on his shoulders.

It is noteworthy that the call sign of Utkin, Wagner, is in commemoration of Adolf Hitler's favorite composer. Yes, the Wagner group is named after Utkin, who styled himself after Richard Wagner.

There is a photo of a man resembling Utkin with tattoos or drawings on his body in the form of SS Obersturmbannführer loops

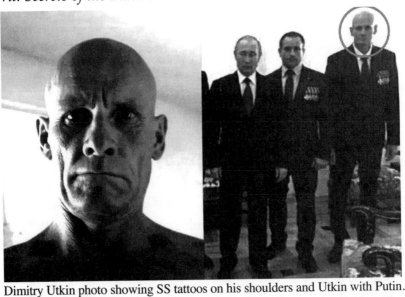

Dimitry Utkin photo showing SS tattoos on his shoulders and Utkin with Putin.

and the Wehrmacht emblem. In another photo, someone in profile resembling Utkin is wearing a bergmütte (a German military hat) with an SS eagle. On some of his documents, Utkin signs his initials "D.A.," while on other documents he signs with the SS sign and the sig runes. In other words, Utkin would often sign his name "SS" in the runic style. In addition, he used the address "Heil Petrovich," referring to Prigozhin.

Journalists learned that Utkin was born on June 11, 1970 in Asbest, Sverdlovsk Oblast, RSFSR. He finished school in Ukraine, in the village of Smolino in the Kirovohrad region, where he moved with his mother. As late as 2017, Utkin's mother lived in Smolino, in an ordinary apartment in a Soviet five-story building.

According to Censor.net, Utkin did not live in Smolino after school, although he sometimes visited. The media outlet's interlocutors recounted rumors that his two children from different wives live in the village. Censor.net also wrote that Utkin allegedly visited his mother in 2016, when the fighting was already ongoing in southeastern Ukraine and he was in command of a unit of Russian mercenaries.

After school, Utkin entered a military

The SS Sig runes.

school (presumably the Kirov Higher Combined Arms Command School) in Leningrad. Utkin retired in 2012 with the rank of lieutenant colonel, but continued to make a living in the military. At first, he joined the Russian PMC Moran Security Group (based abroad), and in the early summer of 2014, Prigozhin's private military company was born.

Before he met Prigozhin Utkin had received at most one award—the Order of Courage. "By the end of 2016, he had four Orders of Courage on his chest, and Vladimir Putin received him in the Kremlin. Soon, Utkin became a hero of Russia," the article says.

According to a BBC article published on August 24, 2023 entitled "Who is Dmitry Utkin and who else was reportedly on the plane?":

Nine other people were on the plane alongside Wagner boss Yevgeny Prigozhin when it crashed, according to flight details released by the Russian aviation authorities.

They include Dmitry Utkin, who is believed to have given the mercenary group its name.

Russia also says Valery Chekalov, who is believed to have been crucial to the group's finances, was on board.

Three crew members were on the flight alongside the Wagner members. Here's what we know about them.

Dmitry Utkin

The history of the Wagner Group is murky but follow the trail back far enough and Dmitry Utkin's name will inevitably crop up. The 53-year-old veteran of Russia's two wars in Chechnya in 1994-2000 is believed to have been involved in the private army since its early days in 2014.

The group itself is named after his call sign Wagner. It is seemingly a reference to composer Richard Wagner, who was Adolf Hitler's favorite composer.

In recent years, Utkin is reported to have been Prigozhin's right-hand man, responsible for overall command and combat training.

There are few photographs of Utkin but one of those in circulation is a selfie which reveals neo-Nazi tattoos on his body.

According to Utkin's online CV, which appears to be from around 2013 and was unearthed by the investigative website Bellingcat, he served in the GRU—Russia's military intelligence division—from 1988 to 2008. It says his involvement in combat operations led to government awards, and lists weapons skills among his professional qualities.

Utkin became a gun for hire after leaving military intelligence and gained influence in Wagner when the group fought on the side of pro-Russia separatists in eastern Ukraine in 2014. He is also thought to have been involved in the group's operations in Syria and Africa. A BBC investigation in 2021 linked him to documents which exposed Wagner's involvement in the Libyan civil war.

A picture thought to be taken in 2016 shows Utkin alongside Russian President Vladimir Putin at a Kremlin reception, at a time when the Russian government was denying links to Wagner. Mr Putin has since said the Russian government funded the group to the tune of billions of dollars.

Valery Chekalov

Chekalov is believed to be a close Prigozhin associate with business links to the Wagner leader stretching back to the 2000s. The 47-year-old appears to have been involved in running Prigozhin's non-military business interests, which Western governments say are used to finance the mercenary group.

Chekalov was linked with Evro Polis, a company associated with Prigozhin, which signed contracts for the production of gas and oil in Syria in 2017. According to the US Treasury, the company was contracted by President Bashar al-Assad's government "to protect Syrian oil fields in exchange for a 25% share in oil and gas production from the fields." The finances raised from the deal were used to pay Wagner fighters and procure arms, the US Treasury said. Chekalov is also believed to have been in charge of Wagner's business projects across Africa.

He had been targeted by US and Ukrainian sanctions over his links with Prigozhin, and Evro Polis has also been sanctioned by a number of governments, including the UK.

Yevgeny Makaryan, Sergei Propustin, Alexander Totmin and Nikolai Matuseyev

The other five men listed as passengers all appear to be Wagner fighters. Unlike Utkin and Chekalov, they do not appear on international sanctions lists and so have not been deemed to be senior figures by Western governments. Given that we know Prigozhin was surrounded by close protection—and even more so after his rift with Vladimir Putin deepened—they may have been travelling as bodyguards.

The names of three of the men appear in a database of alleged Wagner fighters which has been compiled by pro-Ukrainian activists: Yevgeny Makaryan, Sergei Propustin and Alexander Totmin. Another man identified by the Russian authorities as Nikolai Matuseyev does not appear in the database. One Russian Telegram channel says it could have been Nikolai Matusevich, a member of Wagner's assault unit.

So why did Utkin have SS tattoos on his shoulders and frequently sign his name as "SS"? Was he enamored with the Nazis and the SS? Was it because he was born in the Ukraine? It would seem unusual for a Russian military operative to has SS tattoos on their body, but maybe it is not that unusual, we just do not know. He was clearly someone who identified with the ruthlessness of the SS, but aren't the Nazis in Ukraine the enemy? What gives? Who are these "SS men" working as mercenaries for Russia against the "Nazi Ukrainian" government? Is this just a war to have a war? Caught in the middle are the Ukrainian people who suffered greatly during WWII. Was this somehow a continuation of WWII?

What we are seeing here is that the SS and their symbols are popular in the Ukraine, as well as among mercenary types, including French-allied fighters in the Sahel area of Africa. The skull and crossbones "Totenkopf" symbol is a popular one among paramilitary groups, bikers, and heavy metal enthusiasts. It is also the symbol of the pirates in the Caribbean, often called the Jolly Roger. This came from early masonic symbolism.

Once again, we see how elements of WWII were a clash between secret societies. On the British, French and American side were the strong Masonic elements that pervaded life at the time, before television became the typical pastime. On the other side was the Teutonic Knights of the crusades and secret societies in Germany that started with the Thule Society and morphed into the Vril Society and the SS with its sacred castle at Wewelsburg. The SS then morphed into the Black Sun group because the use of the swastika was essentially stopped.

So, who is Dmitry Utkin? Why does he have SS tattoos on his shoulders? Is he really a member of a latter-day SS—the Black Sun—who are mercenaries and will fight for any "right wing" cause? Why would a mercenary working for Putin's Russia—against a supposed Nazi government in the Ukraine—be having such a permanent symbol as SS runes on his shoulders? Does he not realize that the SS and Nazis in Ukraine are the enemy? Who was this bizarre traitor and double agent? Is he part of a Black Sun international mercenary group that is involved in various criminal activities including arms smuggling, drug smuggling, plus gold and money laundering? Is the Wagner Group—now minus its founding members—part of some extraterritorial Black Sun group that continues from its bases in Tierra del Fuego and Argentina?

The Wolfsangel and the SS

Another SS sign that was used in Nazi Germany and is commonly used in Ukraine today is the Wolfangel. The Wolfsangel ("wolf's hook") was inspired by medieval European wolf traps that consisted of a Z-shaped metal hook called the Wolfsangel that was hung by a chain from a crescent-shaped metal bar called the Wolfsanker. Wikipedia says that the stylized symbol of the Z-shape (also called the Doppelhaken, meaning the "double-hook") can include a central horizontal bar to give a Z-symbol, which can be reversed and/or rotated. It is sometimes mistaken as being an ancient rune due to its similarity to the "gibor rune" of the pseudo Armanen runes.

The Wolfsangel device was to catch and kill wolves and

314

The Wolfsangel hook, chain, and crossbar for hanging from a tree.

consisted of the hook attached via a chain or rope to a larger bar that was lodged between the overhanging branches of a tree. This would encourage the wolf to jump up to gulp the hanging chunk of meat (with the hook concealed inside), thus further impaling itself in the manner of a fish caught on a fishing hook.

Early medieval pagans believed that the Wolfsangel symbol possessed magical powers, and could ward off wolves. It became an early symbol of German liberty and independence after its adoption as an emblem in various 15th-century peasant revolts, and also in the 17th-century Thirty Years War. The Thirty Years' War was one of the longest and most destructive conflicts in European history, lasting from 1618 to 1648. Fought primarily in Central Europe, an estimated 4.5 to 8 million soldiers and civilians died as a result of battle, famine, and disease.

In prewar Germany, interest in the Wolfsangel was revived by the popularity of the 1910 novel *Der Wehrwolf*, which follows a hero in the Thirty Years War. According to Wikipedia in Nazi Germany, the Wolfsangel symbol was widely adopted by both the Wehrmacht and the Waffen SS.

The Wehrmacht ("defense force") were the unified armed forces of Nazi Germany from 1935 to 1945. It consisted of the Heer (army), the Kriegsmarine (navy) and the Luftwaffe (air force). The designation "Wehrmacht" replaced the previously used term Reichswehr and was the manifestation of the Nazi regime's efforts to rearm Germany to a greater extent than the Treaty of Versailles permitted.

After the Nazi rise to power in 1933, one of Adolf Hitler's most overt and audacious moves was to establish the Wehrmacht, a modern offensively-capable armed force, fulfilling the Nazi regime's long-term goals of regaining lost territory, gaining new territory,

The Wolfsangel symbol.

and dominating its neighbors. This required the reinstatement of conscription and massive investment and defense spending on the arms industry.

The Wolfsangel symbol was used in the Wehrmacht's 19th Infantry Division, the 19th Panzer Division, the 33rd Infantry Division, the 206th Infantry Division, and the 256th Infantry Division.

The Wolfsangel symbol was also used by the Waffen SS, a separate military division of Nazi Germany. As we have seen, the Waffen-SS was the combat branch of the Nazi Party's paramilitary Schutzstaffel (SS) organization. Formations included men from Nazi Germany, along with volunteers and conscripts from both Axis occupied and unoccupied lands.

Initially, in keeping with the racial policy of Nazi Germany, membership was open only to people of Germanic origin (so-called "Aryan ancestry"). The rules were partially relaxed in 1940, and after the invasion of the Soviet Union in June 1941, Nazi propaganda claimed that the war was a "European crusade against Bolshevism" and subsequently units consisting largely or solely of foreign

Coat of Arms for Burgwedel.

316

volunteers and conscripts were also raised.

These Waffen-SS units were made up of men mainly from among the nationals of Nazi-occupied Europe such as Ukraine. Despite having relaxed the rules, the Waffen-SS was still based on the racist ideology of Nazism, and ethnic Poles were specifically barred from the formations. This is because they were viewed as "Untermensch" or "subhumans."

2nd SS Panzer Dvision symbol.

Untermensch literally means "underman," or "subhuman," and was extensively used by Germany's Nazi Party to refer to non-Aryan people they deemed to be inferior. It was mainly used against "the masses from the East," that is Jews, Roma (Gypsies), and Slavs (mainly ethnic Poles, Belarusians, Ukrainians, and Russians).

The Waffen SS used the Wolfsangel symbol on the 2nd SS Panzer Division Das Reich, the 4th SS Polizei Panzergrenadier Division, the 34th SS Volunteer Grenadier Division Landstorm Nederland, the Sturmabteilung "Feldherrnhalle" (SA "Warlord's Hall" Guard Regiment), and others. It was also used by the Dutch Nazi fascist party whose magazine was *De Wolfsangel*. There was also the "Werwolf" plan of resistance against Allied occupation which was intended to use the Wolfsangel symbol.

After World War II, Germany made public exhibition of the Wolfsangel symbol illegal in Germany. On August 9, 2018, Germany lifted the ban on the usage of swastikas, the sonnenrad and other Nazi symbols in video games. However, the general use of such symbols as the swastika, Totenkopf, sonnenrad, and Wolfsangel is still banned in Germany. So are the Revell

34th SS Division logo Nederland.

317

models of the Haunebu craft.

In Italy, the Wolfsangel was the symbol used by the far right movement Terza Posizione. Outside of Europe, the Wolfsangel symbol has been used by some Neo-Nazi organizations such as in the United States where the Aryan Nations organization uses a white Wolfsangel-like symbol with a sword replacing the cross-bar in its logo.

In Ukraine, far-right movements like the Social-National Party of Ukraine and the Social-National Assembly, as well as the Azov Regiment of the Ukrainian army, have used a similar symbol of ᚺ (an elongated center bar and the Z being rotated but untypically not reversed) for their political slogan "National Idea," where the symbol is a composite

The Azov Battalion logo.

of the "N" and the "I"); they deny any connection or attempt to draw a parallel with the regiment and Nazism. Political scientist Andreas Umland told *Deutsche Welle*, that though it had far-right connotations, the Wolfsangel was not considered a fascist symbol by the general population in Ukraine.

The Karelian National Battalion, which is a pro-Ukrainian volunteer battalion formed in January 2023 by members of the Karelian National Movement, notably features a Wolfsangel in the middle of the battalion's insignia. The Karelian National Battalion was proclaimed a voluntary military unit consisting of ethnic Karelians, functioning as part of the International Legion of Territorial Defense of Ukraine. They are for liberating the area along the Russian and Finnish borders which consists of Karelians, who are ethnic Finns but are "occupied" by Russia.

While they are an ethnically Finnish resistance movement their base is in the Ukraine. The other major Finnish language area outside of Finland is Estonia, an independent nation since 1989 with the collapse of the Soviet Union. Like other Baltic nations occupied by the USSR after WWII, the Estonians consider Russia as their enemy.

So we see how Ukraine is the focus of anti-Russian activity, which includes Finnish separatists who are allied with what appears to be SS-Black Sun units in the Ukraine.

Karelian National Battalion logo.

The Waffen-SS Indian Legion

A little-known Waffen-SS regiment was made up of fighters from India who were to ultimately invade British-controlled India. The India Legion or 950th (Indian) Infantry Regiment was a military unit raised during the Second World War, initially as part of the German Army and later the Waffen-SS from August 1944, intended to serve as a liberation force for British-ruled India. Due to its origins in the Indian independence movement, it was known also as the "Tiger Legion," and the "Azad Hind Fauj." As part of the Waffen-SS it was known as the Indian Volunteer Legion of the Waffen-SS.

Indian independence leader Subhas Chandra Bose initiated the legion's formation, as part of his efforts to win India's independence by waging war against Britain, when he came to Berlin in 1941 seeking German aid. The initial recruits in 1941 were volunteers from the Indian students resident in Germany at the time, and a handful of the Indian prisoners of war who had been captured during the North African campaign. It later drew a larger number of Indian prisoners of war as volunteers. The special India unit was trained by the German Army's special forces, called the Brandenburgers.

Though it was initially raised as an assault group that would form a pathfinder to a German–Indian joint invasion of the western frontiers of British India, only a small contingent was ever put to its original intended purpose.

About 100 members of the Indian Legion were parachuted into eastern Persia in January 1942 tasked with infiltrating the Baluchistan Province of British India in what was called Operation Bajadere. The German Abwehr had actively sought out Hindu,

319

Subhas Chandra Bose meeting with SS head Heinrich Himmler.

Sikh, and Muslim recruits for a planned strike through the oilfields at Baku, Azerbaijan into Iran, Afghanistan, and India.

The unit did indeed infiltrate India. They engaged in sabotage, attempted to create dissent and worked towards a popular revolt against British rule. However, the defeat of the Germans at Stalingrad meant that no major offensive towards India would take place, and the Germans would not be able to capture the all-important oilfields at Baku.

The majority of the troops of the Indian Legion headquartered in Berlin were given only non-combat duties in the Netherlands and in France until the Allied invasion. The legion saw action in the retreat from the Allied advance across France, fighting mostly against the French Resistance. One company was sent to Italy in 1944, where it saw action against British and Polish troops.

On August 8, 1944 Himmler authorized the legion's control to be transferred to the Waffen-SS, as was done with every other foreign volunteer unit of the German Army. The unit was renamed the Indische Freiwilligen Legion der Waffen-SS. It was now a division of the SS and was under the control of Heinrich Himmler.

At the time of the surrender of Nazi Germany in 1945, the remaining men of the Indian Legion made efforts to march to neutral Switzerland over the Alps, but they were captured by American and French troops and eventually shipped back to India to face charges of treason.

Flag of the Free India Legion.

The Indian Legion is interesting because it shows the far-reaching scope of German plans for Persia, Afghanistan and British India. The Germans hoped to create a spearhead army out of the Indian Legion which would allow the German army to move through Baku in Azerbaijan, having captured the oilfields there, and continue on through Tehran to Baluchistan on the western edge of the British Indian Empire. However, this was never to happen.

It is interesting to note that some of men in the India Legion were SS officers. We aso know that a large number of Tibetans were found in Berlin at the end of the war. Depending on how high up in the SS the Indian Legion officers rose, they might have been part of a special cadre of SS officers who were taken to the secret bases in Norway, Greenland, Antarctica and elsewhere. Landig describes a meeting at a secret base in Greenland where many of the members were from different parts of the world wearing their

Fighters of the Free India Legion on the beaches on Normandy.

321

traditional costumes. It is possible that Sikh or Hindu SS officers, wearing turbans, were part of this group.

The Black Sun Resurfaces

In the over seven decades since the end of WWII the subject of the Black Sun and their secret craft is still in the news. If it is not in the media because of the proliferation of SS symbols in Ukraine it is about the Vril and Haunebu saucers.

A Sikh of the Free India Legion in Berlin.

As previously noted, a CNN news story in the summer of 2023 featured a wounded Ukrainian soldier was being interviewed. He was sitting up in his hospital bed with bandages on his head and left hand. He was wearing a t-shirt that depicted the schematics for two flying saucers: the familiar schematics for the Vril flying saucer and the Haunebu flying saucer. The Vril craft was above the Haunebu craft. This indicates that the SS and Black Sun believers in Ukraine are very familiar with the Nazi flying saucer mythos and believe in it.

In the US, where UFOs are hotly debated in Congressional panels, the idea of Nazi flying saucers and secret SS bases in South America are hardly considered. But in Europe, especially in Eastern Europe including Czech, Austria, Poland, Ukraine and Finland, the knowledge and acceptance of the Haunebu and Vril saucers is widespread. This is especially true of the small Baltic countries of Estonia, Latvia and Lithuania where book publishers have focused quite a bit on this subject.

The Nazi flying saucer mythos has been used in a number of popular books and movies including *Iron Sky, Nazis at the Center of the Earth* (both from 2012), *Sky Sharks*, and other movies. The mythos of Nazis, flying saucers, Antarctica and the concept of the hollow earth are now familiar to millions of people, especially in Eastern Europe.

The release of a number of declassified CIA files in August of

2018 showed how in 1952 the CIA was getting information on the Haunebu and Vril saucers. Descriptions of the large Andromeda craft do not seem to occur.

The *Daily Star* of the UK said on August 6, 2018 that one of the CIA files was about interviews with a German engineer named George Klein from between March 11 and May 20, 1952. Said the *Daily Star*:

> In these interviews Klein claimed that the Nazis had a flying saucer that was capable of reaching heights of 12,400 meters in three minutes—with speeds of up to 2,500 mph. Nazi flying saucers appear twice in the CIA's trove of documents as part of their investigations into UFOs. The Klein testimony was published in newspapers in Greece, Iran and the Congo.
>
> Klein said he was an engineer in the Ministry of Speer (i.e.: Albert Speer, Reich Minister of Armaments and War Production for Nazi Germany) and was present in Prague on February 14, 1945, at the first experimental flight of a flying saucer. Klein claims the Third Reich actually successfully carried out a test of their "flying saucer" in Prague on Valentine's Day, 1945, only months before the Czech capital was liberated by the Soviet Union's advancing Red Army.
>
> Exceeding 2,500 mph (Mach 3) would make the Nazi saucer almost twice as fast as the state-of-the-art F-35 warplane being rolled out in the US and UK during World War II. Klein claimed the saucer could takeoff vertically like a helicopter, and had been in development since 1941.
>
> The CIA document alleges the saucers were constructed at the same slave-labor driven factories which made the dreaded V2 rockets. Nazi engineers were reportedly evacuated from Prague as the Red Army bore down upon them. Klein claims one team failed to be notified of the order to escape—and they were captured by the Soviets.
>
> ...Claims about the Nazis' advanced technology are often tied to alleged links between Hitler and the occult. Conspiracy theorists claim that remnants of the Third Reich

fled to South America under the guidance of SS commander Hans Kammler. The Nazis are claimed to have continued testing their experimental weapons from secret bases in the Antarctic. UFO sightings from the era are alleged to be secret tests of experimental technology by the Nazis— and the US and Soviets. Theories persist to this day about advanced Reich technology—and still cause controversy.

It is interesting that they mention Hans Kammler as a chief architect of the Nazi presence in South America. It seems that he did spend quite a bit of his time in Argentina and other South American countries—while being officially dead. He also apparently spent time in Prague after the war, probably advancing the mission of the SS in Czechoslovakia somehow. It would seem that he was also active in the Ukraine, but no one really knows what he did or where he went.

We see how the SS and the Third Reich had no beliefs in territorial integrity and were happy to put their secret facilities—many of them quite astonishing—in foreign countries and territories, even those of their adversaries such as Norway or Canada.

And, astonishing as many of the suppositions in this book have been, one of the most astonishing is that the Nazis, the SS, and the Thule/Vril Society had been working on these bases and technologies starting in the early 1930s with careful planning and lots of financing, some of it from stolen gold and art. They have been accused of drug smuggling as well.

Indeed, the remnants of the SS, the Black Sun community of super-mystics as described by Landig must still exist in some form. With the oil companies fading on the world stage and electric cars and trucks becoming the norm, maybe it is time for the technology behind the Haunebu, Vril and Andromeda craft to be brought to the public.

Unfortunately, one reason that this will not happen is that the secret space program, now called the Space Force, is using this technology and wants to keep it a military secret. For all the researchers into the secret German saucer programs and their aftermath the question has been: "Just how integrated into the American secret space program was the Nazi technology that we

SS General Hans Kammler (center) during World War II.

have chronicled in this and other books?"

The main enemy of the SS during WWII was not Britain and the US it was Russia. Hitler wanted to annex much of western Russia into the Third Reich and Himmler tried to negotiate a separate peace with Britain at the end of the war—so they could keep fighting Russia.

And so SS and Black Sun symbolism resurfaces in Ukraine among those fighting the Russians. These fighters are not unaware of the source of these symbols and use them with pride as symbols of "fanatical fighters" and "deadly special forces." The skull and cross bones of the American pirate era are similarly used by certain US military units as a symbol.

So, it seems that history is coming full circle. For many decades the US military and other governments tried to suppress the reality of flying saucers by saying that they just don't exist. The military has looked into flying saucer reports but has concluded that they are not real. Now the government is saying that UFOs are real—and they are openly looking into it.

That the Germans developed this technology before and during WWII and the SS-Black Sun continued to fly them around the world for many decades, often trying to be noticed and photographed—has to be the greatest cover-up in modern times. At what point did the British and American militaries realize that the Germans had secret bases in Antarctica and elsewhere that they continued to operate after the war? By 1946 they must have realized this and in 1947 the US Navy invaded Antarctica with Project Highjump.

Why has all this been kept secret for all these years? Britain is

325

notorious for holding onto state and intelligence secrets and still retains many secrets from WWII. The Americans have been forced to release various CIA and FBI documents that corroborated in many ways the entire scenario of SS survival and secret bases. However, Naval Intelligence documents remain secret and the US Navy is the primary holder of many of our military's secrets. We will never know what is in their files but it is likely to be pretty amazing.

Sometimes they say that "truth is stranger than fiction" and that may be what is

A Vril craft photographed in Peru in 1967.

happening here. Over the decades there has been this creep—and creep—drip—and drip of information concerning Nazi survival and man-made UFOs. Movies and serials began immediately bringing this out and popularizing flying saucers—much to the chagrin of the US military who wanted to dampen any fantasies of flying saucers. The military then persuaded Hollywood to make alien invasion movies. They wanted it all to be science fiction about a UFO phenomenon that did not exist.

However, the SS-Black Sun operatives wanted to be seen and therefore made large UFO displays around Buenos Aires and other major cities in South America. One display over Buenos Aires lasted for hours and included two of the large cylindrical Andromeda craft. Haunebu and Vril saucers flew around the Andromeda craft for hours before they all departed.

South America was a hotbed of UFO activity during the 50s, 60s, 70s, and 80s. UFO activity continues in South America today and one has to wonder who is flying these craft? Extraterrestrials? Black Sun operatives from secret SS bases? It has been suggested that the military of Chile has built some craft of their own and are flying them around Chile. Did they have help from the Black Sun?

And so we have to leave it there. Flying saucers are real. Huge flying cigar-shaped craft are real. Some might be from another planet but it seems that some were built right here on planet Earth. The technology remains a secret and the oil companies continue to drill for oil for our airplanes, submarines, ships and cars. WWII was an oil war that the Germans lost. They had hoped that by expanding Germany through the Ukraine to the Caucasus countries of Georgia and Armenia to the oilfields at Baku in Azerbaijan, they would get the oil they needed to keep their war machine going.

The Black Sun SS officers were now in possession of the Tesla technology of electric flying craft. With the technology used in the Vril, Haunebu, and Andromeda craft, they knew that they could continue the "fight" without controlling any oilfields. Indeed, today the Black Sun must be very different from the SS officers that comprised it immediately after WWII. Far more modern and hip— they know Beatles songs—and they are promoters of a "flying saucer" future.

While dying fighters on the front lines of the war in Ukraine are wearing their Vril and Haunebu t-shirts, Russian mercenaries with SS tattoos are dying as well. The Totenkopf and the Wolfsangel are popular symbols of death-dealing soldiers on any side of a war. Does the Black Sun organization in Tierra del Fuego have a dog in this fight? They may well have.

A Vril craft photographed over Hampton, Virginia on January 25, 1967.

A Vril craft photographed near power lines in St. Paul, Minnesota on December 27, 1966. It seems that these craft are able to draw power from power lines.

FOOTNOTES & BIBLIOGRAPHY

1. *UFOs Before Roswell*, Graeme Rendall, 2021, Reiver Country Books, UK.
2. *Hess and the Penguins,* Joseph P. Farrell, 2017, Adventures Unlimited Press, Kempton, IL.
3. *UFO Contact from Undersea*, Wendelle Stevens, 1982, UFO Photo Archives, Tucson, AZ.
4. *Grey Wolf: The Escape of Adolf Hitler*, Simon Dunstan and Gerrard Williams, 2011, Sterling Press, New York.
5. *Hitler's Terror Weapons: From VI to Vimana*, Geoffrey Brooks, 2002, Pen and Sword Books, Barnsley, UK.
6. *UFOs: 1947-1987:The 40-Year Search for an Explanation*, compiled and edited by Hillary Evans with John Spencer, 1987, Fortean Times, London.
7. *UFOs and Nukes*, Robert Hastings, 2017, self-published on Amazon.
8. *Hitler in Argentina,* Harry Cooper, 1984, updated 2014, Sharkhunters International, Hernando, FL.
9. *Ratline*, Peter Levenda, 2012, Ibis Press, Lakeworth, FL.
10. *Antarctica and the Secret Space Program*, David Childress, 2020, Adventures Unlimited Press, Kempton, IL.
11. *UFO Odyssey*, Brad and Sherry Steiger, 1999, Ballantine Books, New York.
12. *Nazi International*, Joseph P. Farrell, 2008, Adventures Unlimited Press, Kempton, IL.
13. *The SS Totenkopf Ring,* Craig Gottlieb, 2008, Schiffer Publishing, Atglen, PA.
14. *Hunt for the Skinwalker*, Colm Kelleher, Ph.D. and George Knapp, 2005, Pocket Books, New York.
15. *Vimana*, David Hatcher Childress, 2013, Adventures Unlimited Press, Kempton, IL.

16. *Man-Made UFOs,* Renato Vesco and David Childress, 1994, Adventures Unlimited Press, Kempton, IL.

17. *Flying Saucers: The Startling Evidence of the Invasion from Outer Space*, Coral Lorenzen, 1962, 1966, Signet Books, New York.

18. *The Lubbock Lights,* David R. Wheeler, 1977, Award Books, New York.

19. *Hitler est vivo,* Ladislao Szabo, 1947, El Tábano, Buenos Aires. In Spanish.

20. *La Antárctica y otros Mitos (The Antarctic and other myths)*, Miguel Serrano, 1948, Santiago (52 page booklet). In Spanish.

21. *UFO—Das Dritte Reich schlägt zurück? (UFO—The Third Reich Strikes Back?)*, Norbert Jürgen Ratthofer and Ralf Ettl, 1989, self-published. In German.

22. *Das Vril-Projekt. Der Endkampf um die Erde,* Norbert Jürgen Ratthofer and Ralf Ettl, 1992, Self-published. In German.

23. *Die Dunkle Seite Des Mondes (The Dark Side of the Moon)*, Brad Harris, 1996, Pandora Books, Germany. In German.

24. *The Mysteries of the Andes,* Robert Charroux, 1977, Avon Books, New York.

25. *Yo He Estado en Marte,* Narciso Genovese, 1958, Editorial Posada, Mexico City.

26. *UFO: Evaluating the Evidence,* Bill Yenne, 1997, Grange Books, London.

27. *SS Brotherhood of the Bell,* Joseph P. Farrell, 2006, Adventures Unlimited Press, Kempton, IL.

28. *Black Sun: Aryan Cults, Esoteric Nazism, and the Politics of Identity*, Nicholas Goodrick-Clarke, 2002, New York University Press, New York.

29. *The Morning of the Magicians*, Jacques Bergier and Louis Pauwels, 1960, 1963, English edition, Stein and Day, New York.

30. *Reich of the Black Sun,* Joseph P. Farrell, 2009, Adventures Unlimited Press, Kempton, IL.

31. *Casebook on the Men in Black*, Jim Keith, 1997, Adventures Unlimited Press, Kempton, IL.

32. *Flying Saucers Uncensored*, Harold T. Wilkins, 1955, Citadel Press, New York.

33. *The Humanoids*, edited bybCharles Bowen, 1969, Henry Regnery, Chicago.
34. *Hitler's Flying Saucers*, Henry Stevens, 2003, Adventures Unlimited Press, Kempton, IL.
35. *Arktos: The Polar Myth*, Joscelyn Godwin, 1996, Adventures Unlimited Press, Kempton, IL.
36. *Andromeda: The Secret Files*, David Childress, 2022, Adventures Unlimited Press, Kempton, IL.
37. *Haunebu: The Secret Files*, David Childress, 2021, Adventures Unlimited Press, Kempton, IL.
38. *Saucers, Swastikas and Psyops*, Joseph P. Farrell, 2011, Adventures Unlimited Press, Kempton, IL.
39. *Roswell and the Reich,* Joseph P. Farrell, 2010, Adventures Unlimited Press, Kempton, IL.
40. *The CIA UFO Papers,* Dan Wright, 2019, MUFON-Red Wheel-Weiser, Newburyport, MA.
41. *I Read the News Today, Oh Boy*, Paul Howard, 2016, Picador Books, London.
42. *Underwater and Underground Bases*, Richard Sauder, 2001, AUP, Kempton, IL.
43. *The Great Heroin Coup: Drugs, Intelligence and International Fascism,* Henrik Kruger, 1980, South End Press, Boston.
44. *Dark Fleet*, Len Kasten, 2020, Bear & Company, Rochester, VT.
45. *Vimana: Flying Machines of the Ancients*, David Childress, 2013, Adventures Unlimited Press, Kempton, IL.
46. *Dark Star*, Henry Stevens, 2011, Adventures Unlimited Press, Kempton, IL.
48. *The German Saucer Story*, Michael Barton, 1968, Future Press, Los Angeles.
49. *We Want You: Is Hitler Still Alive?,* Michael Barton, 1960, Future Press, Los Angeles.
50. *Inside the Allgemeine SS: 1925-1945*, Ulric of England, 2012, Andrea Press, Madrid, Spain.
51. *Il Deutsche Flugscheiben und U-Boote Ueberwachen Die Weltmeere,* O. Bergmann, 1989, Hugin Publishing, Germany.

331

52. *Anti-Gravity & the World Grid*, David Hatcher Childress, 1987, AUP, Kempton, IL.
53. *Vril, The Power of the Coming Race*, Sir Edward Bulwer-Lytton, 1871, Blackwood and Sons, London.
54. *The UFO-Nauts*, Hans Holzer, 1976, Fawcett Books, Greenwich, CT.
55. *The Real Odessa*, Uki Goni, 2003, Granta Press, London.
56. *War in Ancient India*, V. R. Dikshitar, 1944, Oxford University Press (1987 edition published by Motilal Banarsidass, Delhi).
57. *Invisible Residents*, Ivan T. Sanderson, 1970, Adventures Unlimited Press, Kempton, IL.
58. *The Philadelphia Experiment*, William Moore and Charles Berlitz, 1979, Grosset & Dunlap, New York.
59. *UFO Photographs Around the World*, edited by Wendelle Stevens, 1986, UFO Photo Archives, Tucson, AZ.
60. *UFO Photographs Around the World, Vol. II*, edited by Wendelle Stevens, 1986, UFO Photo Archives, Tucson, AZ.
61. *UFO Photographs Around the World, Vol. III*, edited by Wendelle Stevens, 1986, UFO Photo Archives, Tucson, AZ.
62. *Bariloche Nazi: Sitios Historicos Relacionados Al Nacionalsocialismo*, Abel Basti, 2004, Guia Touristeca, Buenos Aires.
63. *UFOs: A Pictorial History from Antiquity to the Present*, David Knight, 1979, McGraw-Hill Book Company, New York.

Get these fascinating books from your nearest bookstore or directly from:
Adventures Unlimited Press
www.adventuresunlimitedpress.com

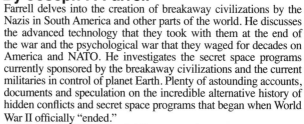

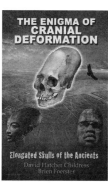

ANTARCTICA AND THE SECRET SPACE PROGRAM
Hatcher Childress
David Childress, popular author and star of the History Channel's show *Ancient Aliens*, brings us the incredible tale of Nazi submarines and secret weapons in Antarctica and elsewhere. He then examines Operation High-Jump with Admiral Richard Byrd in 1947 and the battle that he apparently had in Antarctica with flying saucers. Through "Operation Paperclip," the Nazis infiltrated aerospace companies, banking, media, and the US government, including NASA and the CIA after WWII. Does the US Navy have a secret space program that includes huge ships and hundreds of astronauts?
392 Pages. 6x9 Paperback. Illustrated. $22.00 Code: ASSP

HAUNEBU: THE SECRET FILES
The Greatest UFO Secret of All Time
By David Hatcher Childress
Childress brings us the incredible tale of the German flying disk known as the Haunebu. Although rumors of German flying disks have been around since the late years of WWII it was not until 1989 when a German researcher named Ralf Ettl living in London received an anonymous packet of photographs and documents concerning the planning and development of at least three types of unusual craft. Chapters include: A Saucer Full of Secrets; WWII as an Oil War; A Saucer Called Vril; Secret Cities of the Black Sun; The Strange World of Miguel Serrano; Set the Controls for the Heart of the Sun; Dark Side of the Moon; more. Includes a 16-page color section. Over 120 photographs and diagrams.
352 Pages. 6x9 Paperback. Illustrated. $22.00 Code: HBU

ANDROMEDA: THE SECRET FILES
The Flying Submarines of the SS
By David Hatcher Childress
Childress brings us the amazing story of the Andromeda craft, designed and built during WWII. Along with flying discs, the Germans were making long, cylindrical airships that are commonly called motherships—large craft that house several smaller disc craft. It was not until 1989 that a German researcher named Ralf Ettl, living in London, received an anonymous packet of photographs and documents concerning the development of three types of craft—including the Andromeda. Chapters include: Gravity's Rainbow; The Motherships; The MJ-12, UFOs and the Korean War; The Strange Case of Reinhold Schmidt; Secret Cities of the Winged Serpent; The Green Fireballs; Submarines That Can Fly; more. Includes a 16-page color section.
382 Pages. 6x9 Paperback. Illustrated. $22.00 Code: ASF

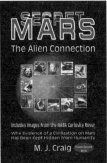

SECRET MARS: The Alien Connection
By M. J. Craig
While scientists spend billions of dollars confirming that microbes live in the Martian soil, people sitting at home on their computers studying the Mars images have found the possible archaeological remains of an extraterrestrial civilization. Hard to believe? Well, this challenging book invites you to take a look at the astounding pictures yourself and make up your own mind. *Secret Mars* presents over 160 incredible images taken by American and European spacecraft that reveal possible evidence of a civilization that once lived, and may still live, on the planet Mars... powerful evidence that scientists are ignoring! A visual and fascinating book!
352 Pages. 6x9 Paperback. Illustrated. $19.95. Code: SMAR

THE GIZA DEATH STAR REVISITED
By Joseph P. Farrell

Join revisionist author Joseph P. Farrell for a summary, revision, and update of his original *Giza Death Star* trilogy in this one-volume compendium of the argument, the physics, and the all-important ancient texts, from the Edfu Temple texts to the Lugal-e and the Enuma Elish that he believes may have made the Great Pyramid a tremendously powerful weapon of mass destruction. Those texts, Farrell argues, provide the clues to the powerful physics of longitudinal waves in the medium that only began to be unlocked centuries later by Sir Isaac Newton and his well-known studies of the Great Pyramid, and even later by Nikola Tesla's "electro-acoustic" experiments. Chapters and sections include: The Hypothesized Functions of the Great Pyramid's Topological-Analogical Code of Ancient Texts; Greaves, Gravity, and Newton; Meta-Materials, Crystals, and Torsion; The Top Secret Cold War Soviet Pyramid Research, and much, much more!
360 Pages. 6x9 Paperback. Illustrated. $19.95. Code: GDSR

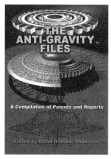

THE ANTI-GRAVITY FILES
A Compilation of Patents and Reports
Edited by David Hatcher Childress

With plenty of technical drawings and explanations, this book reveals suppressed technology that will change the world in ways we can only dream of. Chapters include: A Brief History of Anti-Gravity Patents; The Motionless Electromagnet Generator Patent; Mercury Anti-Gravity Gyros; The Tesla Pyramid Engine; Anti-Gravity Propulsion Dynamics; The Machines in Flight; More Anti-Gravity Patents; Death Rays Anyone?; The Unified Field Theory of Gravity; and tons more. Heavily illustrated. 4-page color section.
216 pages. 8x10 Paperback. Illustrated. $22.00. Code: AGF

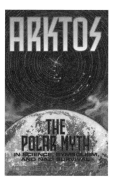

ARKTOS
The Polar Myth in Science, Symbolism & Nazi Survival
by Joscelyn Godwin

Explored are the many tales of an ancient race said to have lived in the Arctic regions, such as Thule and Hyperborea. Progressing onward, he looks at modern polar legends: including the survival of Hitler, German bases in Antarctica, UFOs, the hollow earth, and the hidden kingdoms of Agartha and Shambala. Chapters include: Prologue in Hyperborea; The Golden Age; The Northern Lights; The Arctic Homeland; The Aryan Myth; The Thule Society; The Black Order; The Hidden Lands; Agartha and the Polaires; Shambhala; The Hole at the Pole; Antarctica; more.
220 Pages. 6x9 Paperback. Illustrated. Index. $16.95. Code: ARK

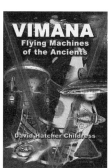

VIMANA:
Flying Machines of the Ancients
by David Hatcher Childress

According to early Sanskrit texts the ancients had several types of airships called vimanas. Like aircraft of today, vimanas were used to fly through the air from city to city; to conduct aerial surveys of uncharted lands; and as delivery vehicles for awesome weapons. David Hatcher Childress takes us on an astounding investigation into tales of ancient flying machines. In his new book, packed with photos and diagrams, he consults ancient texts and modern stories and presents astonishing evidence that aircraft, similar to the ones we use today, were used thousands of years ago in India, Sumeria, China and other countries. Includes a 24-page color section.
408 Pages. 6x9 Paperback. Illustrated. $22.95. Code: VMA

ORDER FORM

10% Discount When You Order 3 or More Items!

One Adventure Place
P.O. Box 74
Kempton, Illinois 60946
United States of America
Tel.: 815-253-6390 • Fax: 815-253-6300
Email: auphq@frontiernet.net
http://www.adventuresunlimitedpress.com

ORDERING INSTRUCTIONS

✓ Remit by USD$ Check, Money Order or Credit Card

✓ Visa, Master Card, Discover & AmEx Accepted

✓ Paypal Payments Can Be Made To:

   info@wexclub.com

✓ Prices May Change Without Notice

✓ 10% Discount for 3 or More Items

SHIPPING CHARGES

United States

✓ POSTAL BOOK RATE

✓ Postal Book Rate { $5.00 First Item / 50¢ Each Additional Item

✓ Priority Mail { $8.50 First Item / $2.00 Each Additional Item

✓ UPS { $9.00 First Item (Minimum 5 Books) / $1.50 Each Additional Item

   NOTE: UPS Delivery Available to Mainland USA Only

Canada

✓ Postal Air Mail { $19.00 First Item / $3.00 Each Additional Item

✓ Personal Checks or Bank Drafts MUST BE US$ and Drawn on a US Bank

✓ Canadian Postal Money Orders OK

✓ Payment MUST BE US$

All Other Countries

✓ Sorry, No Surface Delivery!

✓ Postal Air Mail { $29.00 First Item / $7.00 Each Additional Item

✓ Checks and Money Orders MUST BE US$ and Drawn on a US Bank or branch.

✓ Paypal Payments Can Be Made in US$ To: info@wexclub.com

SPECIAL NOTES

✓ RETAILERS: Standard Discounts Available

✓ BACKORDERS: We Backorder all Out-of-Stock Items Unless Otherwise Requested

✓ PRO FORMA INVOICES: Available on Request

✓ DVD Return Policy: Replace defective DVDs only

ORDER ONLINE AT: www.adventuresunlimitedpress.com

10% Discount When You Order 3 or More Items!

Please check: ☑

☐ This is my first order   ☐ I have ordered before

Name

Address

City

State/Province   Postal Code

Country

Phone: Day   Evening

Fax   Email

Item Code	Item Description	Qty	Total

Please check: ☑

	Subtotal ▸	
	Less Discount-10% for 3 or more items ▸	
☐ Postal-Surface	Balance ▸	
☐ Postal-Air Mail (Priority in USA)	Illinois Residents 6.25% Sales Tax ▸	
	Previous Credit ▸	
☐ UPS (Mainland USA only)	Shipping ▸	
	Total (check/MO in USD$ only) ▸	

☐ Visa/MasterCard/Discover/American Express

Card Number:

Expiration Date: Security Code:

✓ SEND A CATALOG TO A FRIEND: